Charles Dickens

A CRITICAL INTRODUCTION

K. J. FIELDING

SECOND EDITION
ENLARGED

LONGMANS

LONGMANS, GREEN AND CO LTD
48 Grosvenor Street, London W.1
Associated companies, branches and representatives throughout the world

First published 1958
Second impression by photolithography, 1960
Second edition 1965

PRINTED IN GREAT BRITAIN
BY WESTERN PRINTING SERVICES LTD, BRISTOL

CONTENTS

1. Early Years: 'Sketches by Boz' *page* 1
2. 'Pickwick Papers' and After 13
3. 'Oliver Twist' 32
4. 'Nicholas Nickleby' 47
5. 'Master Humphrey's Clock'—'The Old Curiosity Shop'; 'Barnaby Rudge' 59
6. America—1842: 'Martin Chuzzlewit' 80
7. 'Christmas Books' and 'Dombey and Son' 100
8. Actor, Editor, and Author: 'David Copperfield' 124
9. 'Bleak House' and 'Hard Times' 144
10. Political Views and 'Little Dorrit' 172
11. Separation—and 'A Tale of Two Cities' 189
12. 'Great Expectations' 207
13. 'Our Mutual Friend' 224
14. Last Years and 'Edwin Drood' 236

Select Annotated Bibliography 253

Index 263

NOTE TO THE REVISED EDITION AND ACKNOWLEDGEMENTS

The present edition has been considerably lengthened in its revision, but I have still tried to bear in mind that it is meant to be introductory: that is to say, it attempts to trace Dickens's development as a novelist in the light of his intentions, his general development, the life of his times and the expectations of his readers, and I have tried to write and arrange it as clearly as I can with both the general reader and the student in mind. It owes much to almost all the works on Dickens mentioned in the text and listed in the bibliography. It is also founded on contemporary records and papers, published and unpublished, which it would be impossible to particularize.

Especial thanks are due to Mr. H. C. Dickens, O.B.E., for copyright permission to quote from anything of Dickens's previously unpublished; also to the authorities of the J. Pierpont Morgan Library for the letters of Mrs. Dickens, and Wilkie Collins (quoted in chapter six), and of Maclise in chapter seven, to those of the Houghton Library, Harvard University, for those to the Norton family at the end of chapter fourteen, and to those of the Berg Collection, New York Public Library, for permission to consult and confirm the text of their Dickens letters and papers.

I am also very grateful for the kindness of many private and institutional owners of manuscripts, and to friends who have been most helpful.

K.J.F.

Chapter One

EARLY YEARS: *SKETCHES BY BOZ*

THIS is not an attempt to give the full story of Dickens's life, but to provide an account of his career as an author. There have been enough biographies which tell us everything about what he did in the intervals of writing, but which almost leave out of account the nature of his greatness as a novelist. In his Will, Dickens wrote, 'I rest my claims to the remembrance of my country on my published works.' In a memoir written just after Dickens's death Anthony Trollope said of him that for 'other matters he seemed to have a disregard', but 'to literature in all its branches his attachment was deep, and his belief in it was a thorough conviction'. Though possibly no author offers more from a chronological approach to his books and a comparison between his life and his writings, the emphasis in this study is laid on his works.

Charles Dickens was born on 7 February 1812, the second child and eldest son of John and Elizabeth Dickens. His father was an improvident clerk in the Navy Pay-Office, then stationed near Portsmouth; his mother came of a slightly better class of respectable civil servants. They were a young couple in their twenties, light-hearted, energetic, and unliterary. Dickens probably owed them a good deal, but he confessed to no more than Mr. Micawber as his sole inheritance from his father, and Mrs. Nickleby from his mother.

We know little of Mrs. Dickens except that she was

ladylike and a good mimic. She taught her children their letters, and was later ready to have set up a school if she could have obtained any pupils. John Dickens was the child of upper-class servants, with a fatal leaning to the genteel: he was affectionate, hard-working, and generous, but so easy-going that he spent money and borrowed it with the same happy facility, and without a thought of the future. As a rich man he would have been an ideal father; on a salary of from £200 to £350 he wore out the patience of both his friends and family.

Yet while the family was small they seem to have been happy. From Portsmouth they went up to London, and by the time that Charles Dickens was five they moved again to Chatham. Here he was looked after by a nurse named Mary Weller, learned comic songs, was told horrific stories, played with the next-door children, and grew up 'a very queer small boy', with the habit of noticing everything about him. He was rather delicate, lively, good-tempered and cheerful, and most decidedly precocious.

When the time came for him to go to school, he at first went with his sister, and then to one run by the son of a neighbouring minister. William Giles was a good teacher who made a favourite of the boy and gave him special attention, but more important than this was what Dickens learnt at home. In a little room in the attic, he discovered a long series of novels, and he crept up there to read—and to go on 'reading as if for life'.

'From that blessed room,' he wrote, 'Roderick Random, Peregrine Pickle, Humphrey Clinker, Tom Jones, the Vicar of Wakefield, Don Quixote, Gil Blas, and Robinson Crusoe came out, a glorious host to keep me company. They kept alive my fancy . . . they and the *Arabian Nights* and the *Tales of The Genii*'; and, one might add, *The Tatler*, *The Spectator*, Johnson's *Idler*, Goldsmith's *Citizen of the World*, and the works of Shakespeare. They and the performances at the Theatre Royal (where he saw *Richard III* and *Macbeth*) stamped his imagination and sympathies in a way that was to leave a mark on everything he wrote.

Life in Chatham was Dickens's golden age. Whenever afterwards he was in difficulties with a novel, he would put his characters into a coach and send them off to Chatham or to the adjoining Rochester. When he was a boy he was once out with his father on the road to Gravesend as they passed a great house at Gad's Hill. 'When you are a man', said his father, 'you might live there if you work hard enough.' When he was a man he bought it. Rochester and Chatham, and the countryside around, were a background against which he set some scene or other in almost every book he wrote. Chatham was the birthplace of his fancy, and he hardly knew how to value it until he 'saw the falling cloud which was to hide its pictures from him for ever'.

The scene darkened when his father was recalled to London. The family went off, leaving him behind for a time to finish the school term; and then, one cold wet day, he was packed up 'and forwarded like game' by coach to join them. Before he left, William Giles came 'flitting among the packing cases' to give him a copy of Goldsmith's *Bee*; and away he went, in solitude and dreariness; the only inside passenger.

In London Dickens found that his family were living in a little house in Camden Town. The conversation was all about the financial difficulties which his father had got into by over-spending. His sister went to the Royal Academy of Music and the boy wanted to go to school, but he was kept at home to do odd jobs. He had no friends and nothing to do but to find his way round north London. His greatest treat was 'to be out for a walk into the real town', to the Strand, or Covent Garden and the neighbouring Seven Dials. He began by writing little plays and essays, visited a godfather in Limehouse, and had fun with a toy-theatre; yet all the while he felt neglected, for, as he afterwards said, he understood things then as well as he did later.

Then the blow suddenly fell and his father was arrested. The boy ran messages for him while he was held at the sponging-house, and said good-bye when he was taken off to the debtors' prison declaring, like Micawber, that the sun had set on him for ever. 'I really believed at the time', Dickens said, 'that they had broken my heart.' In the Marshalsea, John Dickens was allowed to be visited by his family, and he was not too badly off since he still had his salary, which his creditors could not touch. At home everything they had was pawned. The boy took the things to the shop, including his books; and then, two days after his twelfth birthday, his mother thought it was time to find him a job.

He went as a boy-assistant in a blacking-factory, where he was employed by favour of the manager, a relative on his mother's side. He was paid six or seven shillings a week, and was set to work in the dirty, rat-ridden warehouse, covering and labelling pots of blacking. Two other boys, one of whom was called Bob Fagin, did the same work. At first young Dickens was kept apart from them, but afterwards they went on side by side. When his mother and the younger children joined his father in prison, he was found lodgings somewhere in Camden Town. On Sundays he would call for his sister at the Royal Academy of Music, and they would visit the rest of the family. For the other six days he was left to look after himself, with 'no advice, no counsel, no encouragement . . . no support, from any one that I can call to mind'.

In after years Dickens was bitterly ashamed of having had to work for his living as a child, and never confessed it to anyone in his family but his wife. Not only this, but his parents never afterwards mentioned it to him, and his children and other members of the family were upset when the story came out after his death. In fact, it might never have been known at all, if a friend of his father's had not casually mentioned that he had once met Dickens when he was in employment, as a boy, in a warehouse in the Strand. This remark was made to Dickens's friend and biographer, John Forster; and it was to Forster (who had passed it on to him) that Dickens hesitantly repeated the whole story. It stirred him so profoundly that he wrote it out—with much else about his childhood—in an account which he thought it would be easier for his friend to read than for him to tell.

Ultimately Dickens decided to make use of the account for some of the earlier chapters of *David Copperfield*, in which he described how David was employed by a wine-merchant's, Murdstone and Grinby; and this story of David's childhood in London is a true account of what happened to Dickens himself.

The difference between them was that David was made to put the responsibility on his ogre of a stepfather, while Dickens blamed his parents. He could never understand how they could see their son off to work in the blacking-factory as satisfied as if they were sending him to Cambridge. He was a child of marked abilities, eager and quick and, strange as it may seem, already ambitious to grow up 'a learned and distinguished man'. Yet, he wrote, 'I know that, but for the mercy of God, I might easily have been, for any care that was taken of me, a little robber or a little vagabond.'

'I have no idea how long it lasted', Dickens wrote. It went on for four or five months. John Dickens was left a fair-sized legacy and released, but he never thought of releasing his son from the factory. Then, at last, he had a slight quarrel with the manager, and took him away. Mrs. Dickens was for arranging for his return, while his father 'said I should go back no more, and should go to school. I do not write resentfully or angrily,' said Dickens, 'but I never afterwards forgot, I never shall forget, I never can forget, that my mother was warm for my being sent back.'

Dickens never recovered from his experience. Not even the account of his childhood as Forster printed it, gives a tenth part of what he meant to write or a hundredth of his grief and shame. Yet to understand what lies at the heart of Dickens's feeling for children, the poor, debtors, and the unloved and outcast, one should read in Forster's pages all that is left of the strange document that Dickens once designed for his autobiography. As a consequence, there developed in him side by side a stern self-reliance, a liking for sympathy, and a burning desire to help others.

He now had his wish, as he was sent to school at Wellington House Academy, a private establishment run by a Mr. Jones, 'by far the most ignorant man I have ever had the pleasure to know', and 'whose business was to make as much out of us and to put as little into us as possible'. Fellow-pupils afterwards remembered Dickens as a smart lad, 'with a more than usual flow of spirits' and no special academic attainments. They had no idea, however, that he had had a very different kind of schooling for the past two years; and, as he kept up with the rest and even carried off a Latin prize, he was probably right in telling Wilkie Collins that at school he had 'distinguished' himself 'like a brick'.

At home his father was compulsorily retired from the civil service, but allowed a pension; and he seems to have managed on this and his legacy while he taught himself shorthand and devoted himself to journalism. They had six children by now, so that by the time Charles was fifteen it was necessary for him to think of leaving school and once again going out to work.

About May 1827, therefore, he was found a position as a clerk in a solicitor's office. He 'didn't much like it', he said afterwards, as it was not much better than being an office-boy, and after eighteen months he got out. Even at that time he was ambitious, for he either persuaded his parents to support him, or utilized a small legacy that he and the other children had been left, while he set to work to qualify himself to become 'a first-rate parliamentary reporter'.

There is no doubt that he must have been influenced by the example of his uncle, John Henry Barrow, who had formerly been a reporter for *The Times*, and who had just published a novel, deserted his wife, and founded a journal recording the parliamentary debates as a rival to Hansard. Like David Copperfield, Dickens set to work to learn the Gurney system of shorthand, 'about equal in difficulty to the mastery of six languages'. In time he gained a complete command. His friend, Thomas Beard, said of him, 'there never *was* such a shorthand writer', and many years later Dickens, himself, half-seriously wrote, 'I daresay I am at this present writing . . . the best in the world'!

At first, he was confined to reporting cases in the

ecclesiastical courts of the Doctors' Commons; he then graduated to the Law Courts, including the Court of Chancery, where he may well have heard cases which were still continuing when he began writing about Jarndyce *v.* Jarndyce in *Bleak House*; and, at last, when he was only nineteen, he was admitted to Parliament as a reporter. 'I have worn my knees', he said afterwards, 'by writing on them on the old back row of the old House of Commons; and I have worn my feet by standing to write in a preposterous pen in the old House of Lords, where we used to be huddled together like so many sheep.'

All this while he was preparing himself in other ways. His father was once asked, 'Pray, Mr. Dickens, where was your son educated?' 'Why, indeed, Sir—ha! ha!—he may be said to have educated himself.' He went regularly to the theatre, studied hard to be an actor, and would have attended an audition for an engagement but for being prevented by a bad cold; as soon as he was eighteen he took out a reader's ticket for the British Museum and settled down to a course of reading; and he got to know all the ins-and-outs of London. 'I thought I knew something of the town,' said a fellow-clerk, 'but after a little talk with Dickens, I found that I knew nothing.'

Meanwhile, he had fallen in love with a girl named Maria Beadnell. She was flattered by his devotion, but did not take him seriously. Her father, who was a bank manager, had somehow learnt of John Dickens's bankruptcy, and disapproved of the young reporter as a prospective son-in-law. Dickens, himself, was desperately in love, and even twenty-five years later he was quite annoyed when his friend Forster refused to take seriously what he wrote about it:

> I don't quite apprehend what you mean by my over-rating the strength of the feeling. . . . If you mean of my own feeling, and will only think what the desperate nature of my intensity is . . . that it excluded every other idea from my mind for four years . . . and that I went at it with a determination to overcome all the difficulties, which fairly lifted me up . . . and floated me away over a hundred men's heads: then you are wrong, because nothing can exaggerate that.

She was the Dora of his *David Copperfield*. 'And just as I can never open that book, as I open any other book', he went on, he could never see her again even so many years later, 'without going wandering away over the ashes of all that youth and hope in the wildest manner'. On her side the romance fizzled out; on Dickens's, he made a determined effort to see that it was forcibly extinguished and turned his back on the affair. He went at his work harder than ever, but he afterwards wrote to her, when they were both middle-aged, that the effort had left him 'with a habit of suppression which now belongs to me . . . which makes me chary of showing my affection even to my children'.

As a reporter he was engaged on the *True Sun* and his uncle's *Mirror of Parliament* and then, in 1834, on the *Morning Chronicle*. His editor was James Black, a bluff Scot, who soon became Dickens's 'first hearty out-and-out appreciator'. In return, Dickens evidently respected Black, a man of marked independence of mind, and 'the first journalist', according to Mill, to carry 'criticism and the spirit of reform into English institutions'. For the time being Dickens simply continued his work as a reporter, in Parliament when it was in session, and in the country when it was not. 'I have pursued the calling', he once said, 'under circumstances of which

. . . my modern successors can form no adequate conception. I have often transcribed for the printer . . . writing on the palm of my hand, by the light of a dark lantern, in a post chaise and four, galloping through wild country.'

Already, however, he had begun writing original pieces, and his first published work, which was a little sketch entitled 'A Dinner at Poplar Walk', was printed in the old *Monthly Magazine* in December 1833. Dickens bought in the Strand a copy of the number in which it appeared, and hurriedly turned into Westminster Hall to read it, 'my eyes so dimmed with pride and joy that they could not bear the street, and were not fit to be seen'. He contributed eight more sketches to the *Monthly*, in which they appeared without payment, including the first to be signed with his pseudonym of 'Boz'. This was taken from a facetious pronunciation of the name 'Moses' (from the character in *The Vicar of Wakefield*)—altered to 'Boses', and then shortened—which had been given to Dickens's youngest brother Augustus.

His talent for descriptive writing was soon recognized by his new employers, and when they launched an *Evening Chronicle*, early in 1835, Dickens was invited to contribute a series of 'Sketches of London'. The editor of the evening paper was George Hogarth, a man of some cultivation, journalist, former Writer to the Signet and friend of Sir Walter Scott. Dickens was invited to his home, where he met his eldest daughter, Catherine, a pretty pink-and-white girl, with whom he soon fell in love—and she with him. The agonies of the Beadnell period were over: Dickens took the dominant role, lectured her on her behaviour, and insisted that she leave him time for his 'pursuits and labours' which were all undertaken with a view to her future happiness.

They were genuinely in love, but there was a new reserve about Dickens which shows through all the jokes and endearments in his letters.

His writing and reporting certainly took up much of his time, for by August he had contributed twenty sketches to the *Chronicle* and was ready to start on a series in another magazine and to listen to a publisher's proposal that they should be collected. Dickens had been introduced to John Macrone by William Harrison Ainsworth, and he readily accepted the young publisher's offer of £150 for a volume to be illustrated by George Cruikshank. He set to work to write extra sketches, hoping that it would be out by Christmas, but it was not published until 6 February 1836, the day before its author's twenty-fourth birthday.

The new *Sketches by Boz* were something remarkable for their time, and were received with great enthusiasm. They were new to the experience of his readers, and in spite of their origins and all that is often written about the effect of Dickens's early training as a journalist, it is quite wrong to think of Dickens as really owing anything to it. They were literary sketches, and apart from these and some reviewing his other work for his newspaper had been as a mere reporter of speeches. Descriptive journalism hardly existed at the time, and where it did it was swaddled in leader-writers' clichés. These were written with freshness of phrase and quickness of fancy. There is a sameness about them when they are read as a book, but they earned Dickens for the first time the recognition that he was 'inimitable' and unsurpassed in his quickness of perception.

Today, their interest is chiefly in the way in which they foreshadow the works to come; yet they are much more detached than the novels. At the time, they were praised for their sharpness of observation, 'point and shrewdness'. Trollope was later to protest that none knew better than 'Mr. Sentiment', or Dickens, that 'the artist who paints for the million must use glaring colours'; but the *Sketches* are in graphic black-and-white.

His contemporaries recognized that in his aspiration 'to present little pictures of life and manners as they really are' (*Preface*), he was justified. The *Metropolitan Magazine* praised their 'startling fidelity'. '"Boz"', said another reviewer, 'is a kind of Boswell to society.' *Sketches by Boz*, in both the first and the second series, published later the same year, was a work which might have stood alone, but which—skipping over his next book—was to lead directly to the world of *Oliver Twist*.

Chapter Two

PICKWICK PAPERS AND AFTER

It is clear that Dickens already meant to be much more than a journalist, just as he had been determined to be more than a reporter. He was proud to be an author, and, early in February, just a week after the publication of the *Sketches*, he had a further opportunity. There was something auspicious about it from the start. When, one morning, Dickens answered the door to let in William Hall (then partner in the youthful firm of Chapman and Hall, the publishers) he recognized the man who had sold to him, over the counter, the copy of the *Monthly Magazine* which had contained his first published piece of writing.

Edward Chapman and William Hall were anxious to publish a humorous account of a sporting club, to accompany a series of sketches by a well-known sporting illustrator, Robert Seymour. They had been looking round for someone to write it, wanting a sort of Surtees on the cheap. They had proposed it to a minor writer, Charles Whitehead, and let him down; and then, according to Dickens, attracted by what they remembered of the 'Sketches' in the *Chronicle*, they decided to call on their author. They were young men of ideas, and they made the surprising proposal that the work should be brought out in shilling numbers, 'then only known to me', wrote Dickens, 'or, I believe to anyone else, by a dim recollection of certain interminable novels in that form, which used to be carried around the country by pedlars'.

Dickens saw his chance—mainly a financial one as it seemed to him at the time—and there was a brisk discussion about the sort of work it was to be. A point that Dickens wanted to make clear was that while he would be happy to have Seymour as an illustrator, he would not think of merely producing a text for Seymour's sketches. Nor did he wish to be confined to the adventures of a group of sportsmen in the country, but wanted to take 'his own way with a freer range of English scenes and people'; on the other hand he would be quite happy to have the work published serially, in monthly numbers of twenty-four pages (later thirty-two) at a time. There was never a written contract. They shook hands on the agreement; confirmed it after consultation with Chapman and Seymour; and that was that. 'My views being deferred to,' Dickens said later, 'I thought of Mr. Pickwick, and wrote the first number.'

Yet, for the time being, it was easier said than done. When the agreement was confirmed, the publishers offered Dickens fourteen pounds a month, and he at once wrote to Catherine to say, 'The work will be no joke, but the emolument is too tempting to resist.' His letters to her report progress frequently, for now that their marriage was so near both of them were interested in his success. About a fortnight later he wrote, 'I have at this moment got Pickwick, and his friends, on the Rochester coach, and they are going on swimmingly, in company with a very different character from any I have yet described [Alfred Jingle], who I flatter myself will make a decided hit.' He spent his days in reporting, and his nights in writing. He had to tell her, 'Pickwick must be attended to', and again, 'The sheets are a weary length—I had no idea there was so much in them.' Still, by 15 March he had managed to complete two numbers in time for the first to be published at the end of the month; and on 5 April he and Catherine were quietly married at a church in Chelsea. Years later, his brother-in-law wrote, 'As for the wedding, even Boswell could have had nothing to say—unless he had invented it.' There were few but relatives present. Catherine was described as 'a bright, pleasant bride, dressed in the simplest and neatest manner', and everyone seemed very happy. Having given up the idea of following the Pickwickians to Rochester, they spent a week's honeymoon at a cottage in Chalk, near Gravesend, and then returned to London.

Pickwick, meanwhile, was in difficulties. It sold only about four hundred copies, it had few notices, and James Grant (of the *Monthly Magazine*) even called it a 'signal failure'. To crown everything, after a minor difference with Dickens and the publishers, Robert Seymour retired to the summer-house at the bottom of his garden and shot himself. Fortunately, Chapman and Hall decided to continue, and Dickens interviewed candidates for the post of illustrator, turning down both John Leech and Thackeray. The publishers took on quite a successful artist, and then abruptly switched their choice to Hablot K. Browne ('Phiz'). With the exception of *Oliver Twist*, which Cruikshank undertook, Browne henceforward remained Dickens's chief illustrator until after *Little Dorrit*.

Success came after only a few months, when the sales began to rise with the fourth number. By the fifth it was a triumph. The credit is often given to Sam Weller, but in fact he was introduced only after the book was already beginning to catch on. Mr. Jingle, the Fat Boy and Mr. Wardle, the Ball at Bath, the military review, Dingley Dell and the cricket-match with the Muggletonians

—not to mention the Pickwickians themselves—had all contributed to its eventual popularity. *John Bull* thought it 'irresistibly good', and Captain Marryat's magazine, *The Metropolitan*, reviewed the fifth number, saying, '"Boz" marches on triumphantly, and has completely taken possession of our ear, and the hearts, too, of his countrymen.' The chorus of praise began to swell.

When it reached the tenth number, Dickens issued an 'Address' explaining that he meant to keep to his original plan of only another ten numbers, because if it were prolonged it might suffer as 'a complete work'. He subsequently followed the same scheme when publishing almost all the serials that appeared in monthly parts. By this time everyone was reading *Pickwick*, and the sales were shooting up to forty thousand. As it was drawing to a close, in October 1837, even the conservative *Quarterly* was forced to pay tribute: 'In less than six months from the appearance of the first number', it said, 'the whole reading public was talking about it . . . a new and decidedly original genius has sprung up'; and it declared that Dickens had taken his place as the first of all English comic writers. 'Judges on the bench and boys in the street,' said Forster, 'gravity and folly, the young and the old, those who are entering life and those who are quitting it' were all found to be reading *Pickwick*.

'Phiz' sketched its hero, crowned king, on a throne resting on the works of Fielding, Smollett and Sterne. Miss Mitford sent a letter to Elizabeth Barrett saying that she held Dickens to be 'the next great benefactor of the age to Sir Walter Scott'; and Dickens, himself, wrote to Chapman and Hall, 'if I were to live a hundred years, and write three novels in each, I should never be so proud of any of them, as I am of Pickwick, feeling as I do, that it has made its own way, and hoping . . . that long after my hand is withered as the pens it held, Pickwick will be found on many a dusty shelf.' Though not everyone welcomed his success, *Pickwick* was recognized as literature and its author took his place among the greatest English novelists.

Yet it is when one comes to consider *Pickwick* as a novel that the trouble arises. Professor Sylvère Monod has said that it is not *un véritable roman* in the sense in which the word is used today, and G. K. Chesterton declared that 'it is not a novel at all'. Even Forster described it as 'a series of sketches'. Other writers have been content to regard it as an entertainment, or a monstrous kind of periodical; while critics who exult about the place of *Tristram Shandy* in 'the history of the novel' have boggled over the *Pickwick Papers*.

All this is questionable. It is quite as much a 'novel' as most works written in the twentieth century which have exploited all the looseness and freedom of fiction, and it is even more of a novel than many earlier works, also written in the tradition of *Don Quixote* or *Gil Blas*. To judge it by limitations which were not formulated until halfway through the nineteenth century, and which still cannot be applied to most novelists, living or dead, is to nullify one's criticism completely.

Of course the real merits of *Pickwick* have little to do with whether or not one wishes to call it a *novel*. Its bright comedy, its good humour and its raciness of style, are something apart from its form. But these qualities themselves have often been undervalued, just because critics have felt that *Pickwick* was in a class by itself. For as well as the tendency to regard it as outside the range of the novel, there is the feeling that it has little connection with Dickens's more serious work, and is even necessarily inferior. In writing of *Pickwick* in his essay, 'Dickens: The Two Scrooges', Edmund Wilson, for instance, devotes most of his time to the lamentable interpolated stories, and dismisses the humour as 'the aspect . . . that is best known'. Yet, as well as coming at the end of the eighteenth-century tradition, *Pickwick* deserves to be considered seriously as Dickens's first novel.

Of course, this is not to say that the book was not largely improvised, but that improvisation itself may be an art, and that if it produces something permanent it is creative. The form of *Pickwick* was not carpentered but grew. It took shape like a genie from a bottle. It may be clumsy and disjointed, but it has movement, and once it gets under way a controlling mind behind it of immense persuasiveness and definite character. It has direction rather than form, a story rather than a unified plot, and its success is not only due to the impression of abundance it gives, but to a definite sense of completeness.

On the other hand, it has been said that in writing his preface Dickens himself disclaimed the title of 'novelist'. It is true enough that, when he had finished the book, he wrote, 'if it be objected to the Pickwick Papers, that they are a mere series of adventures . . . the same objection has been made to some of the greatest novelists in the English language'—and then, in his proofs, deliberately changed *novelists* to *writers*. This has been thought significant. But before publication he changed the words back again; and if his temporary preference for being styled a writer suggests anything, it may well be that above and beyond being considered as a mere writer of novels, Dickens was even then prepared to court comparison with Shakespeare.

Pickwick, of course, has a plot; or, perhaps, it should be said, that a good one can be carved out of it. Professor Monod has suggested that a better *novel* than we have at present could be made out of *The Case of Bardell* v. *Pickwick* (chapters xii–xlvii); and Quiller-Couch even declared that though the book started without one, the plot 'once found' was admirable. 'What better art', he asks, than its double 'reversal of fortune', or *peripeteia*, 'the charitable turn of Pickwick on Jingle in the debtor's prison, and the incarceration and release of Mrs. Bardell? Consider the first. Insensibly, without premonition of ours, and I dare to say of no long prepared purpose in the author, the story finds a climax:

> "Come here, Sir", said Mr. Pickwick, trying to look stern, with four large tears running down his waistcoat. "Take that, Sir."
>
> 'Take what? In the ordinary acceptation of such language, it should have been a blow. As the world runs it ought to have been a sound, hearty cuff; for Mr. Pickwick had been duped, deceived, and wronged by the destitute outcast who was now in his power. Must we tell the truth? It was something from Mr. Pickwick's waistcoat pocket, which chinked as it was given into Job's hand. . . .'

Yet this was all improvised. This, and the second 'reversal of fortune', when Mrs. Bardell, the prosecutrix, 'herself gets cast into prison by Dodson and Fogg whose tool she has been, and there, confronted by her victim and theirs, finds herself (O wonder!) pardoned . . . all this grew . . . with the story's growth, and grew out of fierce, rapid improvisation.'

No doubt there were tremendous disadvantages in writing the story as a serial, but Dickens soon began to see that they were by no means insuperable. At first, it seemed necessary, he said, 'that every number should be, to a certain extent, complete in itself'; and though it is possible to point out some exceptions, this is generally true. Indeed, even in Dickens's later novels, or those of Wilkie Collins who learnt from him, it is completely wrong to suppose that serialization meant suspense at the end of each number. If there was a climax it usually came in the middle of each part, and the plot ranged on like a viaduct, rather than spanning the whole novel like a single arch.

Mr. Pickwick's character changes and deepens throughout the story, and so does the whole purpose of the book. The two go together. Hood admitted to Dickens that when he first read extracts from the novel, he thought it just a succession of low-life adventures; but when he read it a second time, he saw its originality and recognized in it 'the goodness of Pickwickedness'. Pickwick may be absurdly innocent, and, as Sam says, 'may rayther want somebody to look after you', but though he is often tricked, he is never defeated. He is soft-hearted, but he is never soft. He stands up to blustering magistrate Mr. Nupkins, he is undeterred by prison-life, and at their last interview he even succeeds in piercing the armour-plated hide of Dodson and Fogg. To Jingle he is 'Old Fireworks', and at times he can go off with a bang.

But, above all, Pickwick is benevolent: not simply because it is his 'humour' or his habit, but on principle. In saying that he hoped his book might induce his readers 'to look on the lighter and more kindly side of life' (*Preface*), Dickens was expressing something that ends up as the heart of the book. Even so, he was already artist enough to prevent it from cloying, by balancing it with the comical and macabre comments of the two Wellers. They are both full of stories 'as 'ud penetrate your benevolent heart, and come out on the other side'; and yet, whatever they think of life, they live it as something to be enjoyed,

This, after all, is the secret of the book's popularity and its success: amid everything else that is to be said, one must never forget the breadth and brilliance of its comedy. It is light-hearted, good-humoured, and irreverent. From the first it has a flow of spirits that 'runs on like a new barrow with the wheel greased'. Like Jingle, it has 'an indescribable air of jaunty impudence and perfect self-possession'. From Mr. Pickwick's conversation with the cab-driver, when he sets out on his travels:

> 'How old is that horse, my friend?' enquired Mr. Pickwick, rubbing his nose with the shilling he had reserved for the fare.
>
> 'Forty-two,' replied the driver, eyeing him askant. . . .

—from the outset to his amiable farewell before retiring, it is perpetually entertaining.

It says much for both Dickens and his age that an ambitious young man, determined to make his way in the world, and driven by what often seems an unyielding will, should have chosen a dear old boy like Pickwick for his hero. The people of the time took Pickwick to their hearts; even Dickens was converted, since he had begun by making him rather an old fool. There is neither malice nor envy in *Pickwick*; it has some of the elements of the folk-tale; it is content with old age and old ways as well as with old jokes.

These abound. Old jokes, which are still flourishing on the B.B.C., are part of *Pickwick*. It even smacks rather of scriptwriters' humour, though it has such comparative life and economy of expression that we seldom stop to think of it. One of the main ideas behind Pickwick is that although he is a respectable old gentleman of unsurpassable innocence, he is always getting into the most appalling scrapes with the opposite sex. He finds himself in the wrong bedroom, with a lady, in an inn; he is caught climbing in to a girls' boarding school; and his friends find him embracing his landlady, which leads to the celebrated case for breach of promise. Winkle, too, is publicly accused of an affair with Mrs. Pott, and finds himself shut out of his lodgings, in the middle of the night, in his nightshirt, and taking refuge with another married lady in the confined space of a sedan chair. Sam Weller's courtship of Mary is more straightforward; but even thirty years later it was enough to rouse *The Spectator* to an outrageous protest at Mr. Dickens's 'vulgar good humour', and his 'strong disposition to approve the distribution of punch . . . and kiss pretty women behind doors', as something 'not really English, and tending to modify English family feeling'!

Dickens's humour, at this time, was his greatest quality; but it is extremely hard to criticize and fatal to analyse. Almost all critiques of the novel avoid foundering on Comedy and Humour by steering clear of them; studies of any comic writings end in long series of quotations. Some of the elements of Dickens's humour lie in his ridicule of all he disliked and feared—cruelty, pomposity, self-deception, chicanery, sanctimonious hypocrisy, and the use of forms, institutions and all kinds of restraints to suppress whatever seems free and natural. He exults in anyone's power to rise above his circumstances, even through the extraordinary innocence and gullibility of Pickwick as well as the sharpness of Sam Weller. The dramatic instinct of his comic characters, as Douglas Bush says, is 'a sort of comic existentialism'.

He had the ability, himself, to see things in a new light, and he constantly uses contrast, irony, and a light and airy sarcasm to illuminate life. Above all, he makes us strongly concerned for his characters, so that we care about what happens to them, like and dislike them, and can share in their laughter and good-humour; for Dickens had already begun as the representative (as he was to write in the *Uncommercial Traveller*) of 'the great house of Human Interest Brothers'.

Even in *Pickwick* his humour was concerned with something more than appearances. However farcical his picture of life might be, even his earliest admirers, such as Miss Mitford, could feel that it was not only 'graphic' and 'individual' but 'true'. This truth, both of observation of life and insight into it, is even harder to show, since it may lead to taking something that is true within the novel, established only within its own world in which Dickens has an unrivalled power of command over his readers, and of proclaiming it as universally true. Yet the qualities of the characters that people this world, their generosity, liveliness, wit, loyalty, affections and ability to share and communicate their delight in life, remain quite as universal, as real and at least as important as those expressed within the later novels. Indeed, in many instances they are the same. No doubt it is wrong to praise Dickens's comic situations chiefly because they are partly serious. Even so, Sam Weller's anecdote of the 'dirty-faced' prisoner 'in the brown coat' who was so frightened of being locked out of prison by the turnkey that he cannot enjoy even a limited freedom, implies much that was to be explicit in *Little Dorrit*. Yet the general tone of *Pickwick* is different from what was to come. It is not yet implied that the condition of the dirty-faced prisoner may be the general human condition: we are to laugh at it (chapter xli). The other prisoners who lounge about the racket-ground like 'beasts in a menagerie' are dispirited because they are denied the freedom and life they could find outside. Pickwick consents to his release from obstinate isolation because he is shown how he can help the newly-wed Bella and Winkle; and, as they leave the Fleet, Sam calls out to his master:

> 'Well, Sam,' replied Mr. Pickwick, thrusting his head out of the window.
>
> 'I wish them horses had been three months and better in the Fleet, Sir.'
>
> 'Why, Sam?' inquired Mr. Pickwick.
>
> 'Vy, Sir,' exclaimed Mr. Weller, rubbing his hands, 'how they would go if they had been!'

There is little, therefore, that need be said about the unfortunate interpolated stories. 'Some men', said Dickens, 'like bats or owls have better eyes for the darkness than the light.' These are almost his last words in *Pickwick* and a fair comment on critics who devote too much time to them. This is not to say that they do not indicate that even in the brightest time of his youth, Dickens sometimes felt drawn towards the shadows, when he was possibly still troubled by suppressed fears and feelings of resentment. But they tell nothing that we do not know otherwise, and that is not thrown up and magnified more largely by the greater works to come.

Pickwick is a book that we can turn back to again and again. It has a largeness about it. In the words of the earlier critics of Shakespeare, it deals with Nature. 'He did not need the spectacles of books,' wrote Dryden, 'he looked inwards.' Dickens gives a picture of manners and life. His swift changes from grave to gay can be justified by Dr. Johnson's verdict on Shakespeare's intermingling of comic and tragic scenes; they, too, express the real state of 'the course of the world, in which the loss of one is the gain of another; in which, at the same time, the reveller is hasting to his wine, and the mourner burying his friend; in which the malignity of one is sometimes defeated by the frolick of another; and many mischiefs and many benefits are done and hindered without design.'

Success was now assured for Dickens. He was accepted into literary society, took the chair at authors' club dinners, and was invited to speak in public. He began by making the kind of friends and acquaintances he was to keep to afterwards, Talfourd the lawyer, Macready the actor, Harley the comedian, Ainsworth and Samuel Lover the novelists, Maclise the artist, and Leigh Hunt the man of letters. A little later he was taken up by the smart set at Holland House, where he met Bulwer Lytton, Sydney Smith and Walter Savage Landor, and then among others the dandy Count D'Orsay, the banker-poet Samuel Rogers, and Carlyle. The latter was amused to see that young 'Boz' was unabashed, and not prepared to truckle to rank: 'A fine little fellow, Boz, I think, clear blue intelligent eyes . . . large, protrusive, rather loose mouth, a face of the most extreme *mobility*, which he shuttles about. . . . A quiet, shrewd-looking little fellow, who seems to guess pretty well what he is and what others are.'

Mrs. Dickens played a minor part in entertaining and in being entertained, but she was content to accept that it was her husband that everyone wanted to see. At this time they were quietly happy. Her younger sister

Mary, who was frequently to stay with them, writes to a Scottish cousin in the month after the marriage:

> . . . I have just returned home from spending a most delightfully happy month with dearest Catherine in her own house! I only wish you could see her in it . . . she makes a most capital housekeeper and is as happy as the day is long—I think they are more devoted than ever since their marriage if that be possible—I am sure you [may] be delighted with him if you knew him he is such a nice creature and so clever. He is courted and made up to by all literary Gentlemen, and has more to do in that way than he can well manage.

They had a son, Charles Culliford Boz Dickens, born on 6 January 1837, and a daughter, Mary Dickens, on 6 March 1838. There was another daughter, 'Katey', in October 1839, and eventually ten children over a total of fifteen years. A few months after the birth of the first child they had moved to a small house, 48 Doughty Street, where they remained until December 1839, when they removed to a larger establishment, 1 Devonshire Terrace, near Regent's Park.

Dickens's scope as a writer was now broadening out before him, and in this lay opportunities for trouble. He wanted success, and was ready to strive for it; he wanted to set up a home and family, and establish himself; and he was willing to dedicate himself to writing. Yet he had started on his career, as he realized later, 'without influence, without money, without companions, introducer or adviser'; and although these all came soon enough, he began by making mistakes.

He was doing too much. He did not give up his work on the *Morning Chronicle* until November 1836, and meanwhile he had written a scorching pamphlet on the Sunday observance question, called *Sunday Under Three Heads*; contracted to write a children's book to be ready by Christmas (it never appears to have been started); and had two productions put on at the St. James's Theatre, *The Strange Gentleman* in September, and *The Village Coquettes* not long after. For a bare two hundred pounds he had contracted, in May, to write a three-volume novel for Macrone, which he hoped to have ready by the end of the year; and he set to work to collect, write and prepare for press another volume of *Sketches by Boz* which was actually published in December. No wonder that he burst out to Cruikshank, who was illustrating the *Sketches*, 'I cannot do more than one pair of hands and a solitary head can execute, and really am so hard pressed just now that I must have breathing time.'

Even so, in August, having as he supposed induced Macrone to release him from his agreement about the novel, he had undertaken to write one for the more powerful Richard Bentley, and promised him the next one after that. A short time after he also undertook to become editor of a magazine that Bentley was to bring out early in the new year. For this he was to be paid over forty pounds a month, on the understanding that he contributed sixteen pages to every number himself. *Bentley's Miscellany*, as the new periodical was called, began in January 1837, and in February included the first instalment of Dickens's new serial, *Oliver Twist*. He remained in charge for just over two years, contributing powerfully to the magazine's success, though his career as editor was marred by a series of disputes with Bentley.

A period now began in which Dickens had to fight to secure his independence from his publishers. It would be impossible to trace the exact course of his relations with them within the limits of this book, nor would it be particularly useful to do so. The details of his negotiations, and the contents of the eight different agreements he made with Bentley over four years, do not matter. Yet it is important to understand their general trend, why their disputes were so fierce, and what were Dickens's reasons for acting as he did.

His relations with Chapman and Hall had been perfectly amicable. It has already been noted that there was no written contract for *Pickwick*—a fair indication of the haphazard way in which authors and publishers still dealt with each other. The publishers were said to have made anything from fourteen to twenty thousand pounds out of *Pickwick* in the first two or three years; and, as the idea of the book and the financial risk had been theirs, the share of £2,500 they allotted Dickens was not ungenerous.

But, before realizing that his work was worth so much, or even before he understood that a three-volume novel could not be tossed off in as many months, Dickens had foolishly contracted to write several works for no more than the wages of a clerk. If Bentley had had his way he would have kept him to this—and before he was forty he would have been a worn-out hack. Dickens, on the other hand, had a growing family to support, and saw no good reason why he should spend several years working almost entirely for the benefit of his publisher. He decided, therefore, that he must negotiate his way to independence, buy back his copyrights, and, if necessary, break through his contracts.

If Bentley had been more generous or far-sighted he might easily have retained Dickens—but though a good publisher in many ways, he had a fatal inability to keep his best authors. Dickens, Hood, Ainsworth, Marryat, and Charles Reade all parted from him in exasperation. In those days, authors and publishers (or *booksellers*, as they were called) openly regarded each other as enemies. There was no royalty system, and copyrights were usually sold for cash or a promise to pay. It was not long since Thomas Campbell, the poet, had excused Napoleon's tyranny, amid general applause at a public dinner, on the sole grounds that he had once 'shot a bookseller'! Novelists had no rights over dramatization of their work, no protection from international piracy, and resented the fact that publishers usually held the whip hand. In calling Bentley 'a hound', 'a Brigand', and a 'dog', as he did in his letters, Dickens was only slightly heightening the normal idiom then current among writers.

Thomas Hood, for example, resented the way in which publishers treated Literature as a commodity. Thackeray sneered at them for not being 'gentlemen'. Dickens was exceptional only in realizing that authors were largely to blame for their own misfortunes, and in being determined to fight back. He re-bought *Sketches by Boz* from Macrone for over £2,000, and after placing negotiations in the hands of his lawyers, he eventually struggled free from Bentley. As he later admitted to his solicitor:

> The Oliver agreement was my own making, and so was Pickwick. It was a consequence of the astonishing rapidity of my success and the steady rise of my fame that the enormous profits of these books should flow into other hands than mine. It has always been so (I speak from the knowledge of the lives of eminent and successful writers) and I cannot reasonably hope to be exempt from the curse which has fallen on all Professors of Literature.

He went on to say that although he knew that he could obtain a substantial advance from another firm of publishers, he would not touch it on principle: 'I do not take it, and will not; simply because I wish to free myself by my own exertions, and not by the assistance of "The Trade".'

In extricating himself from these difficulties, he owed much to a friendship he had made with a forceful young critic, John Forster. He was later to be remembered chiefly as Dickens's biographer. At this time, although only about the same age as Dickens, he was already the influential literary and dramatic editor of a weekly periodical, *The Examiner*. He had an energetic character, and a bluff good-nature. Coming from Newcastle and speaking with a Northumbrian burr, he sometimes appeared to his London friends as 'a most unmanageable wild man'. Yet he was prized as an adviser by men whose sensibilities he often jarred on. Tennyson, Browning, and Landor all owed a great deal to him. Bulwer Lytton said of him, 'there is no safer adviser about literary work . . . no more refined critic'. Above all, he was useful to his friends who were writers because, as well as being a thoroughly reliable judge of literature, his shrewd and wary intellect, his clarity of mind, and his aggressive pertinacity made him the ideal representative for an author who was having trouble with his publisher.

He was introduced to Dickens by Ainsworth on Christmas Day 1836. They renewed their acquaintance in April, and in the months that followed they soon became fast friends. Forster first acted for Dickens in negotiations with Macrone, and then represented him in his dealings with Bentley. As well as this, from about the fifteenth number of *Pickwick* there was nothing Dickens published that Forster did not first see and advise on, in either proof or manuscript. Their partnership was not exempt from the sort of embarrassing and hasty outbursts that troubled all Forster's literary friendships; but they always managed to get over them, and they had far more in common than is usually realized. Forster was no bear-leading Boswell; it was a true friendship for well over twenty years, however strained or weakened it may have become in Dickens's last decade.

In January 1839, Dickens wrote to him: 'Believe me . . . I see the value of you and appreciate the sterling openness and honesty of your heart, more and more (if that be possible) as I behold it in contrast with the hearts of other men.' Forster is often accused of exaggerating the importance of their friendship in his biography. This is one of the passages that he suppressed.

Chapter Three

OLIVER TWIST

THE first number of *Bentley's Miscellany* was published in January 1837, and the second number contained the first instalment of *Oliver Twist*. Little is certainly known of how Dickens first thought of it; it is likely that it goes back to the time of his first published sketches. He was probably correct in referring to his 'long-considered intentions and plans' for it. None the less, it was written over a long period for so short a novel (from December 1836 to September 1838), when he was almost submerged by other work and editorial duties that monthly threatened to drive him back 'into a sea of manuscripts'. Yet he enjoyed writing it. Even on holiday, he said, he felt 'great difficulty in keeping my hands off Fagin and the rest of them in the evenings'; and, as it drew to a close, he fell on the story 'tooth and nail'.

It appeared in rather different circumstances from his other novels, since Dickens raced ahead and completed it for publication in three volumes in November 1838, while the serialization continued in the *Miscellany* until the following March. Towards the end he worked faster than he ever attempted afterwards, and found that the story came more easily than his subsequent works. In after years, he was extremely particular about being undisturbed while he was writing; but, while he was working on *Oliver*, his brother-in-law tells that he once came into the sitting-room, and joined in the conversation, 'the feather of his pen still moving rapidly from side to side. . . . It was interesting to watch . . . the mind and muscles working (or, if you please, *playing*) in company, as new thoughts were being dropped upon the paper. And to note the working brow, the set of mouth, with the tongue tightly pressed against the closed lips, as was his habit.'

Yet there is no doubt that the novel had a serious purpose which Forster partly brings out. After the hilarity of *Pickwick*, he explains, Dickens felt that a change had become 'necessary for his own satisfaction'. He had a need to try something new, something more serious than before, and something that might even have a practical effect. He was delighted when his friend mentioned this in a review. But Forster hints at something more. He seems to say, in a somewhat cryptic series of remarks, that the interest aroused by the chapters about Fagin and his gang is due to human sympathies that everyone shares, and that some of the surprise and alarm they caused on their first appearance was because, in much darker scenes of life, readers recognized men and women like themselves. More precisely, he says that the novel showed that 'the result of being above the necessity of depending on other people's opinions, and that of being below it, are pretty much the same', and that 'it would startle both high and low to be conscious of the whole that is implied in this close approximation'. He then shies away from the subject, remarking that it was unnecessary for 'common enjoyment', and that he had better leave Fagin 'in his school of practical ethics', undisturbed. Yet this is precisely the point where criticism of the novel should begin.

Almost everyone who has written about *Oliver Twist* has realized that the most interesting parts of it are those about the criminal underworld. It is not simply that Fagin and Sikes are more exciting than Dr. Losberne and Mr. Brownlow, but that they are described more intelligently. More than this, even, Fagin and his gang are not merely more vigorous and amusing, but they are treated with greater sympathy. This is obviously true of Nancy: Dickens wrote, 'I hope to do great things . . . if I can only work out the idea I have formed of her.' The point about Nancy is that she never had a chance, and that though she might have been different it has become too late. Almost the same point is made by the treatment of the Artful Dodger and Charley Bates, which so moved Dickens's friend Serjeant Talfourd that, as the last chapters were being written, he 'pleaded as earnestly' on their behalf 'in mitigation of judgement as ever at the bar for any client he most respected'. In a sense, as Swinburne declared, even Fagin and Sikes were 'victims of circumstances'; and, as Humphry House said, as Dickens describes them 'they are never despised, though what they do is despicable'.

How far this is consciously brought out in the novel may be open to question. It is interesting that Forster clearly says that Dickens and his friends were well aware of it. Certainly it was to some extent intentional. Indeed, the whole tendency of interest in the 'Newgate novels' of this time (of which *Oliver Twist* was one) was to link fictional crime with radical views of society. It is clear that it was part of Dickens's purpose, for example, to show that the Law was utterly contemptible. Blathers and Duff, the Bow-street runners, are a pair of dunderheads; we know from Mr. Bumble that 'the law is a ass'; and the sketch of the police-magistrate, Mr. Fang, shows it in all its brutality and stupidity. That Fang was drawn from a real magistrate, Mr. Laing, is irrelevant. He was not introduced because Dickens wanted to expose an individual, but because (as he said when discreetly arranging with a friend for admission to Laing's court) the story required a harsh and insolent magistrate, and he preferred to sketch from life. It has fairly been argued that when Dickens described the Artful Dodger's last fling, when he is committed for trial, he was not merely making fun of the Law, but an ironical attack on its very rough justice. From the opening of the novel in the workhouse all institutions are exposed as contemptible; and the chief reason for this seems to be because they are shown to be there merely to keep the lower classes from bothering those above them.

This was not new. From the time of Bulwer Lytton's *Paul Clifford* (1830), in which the hero attacks the Law from the dock as the destructive instrument of the rich, some novelists had expressed their revolt. What is remarkable is that a man as passionate as Dickens should make his tale more than an outcry against society, and the powerful expression of a nightmare sense of evil, and of life's horror, disappointment, mystery and hope. For Dickens's 'main feat' in the novel, writes John Bayley, which is 'surely unique', is that he succeeds in 'combining the genre of Gothic nightmare with that of social denunciation, so that each enhances the other'.

In doing so he had to overcome a central inconsistency in the novel. Dickens's purpose was undoubtedly partly to show that criminals were made not born, and that they took to crime because they knew nothing better. Yet Oliver, himself, brought up on a baby-farm and in a workhouse, is naturally good; he takes no harm from his associates, and he succeeds in spite of the absence of opportunity. He is not even used as a bridge between the underworld and the comfortable surroundings at Chertsey. He is a pawn, who never takes a full part, who is sometimes on the black squares and sometimes on the white. As it happens, however, this seems to matter less than one might at first expect.

In a passage later dropped from his *Preface* Dickens explained that 'in little Oliver' he 'wished to show . . . the principle of Good surviving through every adverse circumstance and triumphing at last'. Oliver is intentionally generalized so that we care little about him as a person. Dickens knew how to turn this sort of convention to account. This absence of individuality, as Arnold Kettle explains (*An Introduction to the English Novel*, I, 1951), only heightens the way in which we feel the book to be less a mere *Parish Boy's Progress*, and more of an allegory—as the echo of Bunyan in the sub-title implies: 'In the famous scene when Oliver asks for more it is not the precise sense of Oliver's feelings and reactions that grips us. . . . We care, not because it is Oliver, . . . but because every starved orphan in the world, and indeed everyone who is poor and oppressed and hungry is involved.'

At the heart of the book is the contrast between two worlds; and it is this which gives it some of its strange power. The criminal underworld seems dangerous. By the end a whole mob has to rouse itself against Sikes with passion and fury. Fagin is described as having fangs like a rat, and crawling forth at night like a 'loathsome reptile . . . in search of some rich offal for a meal'. Dickens certainly meant that Sikes and Fagin were menacing and corrupt, that they were infesting and undermining society, and that the upper classes were right to have the feeling of insecurity.

Yet they are not just representative of a criminal

class, but of how evil mankind may become. G. K. Chesterton felt that Cruikshank's illustration of Fagin and 'the foul-faced Monks', staring through an open window at Oliver asleep, seemed to give him the sense 'of the thieves, as a kind of army of devils compassing earth and sky crying for Oliver's soul and besieging the house in which he is barred for safety'. For their whole purpose is not merely to capture him but to corrupt him. The sensation that the book gives Graham Greene is even one of despair: 'it has the eternal and alluring taint of the Manichee, with its simple and terrible explanation of our plight, how the world was made by Satan and not by God'.

No doubt there is a case for reading it as one of Dickens's 'dark' novels, as if it were a terrifying nightmare in which Oliver searches for his own identity and for hope and purpose in life, and yet one in which all the most forceful scenes are of guilt, loneliness, terror and betrayal. For Oliver is born into a world in which survival is exceptional; antagonism, pain and violence are common; death is ever at hand; life is meaningless and overpowering. This black confusion reaches out towards Oliver even when he seems secure once again with Mr. Brownlow; the forces of evil appear to be as powerful as those of good, only chance defeats them, and they will be renewed as long as conditions that breed them remain unchanged. Even when the happiness of a loving family has just been restored to Oliver, he still learns that 'it is a world of disappointment' for 'poor Dick' (the childhood friend whom he had hoped to help) 'was dead!' And there is the horror of his visit to Newgate, and 'the Jew's last night alive', to come.

It is equally true that the forces of good are tame; they confront wrongdoers only after desperate fictional contrivances; and though they are supported with all the vigour Dickens can command, it is never with the same concentration and skill as evil. On the other hand it is a strained interpretation to see the novel basically as a work of despair rounded off with forced optimism. It is fundamentally optimistic in arguing that crime is caused by circumstance. If the devilishness of Fagin is stressed, Dickens meant to convey that his corruption was due to man and that it can be checked. When Oliver is first taken care of by Dr. Losberne, 'it was a solemn thing to hear . . . the sick child recounting a weary catalogue of evils and calamities which hard men had brought upon him. Oh! if, when we oppress and grind our fellow-creatures, we bestowed one thought upon the dark evidences of human error, . . . if we heard, but one instant, in imagination, the deep testimony of dead men's voices, which no power can stifle and no pride shut out; where would be the injury and injustice, the suffering, misery, cruelty and wrong, that each day's life brings with it!'

Goodness cannot be destroyed. Nancy's love and faithfulness for Sikes is right; Charley has the courage to attack her murderer; within the security of his room, Oliver does not hesitate to leap out of the window to pursue Sikes and Fagin; for he is 'a child of noble nature and a warm heart' in whom, Rose Maylie says, the 'Power which has thought fit to try him . . . has planted . . . affections and feelings' that might honour his elders. And so, Dickens writes, 'men who look on nature, and their fellow-men, and cry that all is dark and gloomy, are in the right; but the sombre colours are reflections from their own jaundiced eyes and hearts. The real hues are delicate and need a clearer vision.' It is the teaching of Henry Fielding, expressed with the power of Dickens, imaginatively concentrated with the intensity of fable in the figure of the child. Its teaching is that it is only in love that humans can live purposefully and happily with each other. It is this which, throughout the novel, holds together Oliver's progress, the tale of his mother's unhappy love, the stories of Harry and Rose and the comic downfall of Bumble, and which makes a tragedy of Sikes's murder of Nancy. Death and violence, within the novel, are common; but the betrayal and murder of Nancy in spite of her love destroy Sikes himself, disrupt Fagin's band, and disorder society.

It is a varied work of frequently terrifying power; and it is not surprising, therefore, that when first published it was given a mixed reception. Yet this has often been forgotten. Mr. Bumble and Oliver, Sikes and Fagin, have somehow come to be accepted as typically English! In his admirable essay on *Oliver Twist*, for example, Arnold Kettle even says that 'it is a curious comment on Victorian civilization that it was considered suitable reading for children'. But as a comment it is curiously inappropriate. To many early Victorians, at least, the suggestion that the book might be fit for children would have been appalling: they hardly considered it suitable for adults.

One of the results of the novel was to reveal something of the realities of life in London to readers who had no conception of them. A contemporary critic explains that 'when *Oliver Twist* came out . . . the most striking thing about the book was that it disclosed . . . an unsuspected gradation of ranks in that great mass which is commonly spoken of as the lower orders' (*Cornhill*, x, 411). Some readers refused to admit its truth, while to others—such as Sir Francis Burdett—it came as an eye-opener. At this time he had been forty years in parliament, but he wrote to his daughter (later Dickens's friend Miss Burdett Coutts) in shocked wonder: 'It is very interesting, very painful, very disgusting, & as the Old Woman at Edinburgh, on hearing a preacher on the sufferings of Jesus Christ said, Oh dear I hope it isn't true. Whether anything like it exists or no I mean to make enquiry for it is quite dreadful, and, to Society in this country, most disgraceful.'

Well might the *Quarterly* write that 'one half of mankind lives without knowing how the other half dies; in fact the regions about Saffron Hill are less known in our great world than the Oxford Tracts: the inhabitants still less. . . .' (LIV, 1839.) Yet others neither knew, nor wished to know. John Lockhart had found even *Pickwick* 'all very well but damned low'. Henry Fox thought it 'painful and disgusting', and Lord Melbourne, the Prime Minister, did not like 'the low debasing style'. Thackeray parodied it in his *Catherine*; and, far from recommending it for children, both the *Edinburgh Review* and the *Quarterly* expressed their consternation at the effect it might have on 'the rising generation'. Dickens, as Mrs. Oliphant said later, was clearly 'a *class* writer . . . one of the advocates of the plea of the Poor *versus* Rich'—and the rich were duly alarmed.

It is often said, quite reasonably, that some knowledge of the historical background is needed if one is fully to appreciate the novel. But it is an awareness of such differences in taste and feeling that is needed, rather than an understanding of the sort of historical question that is usually raised, such as whether the workhouse-scenes were meant to satirize the Old Poor Law or the New. This hardly matters, though it has received a great deal of attention. The novel was never intended as an attack on mere institutions, but on the spirit behind them which remained largely unchanged. Over twenty-five years later, moreover, Dickens referred in the preface to *Our Mutual Friend* to certain reports on workhouse hospitals that had just appeared in *The Lancet* which make it quite clear that the same kind of men were still in charge as in the days of the Bumbles. 'The truth is', wrote the authors, 'that the unfortunate influence of the early traditions of the Poor Law Commissioners lingers with fatal tenacity.' Harriet Martineau's fatuous belief that the evils of the system ended with the New Poor Law of 1834, hardly deserves consideration. Some people neither knew, nor wished to know.

At the same time, it should be made clear that although Dickens's novels were neither works of instruction nor propaganda, they frequently had a close relationship with some of the active public problems of his times. It has recently been said—and it has been accepted without objection—that 'it is a strangely neglected fact that most of the social abuses castigated by Dickens had already ceased to exist when he wrote about them' (A. O. J. Cockshut, *The Imagination of Charles Dickens*, 1961, p. 123). This is rubbish. Do not let us pretend that Dickens was not genuinely and directly concerned about the Chancery prisoner in *Pickwick* and law reform in *Bleak House*; about juvenile crime, prostitution and the poor law in *Oliver Twist*—and with reason; that there was not factual basis for some of the American scenes in *Martin Chuzzlewit*; that class divisions are not one of the concerns of *Dombey and Son*, and that *Our Mutual Friend* was written with no direct reference to its first readers. Dickens and the men of his time were under no such illusion: his concern with public questions was a source of pride to himself and his friends, and of strong offence where his attacks went home. Although, clearly, we can never read the novels in the same way as his contemporaries, these questions cannot be entirely ignored; for though they were never the main subject of his novels, they were among the most effective of many ways in which he communicated with his readers, and they are one which a responsive and fairly well-informed reader can still share today.

Provided that a novelist's references to the life and concerns of his times are entirely relevant to the whole novel, there is no reason why they should detract from it; and, generally speaking, with Dickens's works, they were assimilated. There are glaring exceptions to this: it is certainly less true of the American Eden of *Chuzzlewit* than the Saffron Hill of *Oliver Twist*; yet by now there should be no need to apologize for a writer's concerning himself about his readers or the society of his times. With Dickens the two were the same, for such a concern was part of his nature and of 'the strategy of his fiction'. Being the man he was, a moralist, deeply concerned about men's responsibilities, and choosing to write of society and the interrelations of those who belong to it, his work was often bound to begin in familiar scenes and to concern itself with issues vital to contemporary readers. To Sartre, fiction is a luxury when two-thirds of the world's population is starving, and so it must be if fiction is entirely objective. But Dickens had other aims; and one of the first conditions to be accepted by any reader who wishes to enjoy his work is to be willing to attend to the narrator's voice and to enter the world of his imagination which frequently partly includes a concern with the world of his times.

Even so, for a reader to isolate a concern with this or that 'abuse' apart from the whole novel is one of the most direct ways of giving up his attention, and it is this which has led to such a sharp reaction against any intelligent concern with Dickens's own times. Again, snippets from the novels have so often been used at random to enliven dull histories, that the critic may be driven (as Hillis Miller, in *Dickens Criticism, A Symposium*, 1962, p. 29) to remark, 'It is sometimes hard to remember that if Dickens had not written his novels, he would not justify our attention to the minute details of his life.' Yet it is no less true that if we had everything of Dickens but his novels, he would still have been a phenomenon worth several biographies; his works would fill many volumes; the sharp and streaming consciousness shown in his journalism and the huge range of his letters would still make him a nineteenth-century Pepys or Boswell who erupted into public life. Of course it is always absurd to use the novels simply as a historical scrapbook but it can occasionally be just as wayward to consider Dickens as if he were not a historical as well as a literary phenomenon. When Dickens wrote of the life of his times he wrote of what he knew, of what he felt strongly about, of something in which he played a responsible part, the need for action in which was part of his philosophy, and in which he was an important actor playing an influential role with every page he wrote. There is no comparison to be made with Trollope, for instance, writing about Barchester and the House of Commons from beyond their fringes, nor with Disraeli or Bulwer who put their public lives first. Dickens's works are not a mirror of his times; his relationship with society was a creative one.

Of course there needs to be discrimination in the attention given to this side of Dickens's work. It is still only a means of communication between the author and his public (as in *Hard Times*, for example, see chapter ix below) which, if misinterpreted, can lead to endless petty misunderstandings. Yet, almost alone among novelists, he was able to bring his public figure, his private person, the narrator of his fiction and the 'Charles Dickens' of his journalism effectively into combination.

It is one of Dickens's greatest qualities, however, that although he combined these two voices of novelist and public spokesman, he could face the terrible inhumanity of much of the mid-nineteenth century without being appalled by it or losing his strong concern for fellow-men. Most men had to come to terms with it, like Sir Francis Burdett and the earliest readers of *Oliver Twist*, by ignoring it. A clear impression of the effect that the life of the time might have on a sensibility unhardened by it, and unprepared for it, can be found in the earlier part of Nathaniel Hawthorne's *Journal*. Hawthorne first landed at Liverpool in 1854 and found that the poverty-stricken English street was 'a monstrosity unknown on our side of the Atlantic'. At first he was so fascinated by its squalor that he wrote, 'I often turned aside from the prosperous thoroughfares . . . and went designedly astray among precincts that reminded me of some of Dickens's grimiest pages.' As time went on his journal shows that he did not lose his compassion, but he became unable to see the people of the streets as anything but 'maggots in cheese . . . disgusting', like 'vivacious bugs and insects' under a rotting log; until finally he kept to the beaten path, gave up any attempt to record what he saw, and turned most of his journal into an ordinary tourist's diary. It was a normal response.

Yet Dickens never wrote nor felt about people like this. In contrast to Hawthorne and almost all men of his time, Dickens's extraordinary quality lies not only in his power of observing what was before him and of not recoiling from it, but in his never losing the power of communicating his sense of humanity to his reader. When he died, Arthur Helps wrote, 'We doubt whether there has ever been a writer of fiction who took such a real and living interest in the actual world about him. Its many sorrows, its terrible injustice, its calamities, went to his heart.' If we lose the sense of communicating with such a writer either because of concern with unimportant historical details, or because we ignore them altogether and are concerned exclusively with any limited aspect of Dickens's art, philosophy, or his failures, we experience something much less than he can give.

Meanwhile, no doubt, *Oliver Twist* showed both Dickens and his public that he possessed new powers. At a time when he was still squandering his talent on absurd essays such as the anonymous *Sketches of Young Gentlemen*, and comic operas and burlettas for the stage, he had discovered that he could command a serious public. When he had started the novel he was not above undertaking to edit the memoirs of the famous clown Grimaldi; as it neared completion he began to complain to his publisher that the tasks he had set himself 'would have been beyond Scott himself'. There was now no other comparison.

It was also while he was writing *Oliver Twist* that an event occurred which brought tragedy into his own life. Since he and Catherine had been married, they had often had one of her younger sisters, Mary Hogarth, to stay with them. She was seventeen, naturally charming, sweet-natured and gay; and we know little else about her except through Dickens's eyes and as he described her in his letters. Certainly she was beautiful, and he afterwards declared that it was his solemn belief 'that so perfect a creature never breathed. . . . She had not a fault.' They all three lived in harmony. Then, one evening, early in May 1837, they went together to St. James's Theatre to see a revival of Dickens's comic opera, *The Village Coquettes*, in which his future brother-in-law, Henry Burnett, was taking the main part. Almost immediately after they had returned home Mary was taken ill. Next day she died. 'Of our sufferings at the time . . .', wrote Dickens, 'I will say nothing—no one can imagine what they were. . . . Thank God she died in my arms, and the very last words she whispered were of me.' He slipped a ring from her finger which he wore until his own death; and as long as he lived she had first place in his memory.

Indeed, he did not merely remember her with love and affection, but with an extraordinarily passionate intensity which almost completely mastered him. He brought her character into his books, he wanted to be buried by her side, and for months he dreamed of her every night, until he told his wife—and then the dreams mysteriously stopped. He imagined that her spirit was constantly about him, and when he went to America and visited the Niagara Falls he wrote quite seriously to Forster that, though he wished she were with them, no doubt she had visited the scene many times in spirit since her death. Hardly anything else in Dickens's life (as distinct from his writings) so strongly leaves the impression that his character was completely exceptional.

Chapter Four

NICHOLAS NICKLEBY

THOUGH Mary Hogarth's death caused a break in the novels he was writing he left himself little time to dwell on his grief. In July he went on holiday with Catherine to Belgium, and they spent August and September at Broadstairs, where he went on with *Pickwick* and *Oliver Twist*. Before a dinner to celebrate the completion of *Pickwick* on 18 November, he signed a contract with Chapman and Hall for another novel, on better terms, and after a short break over Christmas this was the next work to demand his attention.

He thought carefully over what the new book should be about, since he knew well how difficult it would be to live up to the popularity of *Pickwick*. He soon hit on the idea of writing about the Yorkshire schools, boy-farms where unwanted children were disposed of, a subject he felt sure he could make tell. He had once heard of them as a child, when someone had told him of a schoolmaster who had operated on a boy's suppurating abscess 'with an inky penknife'. The impression then made had never left him. He at once collected a letter recommending him as an anxious parent looking for a school, invited his illustrator, Hablot K. Browne, to join him and set off by coach through heavy snow to Barnard Castle.

They made a quick survey of some of the schools, taking special note of one kept by a man named William

Shaw in whose school two boys had gone blind from gross neglect. The local solicitor to whom they had been given a letter of recommendation told them not to send a boy there while there was a horse to hold in London or a gutter to lie in. They needed to know no more. Dickens's quick eye had seen enough to give local colour to the tale; Browne had a thumb-nail sketch of the one-eyed William Shaw. They returned to London, and in a few weeks' time Wackford Squeers, the Yorkshire schoolmaster, was introduced to Nicholas Nickleby.

The work was on sale in April, and was an instantaneous success. It sold nearly fifty thousand on the day of publication. It was so astoundingly varied! The grim realities of Dotheboys Hall were presented with an oddity and gusto that left his readers breathless with both horror and laughter. Squeers, as Gissing saw, was treated not as the study of a human being, but 'the representative, pure and simple, of a vile institution'. It was tremendously vigorous and lively, rapidly leading up to the moment when, unable to bear Squeers's brutality to the boys any longer, Nicholas burst out with, 'I will not stand by and see it done', seized the schoolmaster's cane, and 'beat the ruffian till he roared for mercy'.

Nicholas's outcry is in exactly the same words as Nancy's outburst, when Fagin lifts his club against Oliver: it is Dickens's declaration that he means to protest at injustice and cruelty with all his power, and that nothing will prevent him. It was just about this time that a friendly critic who knew him (G. H. Lewes) noticed that 'the vivacity and sagacity which gave a charm to intercourse with him had become weighted with a seriousness which . . . became more and more prominent in his conversation and his writings. He had already learned to look upon the world as a scene where it was the duty of each man in his own way to make the lot of the miserable Many a little less miserable. . . . He was sometimes laughed at for the importance he seemed to attach to everything relating to himself . . . but this belonged to his quality. *Il se prenait au sérieux*, and was admirable because he did so.'

A comic treatment of subjects of grim seriousness and a serious purpose in his comedy, were now the staple of the Dickens novel. Yet it would be a mistake to under-estimate the gaiety of *Nickleby*. It has more fun and amusement in a few pages than most authors in their complete works. The Mantalinis, the Kenwigses, and the Crummleses are almost effortlessly entertaining, and Newman Noggs has a pleasant oddity. Fanny Squeers's letter to Ralph Nickleby is in Dickens's best vein of fanciful humour: 'My pa requests me to write to you, the doctors considering it doubtful whether he will ever recuvver the use of his legs which prevents his holding a pen. We are in a state of mind beyond everything, and my pa is one mask of brooses both blue and green likewise two forms are steepled in his Goar. . . . He assaulted my ma with dreadful violence, dashed her to the earth, and drove her back comb several inches into her head. A very little more and it must have entered her skull.' It is a sign of how little Dickens was appreciated, in spite of his popularity, that Leigh Hunt could exclaim on reading this, 'that it surpassed the best things in Smollett that he could call to mind'.

Brightest and best is Mrs. Nickleby, whose conversation burbles on with refreshing inanities, as fatuous and foolish as a well-intentioned woman can be. She is said to have been drawn from the author's mother; and though even her son-in-law thought the elder Mrs.

Dickens 'was as thoroughly good-natured, easy-going, companionable a body as one could wish to meet with', she and her son were on bad terms just when the story was started, since she objected to certain '"sneering" passages' in his letters. Still, it hurt no one. It was no more than an exaggeration of some slight peculiarities, and, true to character, she never recognized herself to the last. 'Mrs. Nickleby herself,' Dickens once wrote. 'sitting bodily before me . . . once asked me whether I really believed there ever was such a woman!'

The other pair of characters who had definite 'originals' are the Cheeryble brothers, who are founded on what Dickens had heard of two Manchester business-men, Daniel and William Grant. The eldest brother alone was said to have given away more than £600,000 before he died. Perhaps too much has been made of these characters when the book has been criticized. Walter Bagehot, who was editor of *The Economist* as well as being a literary critic, thought that 'the Messrs. Cheeryble are among the stupidest of Dickens's characters', and since then no one has had a good word to say for them. 'The harm they must have done, those two jolly old boys!' wrote Gissing. Yet the whole book is an extravaganza. They are not important; and just as in Dickens's books the villain is said to be present often less as a character than as a danger, so characters like the Cheerybles are introduced just as the expression of his faith in human goodness. Whatever one may think of the later novels, surely everyone must see that *Nickleby* is not a study of society but an entertaining morality? Bagehot objects that Dickens forgot that 'the breadth of platitude is rather different from the breadth of sagacity'. But George Orwell gloried in the fact that Dickens's 'whole "message" is one that at first glance looks like an enormous platitude: If men would behave decently the world would be decent.'

Platitudinous or not, a belief in health and sanity, decency and kindness, is at the core of the whole book. Since this belief is not developed systematically, the pattern is simpler than in the later novels. Nevertheless it expresses fundamentally the same idea as *Little Dorrit* and *Great Expectations*: that those who shut themselves off from their fellows, end by losing all happiness and by bringing a terrible retribution on themselves.

Since *Nickleby* is essentially a young man's novel, this is developed through the theme of Love. It is always *romantic* in the popular sense. Love, true and false, concealed, devoted, disregarded, and fulfilled is its chief theme. The opening paragraph begins by telling how Nicholas's grandparents had married 'out of mere attachment', and how 'thus two people who cannot afford to play cards for money, sometimes sit down for love'. The book ends with an orgy of wedded bliss in which Nicholas is united to Madeline, Frank Cheeryble to Nicholas's sister Kate, and Tim Linkinwater to Miss La Creevy. 'How dare you think, Frank,' cries the elder Cheeryble, 'that we would have you marry for money when youth, beauty, and every amiable virtue and excellence were to be had for love?'—'All love,' thinks Ralph Nickleby, '—bah! that I should use the cant of boys and girls—is fleeting . . . originates in blindness and is fed by vanity.'

Love is seen as essentially ridiculous: Mrs. Nickleby is flattered by the attentions of an escaped lunatic, Madame Mantalini is enslaved by her absurd husband, Fanny Squeers does her best to trap Nicholas, and Mr. Lillyvick insists on putting his head 'in the noose' with Miss Petowker. It may also have a more sinister side:

Kate is pursued by Lord Frederick Verisopht and Sir Mulberry Hawk; the old lord who visits the trying-on room at the gownshop has eyes for no one else; while Smike's eventual happiness is deeply embittered by his hopeless love for her. Above all, the repulsive old miser, Arthur Gride, has an evil, lip-smacking relish for Madeline Bray, 'fresh, lovely, bewitching and not nineteen. Dark eyes, long eyelashes, ripe and ruddy lips that to look at is to long to kiss, beautiful clustering hair that one's fingers itch to play with.'

Even more than in Dickens's other works, the main teaching of *Nickleby* is that there is a virtue in frankness in decent human feelings, and evil perversion when they are thwarted and suppressed. As Dickens meant Oliver Twist to be 'a principle of Good surviving through all adverse circumstances' (*Preface*), so he seems to have intended Kate to be the symbol of tender and attractive purity. Even her uncle sometimes softens towards her. Lord Frederick dies as a result of a quarrel in which he had taken her part. It is significant that Squeers's school is principally successful because it is a place where natural children and stepsons can be sent and forgotten; that Ralph's marriage was a secret one and made for money, that he curses his own offspring, and that he ends by hanging himself 'immediately below the trap-door . . . in the very place to which the eyes of his own son', whom he had helped to hound to death, 'had often been directed in childish horror . . . years before'.

It is not a 'well-written' novel, and many of its tricks are transparent. Some of the scenes with the Vincent Crummles company, for example, help us to understand Dickens's methods and our delight in them. Already, in *Oliver Twist*, he had likened the sudden transitions of the story to those of 'all good murderous melodramas'—which are absurd only if we stand apart from them. One frequent solution was to stand apart, to be absurd, and so arouse the reader's sense of reality. In *Nickleby*, for example, there is nothing so stagey as the serious part of the story, and nothing so comic as the scenes in which we are invited to hold aloof just because they are obviously a life of pretence—those with the Crummles players. Yet when Crummles at last says good-bye to Nicholas, he is seen as fundamentally a man of sincerity and feeling, as 'not a jot of his theatrical manner' remains and he puts out his hand 'with an air which, if he could have summoned it at will, would have made him the best actor of the day in homely parts'. Almost all Dickens's best comedy lies in pretences; and all Dickens's characters involuntarily act out their parts just as Dickens himself (paying tribute to Thackeray) felt that 'every good actor plays direct to every good author, and every writer of fiction, though he may not adopt the dramatic form, writes in effect for the stage'.

He delighted in shams because he saw through them so sharply. They seemed almost necessary to him. In a similar way, the element of sheer escapism was so much higher in the theatre of his time, because men needed to escape urban industrialism and utilitarian philosophy. It is true that Dickens could conscientiously praise the serious drama because it is 'founded on an eternal principle of human nature . . . an inborn delight and interest in a living representation of the actions, passions, joys and sorrows of mankind'. More usually, as he used to say in his *Speeches*, he felt that it was 'cheering', and that it 'afforded relief'. 'I am very fond of the play', he once told his hearers, and 'I dare say the feeling peculiar to a theatre is as well known to everybody here as it is to me, of having for an hour or two quite forgotten the real world, and of coming out into the street with a kind of wonder that it should be so wet, and dark, and cold.' He praises it as a 'fleeting fairyland'; and such, without his comic sense, would have been the tendency of most of Dickens's earlier work in his novels. Comedy often gives him his chance to be serious; for without comic overtones he would never have allowed himself to write of Fagin's den or Dotheboys Hall; they gave him the scope for art which he would have otherwise taken out in 'fine' writing. His view of life is essentially comic in these earlier novels because he sees life as one of necessary but often enjoyable pretences: pretences that are necessary because however much we may decry human nature it is better than the world in which men live; for, so he says, 'it will generally be found that those who sneer habitually at human nature . . . are among its worst and least pleasant examples'. He even goes further, to exult in comedy and pretence for their own sake: Squeers's oddly enjoyable indifference to human suffering, Bumble's pomposity, Mantilini's gentility, all come from the same mould as the self-deceptions of the Pickwickians and the fascinating deceits of Quilp, Pecksniff and Micawber. Comic pretence is Dickens's 'Fancy' in another form, the denial of which in the harsh world of his times he held to be so fatal to the human spirit.

For, considered seriously, the world of the earlier novels is often chaotic and heartless. When Nicholas and Smike reach London at last, they pass into 'streams of people, apparently without end . . . hurrying forward; while vehicles of all shapes and makes, mingled up together in one moving mass like running water'. And, as they dash on, they see a strange procession of objects, all man needs for luxury—and for death:

> . . . guns, swords, pistols, and patent engines of destruction; screws and irons for the crooked . . . drugs for the sick, coffins for the dead, churchyards for the buried—all these jumbled each with the other and flocking side by side, seemed to flit by in motley dance like the fantastic groups of the old Dutch painter, and with the same stern moral for the unheeding, restless crowd.

Squeers's centre of operations, at the Saracen's Head, close by Newgate, is said to be 'at the very core of London'. It is not what the romantic might expect from the name of the inn, but typical of London to Dickens, 'a whirl of noise and motion' from the midst of which men 'have been hurried violently and swiftly from the world, when the scene has been rendered frightful with excess of human life'; a world at times of tragedy, at times of comedy; a life in which there may seem to be no importance but in the individual, yet in which it is all the more necessary to associate in love and friendship, through charity and laughter.

Certainly to understand the Dickens of these earlier novels one must include the interpretation given, most notably, by Hillis Miller in his *Charles Dickens, The World of His Novels*:

> From the point of view of the characters themselves, this kind of life may be defined in a single word, isolation. Each of these novels . . . has at its centre characters who are alienated from society, and the situation of all is to be surrounded by an inimical world, a world which refuses to support or recognize their existence. . . . The happy endings of these novels do not . . . represent an adequate analysis of the complexities of the theme of direct and intimate relations between man and man in society.

This is true of the endings; and what is said of the characters can be abundantly illustrated. Nicholas

Nickleby, himself, can become weary and despondent, not only at his misfortunes but at life, for:

> . . . now, when he thought how regularly things went on, from day to day, in the same unvarying round; . . . how few there were who tenanted the stately houses, and how many those who lay in noisome pens, or rose each day and laid them down each night, and lived and died, father and son, mother and child, race upon race, generation upon generation, without a home to shelter them or the energies of one single man directed to their aid; how . . . in seeking . . . the bare means of a most wretched and inadequate subsistence, there were women and children in that one town, divided into classes . . . and reared from infancy to drive most criminal and dreadful trades; how ignorance was punished and never taught; how jail doors gaped and gallows loomed . . . how many died in soul and had no chance of life . . . how much injustice, misery, and wrong there was, and yet how the world rolled on from year to year, alike careless and indifferent, and no man seeking to remedy or redress it; when he thought of all this, and selected from the mass the one slight case on which his thoughts were bent, he felt, indeed, there was little ground for hope, and little reason why it should not form an atom in the huge aggregate of distress and sorrow, and add one small and unimportant unit to swell the great amount.

Yet true as it undoubtedly is that the happy endings are not enough, no one can question that the spirit of the whole novel checks this tendency. It is not merely the comic spirit: for it cannot be that misfortune is laughable. It is more the conviction that, in *Nickleby* (chapter liii) as in *Oliver*, 'the darkest side of the picture' can be shifted 'at will'; nor does this follow simply because Dickens stops to say that it is so, for this darkness is counterbalanced not only by sentiment but by his strong and outright moral protest and the urgent demand for reform.

To accept 'the darkest side' would lead to despair; but men *can* be helped, children taught, wrongs redressed. Compare Nicholas's passage through the streets with his uncle's return home after he has learnt that he has destroyed his own son, Smike. Ralph passes by a 'mean burial ground . . . a rank unwholesome spot', where lie the 'grisly family', the 'dear departed brothers and sisters of the ruddy clergyman who did his task so speedily when they were hidden in the ground'; he sees a further miming of the Dance of Death, gives a vacant laugh, and then turns home to take his life. Yet Nicholas's decision was 'to act'. Dickens's reformism is not just a social comment on his own times, but part of his fictional philosophy and way of life.

The writing of *Nicholas Nickleby* extended over a full eighteen months, much of it overlapping with *Oliver Twist* and *Barnaby Rudge*. When he went to insure his life at this time the doctors thought he worked too hard, and Dickens himself confessed 'if this were to go on much longer, I should "bust" the boiler'. The book was finished at Broadstairs, in September 1839, when he wrote to Forster, 'the discovery is made, Ralph is dead, the loves have come all right, Tim Linkinwater has proposed, and I have now only to break up Dotheboys and the book together'. He was in tremendously high spirits, and let himself go about George Cruikshank, Ainsworth's *Jack Sheppard*, and the sensationalism of the 'Newgate novelists' in a passage which Forster discreetly suppressed:

> What a strange thing it is that all sorts of things happen in London when I'm away! I almost blame myself for the death of that poor girl who leaped off the Monument—who would never have done it if I had been in town; neither would the two men have found the skeleton in the sewers. If it had been a female skeleton, I should have written to

> the coroner and stated my conviction that it *must* be Mrs. Sheppard. A famous subject for an illustration by George —Jonathan Wild forcing Mrs. Sheppard down the grown-up seat of a gloomy privy, and Blueskin or any such robber, cramming a child (anybody's child) down the little hole— Mr. Wood looking on in horror—and two other spectators, one with a fiendish smile and the other with a torch, aiding and abetting!

The last thing was to dedicate the book to the Shakespearian actor, William Macready, and then to make arrangements to celebrate the occasion with a Nicklebian dinner. Macready, whose friendship with Dickens had grown closer all through the previous year, was deeply touched, and confided to his diary that it was 'as great' an honour 'as a man can receive'. He took the chair at the dinner and, in proposing Dickens's health, 'spoke of him as one who made the amelioration of his fellow-men the object of all his labours'. 'I did not get through it well', he added. A few weeks later he was godfather at the christening of Dickens's third child, Catherine (Katey).

Chapter Five

MASTER HUMPHREY'S CLOCK—THE OLD CURIOSITY SHOP; BARNABY RUDGE

EVEN as *Nicholas Nickleby* had been drawing to a close, Dickens had begun to think of what he should do when it was finished? He wanted greater independence from his publishers, a fair share of the profits, and some relief from the grinding necessity of constantly writing; and now that Forster was well established as his adviser he wrote to ask his opinion of his latest plan to win them.

His new proposal was to bring out a sort of weekly periodical, not all of which he would have to write himself, and which would be a cross between contemporary weeklies like *Hood's Own*, and Addison's *Spectator* or Goldsmith's *Bee*. It would begin, he explained, 'with some pleasant fiction relative to the origin of the publication', introducing 'a little club', the members of which might tell 'their personal histories'. It would introduce new characters and revive old ones—including Sam Weller and Mr. Pickwick—and there would be no continuous story, but simply an entertaining series of papers on all kinds of subjects from articles on Old London to satire on topics of the day. Once it was well established, the editor might even travel abroad, in Ireland and America, and send home descriptive articles about people and places, tales, traditions and legends in the manner of Washington Irving's *Alhambra*.

The idea was not quite so strange as it sounds. Such

magazines were already springing up, and only ten years later Dickens was to show what could be done with *Household Words*. A genuinely new periodical might well have been successful. Where Dickens was at fault was in not having a clear enough idea of what he wanted to do, and in being content to imitate Addison and Irving. Particularly like Irving was his sentimental attitude to the past, for almost everything he suggested was to have had an antiquarian flavour, from a series of stories to be told by the Guildhall giants, Gog and Magog, down to satirical sketches in the manner of *Gulliver's Travels*.

He had a much clearer idea about the financial arrangements for the new publication and, with Forster's help, he soon concluded a favourable agreement with Chapman and Hall. He obtained £1,500 down, as part of his share of the £14,000 that the firm had already made from *Nickleby*, and completely reversed their relations for the future. Under the new scheme his profits were to be more than double theirs, and he was to be completely in charge of the magazine. In its way, this was a triumph, and Dickens looked forward to running the new periodical for perhaps as long as five years.

Meanwhile, he began to think more definitely about the new work, but still on the same lines as before. He had the curious idea, which was actually carried out, of an old man in a queer house, 'opening the book by an account of himself, and, among other peculiarities, of his affection for an old quaint queer-cased clock'. The old man was to have kept a collection of 'odd manuscripts in the old, deep, dark, silent closet where the weights are'. These were to be read and discussed by a small club, and the whole work was to be called either *Old Humphrey's Clock*, or *Master Humphrey's Clock*. Altogether, the antiquity and oddity of the arrangement were a great deal over-emphasized, and the idea of Humphrey's hiding-place for his manuscripts was merely a peculiar device for giving the right atmosphere for the old-world stories that Dickens so curiously wanted to write.

He firmly kept on with his plan, however, throughout March 1840, steadily writing the opening numbers, which have now been completely forgotten. Even Sam Weller and Mr. Pickwick are a disappointment, and the story about a witch that Mr. Pickwick contributes might have been written in his early Tittlebat period. The day of publication drew nearer, and *Master Humphrey's Clock* was announced as 'wound up and going' and ready to strike. 'From week to week,' the announcement continued, 'Master Humphrey will set his Clock, trusting that . . . while it marks the tread of Time, it will scatter a few slight flowers on the Old Mower's path.' Publication was on 4 April; when, according to his custom, Dickens was away from London—on holiday, in Birmingham, with his wife. The day after, Forster hastened down to join them and to announce that the first number had sold seventy thousand copies!

For the moment Dickens was jubilant. 'The clock goes gloriously indeed', he wrote. 'What will the wiseacres say to weekly issues *now*.' But, while no one grudged threepence for the first number, everyone was disappointed when they learnt that it was a mere miscellany. The reviewers did not even care for the idea of Master Humphrey and the clock: 'The veriest abortion', one wrote, 'in the shape of an endeavour to create interest or afford amusement that was ever perpetrated!' Sales fell alarmingly; by the third number their decline was disastrous; and after a hasty conference with his publishers, Dickens set to work to give the public the continuous story it wanted.

Fortunately, he had an idea for one. Towards the end of February he and his wife, with Maclise and Forster, had visited the old poet, Landor, in Bath. He had warmly welcomed them, at his lodgings in St. James's Square, and, one evening, Dickens had sketched out to his companions a fancy which later took the form of the tale of Little Nell. Years afterwards, as Forster tells the story, Landor used to boast of the fact, adding 'that he never in his life regretted anything so much' as his failure to purchase the house and burn it to the ground in order that 'no meaner association should ever desecrate' Nell's birthplace.

It began very hesitantly. Originating in little more than a repetition of the purpose behind *Oliver Twist*, 'to show . . . the principle of Good surviving through every adverse circumstance', it took several weeks before Dickens was able to elaborate sufficient characters to carry on the drama. His first thought had been to make little more than a short story of it, and in that form it had already been introduced in the fourth number, when Master Humphrey had mused on a child he had met, whom he constantly thought of as he had left her, in the keeping of her old grandfather, 'in the midst of . . . lumber and decay and ugly age, the beautiful child in her gentle slumber, smiling through her light and sunny dreams'.

Dickens soon came to realize the possibilities of the idea; and, urged on by Forster and his publishers, set himself again to planning a novel, with all the additional complexity of having to write it in weekly numbers, which he now discovered gave him hardly 'room to turn'. He did not hesitate, however, though it cost him a pang to give up the design of *Master Humphrey's Clock*, which thereby became 'one of the lost books of the earth'.

All that summer Dickens kept on writing, through two seaside holidays at Broadstairs, in June and September. 'Mr. Shandy's clock', he wrote to Landor, 'was nothing to mine, wind, wind, wind, always winding am I; and day and night the alarum is ringing in my ears, warning me that it must not run down.' In July he was at last able to buy back the copyright of *Oliver Twist*, and legally release himself from an agreement to write *Barnaby Rudge* for Bentley. In recognition of Forster's efforts at winning him this freedom, he presented him with a silver claret jug, 'filled to the brim and running over with truth and earnestness'. A month later, he had a fearful scene with him, flew into a violent passion and told him to leave the house! Fortunately Macready (who thought it was Forster's fault) managed to make peace between them, and a week later they were all three sitting round the dining-table after the christening of one of Dickens's children.

The work went on steadily until Christmas, when Dickens was far enough ahead to be able to dwell over the conclusion. Forster says, 'I never knew him wind up any tale with such sorrowful reluctance as this.'—'All night', Dickens told him, 'I have been pursued by the child; and this morning I am unrefreshed and miserable.' He delayed writing about her death until well into the new year, genuinely suffering over the prospect of bringing her to the grave. From the very first, as he openly admitted, he had identified her with Mary Hogarth. He lingered on, refusing all invitations, seeming to luxuriate in the sensation of grief. Although Dickens said that it was Forster who had decided him when he doubted whether or not Little Nell should live, he now seized at the suggestion eagerly, and there can be no doubt that the whole trend of the story had always been towards her death. To Ruskin, she was 'butchered for the market', and Dickens blushed when Macready said 'that he was cruel', but he was quite sincere in his despair at what he had to write. 'Old wounds bleed afresh when I only think of doing it,' he told Forster, 'dear Mary died yesterday when I think of this story.' On 16 January he stayed up until four in the morning, and brought it to an end.

In discussing Little Nell one can only go on to the defensive; yet it is hardly enough to argue that she was enormously popular at the time. Lord Jeffrey, the old critic of the *Edinburgh Review*, declared there was 'nothing so good as Nell since Cordelia'. But, without trying to condemn the whole age, there is something peculiar about almost all Dickens's well-known contemporaries who enlisted as her admirers—Macaulay, Washington Irving, Sydney Smith, Landor, Hans Andersen, Carlyle, Jeffrey, John Forster, and Edward Fitzgerald. They were all quasi-bachelors, sick-at-heart, and denied the love of children. Dickens, himself, had been deeply unhappy since the death of Mary Hogarth. She appealed to a strain of self-pity and the lack of something in these men; and it is this, and the rather monotonous writing which attempts to hide it, that justifies those who dislike her.

On the other hand, there is something to be said in her favour. At the time, she was welcomed as fresh and new. Though Mrs. Oliphant later dismissed her as a 'white smear', she came as a pleasant relief after Sterne's leer, Smollett's chamber-pots, and Fielding's fornication. Little Nell and her grandfather resting in the churchyard were a refreshing change to a generation brought up on *Tom Jones*, with Molly Seagrim and Goody Brown, stripped to the waist and battling with thigh-bones in the burial-ground.

Jane Austen and Scott had created more attractive heroines than Nell; yet Jane Austen was still little known and Scott was falling out of favour. With a new kind of heroine to describe, Dickens returned to an old style of writing. Once he had completed the story Dickens had to return to touch up the opening chapter, and he wrote it to show 'the lonely figure of the child' as one 'who seemed to exist in a kind of allegory'. So he wished to think that he (or Master Humphrey) had originated the story; and so, for once, Dickens went back and wrote in something to account for its development. In the complete tale, as revised, the old man thinks:

> It would be a curious speculation . . . to imagine her in her future life, holding her solitary way among a crowd of wild grotesque companions; the only pure, fresh youthful object in the throng. It would be curious to find—I checked myself here, for the theme was carrying me along with it at a great pace . . . and I resolved to go to bed, and court forgetfulness.

From the moment, therefore, when Master Humphrey goes to bed to dream of the child, to the very end when her grandfather cannot believe that she is not merely sleeping, the story has the atmosphere of a dream. The illustration (by George Cattermole) at the end of the opening number had been of 'The Child in Her Gentle Slumber'. At the end, in a companion-picture, she is shown 'At Rest'. A little earlier than this a new character had been introduced, a child who was continually dreaming of her death; and when they all at last look down upon her, 'on her little bed', we are reminded of how her 'sweet face', though still unchanged, 'had passed like a dream through haunts of misery and care'.

It is strange how the story was developed with such consistency, though at first unplanned. It deliberately went back to the greatest of all tales in the dream convention, by the author who 'dreamed a dream' and saw a man clothed in rags, with 'a book in his hand, and a great burthen upon his back'. As they set out on their journey, the girl and her grandfather are described as 'two pilgrims'; and, when they have their first rest in the countryside, and look back towards London where they can see the cross of St. Paul's glittering above the smoke, Nell thinks of *The Pilgrim's Progress*, and says, 'I feel as if we were both Christian, and laid down on this grass all the cares and troubles we brought with us; never to take them up again.'

The whole course of their journey is emblematical of the changing scenes of life: the graveyard where they meet Punch and Judy, the race-course, the green lanes, the waxworks, the wild journey through the Black Country, and the last procession up the snow-covered path to the churchyard. Thomas Hood, in reviewing the novel, chose the picture of the child asleep, as 'like an allegory of the peace and innocence of childhood in the midst of . . . the hateful or hurtful passions of the world', and, as a companion-piece, the 'Hogarthian' figure of Punch lolling on the tombstone. Age and Youth 'travel afoot through the fields and woods', and, as the grandfather says, trust themselves 'to God in the places where he dwells'. They are like the Shepherd Boy in the Valley of Humiliation, who sings:

He that is down, needs fear no fall,
He that is low, no Pride:

He that is humble ever shall
Have God to be his Guide.

The trouble is that *The Old Curiosity Shop* is never more than *like* an allegory; and that whereas in a genuine one the story and meaning should each have an independent vitality, the tale of the girl and her grandfather has no living belief behind it. With all the references to heaven and the angels, Dickens himself was not convinced; for, in all his sorrow for Mary Hogarth, he told Forster, 'I can't preach to myself the schoolmaster's consolation, though I try.' He was clever enough to make it mean something to others, but only to those who were willing to believe. It was a bold attempt, and for the time being only too successful. But, in the long run, the passages describing Little Nell remain no more than pretty pictures, and now that their novelty has worn off, they leave an impression of hopeless unreality.

The story must be read as a kind of fairy-tale. It is making rather heavy weather to see it in terms of archetypes, primordial symbols, and poetic myths of the ancient world. Fairy-tales share the same world as they do, but as a child sees it. The stock of characters consists of children, dwarfs, midgets, Punch-and-Judy-men and waxwork women; the book's pictures of life, of the churchyard, the factory, the town or country are mainly a child's. Some of this may come from Dickens's limitations once launched on this kind of story, yet he was learning all the time to use technique to fit in with his powers and failings. The appeal of Nell's innocence is to age, and is associated with the old grandfather, the schoolmaster, the younger brother; but elsewhere the tale's horrors, wonders and delights belong to a world of goblins, ogres and giants. Nell's bed, in the written-in first chapter, is one 'a fairy might have slept in'; we are led to the final chapter by 'the magic reel' which at last slackens and stops. Quilp lives in an 'ogre's castle'; 'the Marchioness', says Dick, 'is a Genie'; the Garlands' fairy cottage reminds Kit of giants' castles, princesses and dragons.

Sometimes there is a derivative archness in the writing:[1] Nell pretends to be led on through the woods by the birds:

> 'Come!' . . . She bounded on before, printing her tiny footsteps in the moss . . .; and thus she lured the old man on, with many a backward look and merry beck, now pointing stealthily to some lone bird as it perched and twittered on a branch that strayed across their path, now stopping to listen to the songs that broke the happy silence, or watch the sun as it trembled through the leaves, and stealing in among the ivied trunks of stout old trees, opened long paths of light.

Elsewhere the story is saved from threatening insipidity by sharp observation, satire and comic dramatization. In the scene when Nell is turned away by Miss Monflathers (of the Boarding and Day Establishment), for example, we do not share Nell's tears or know of her 'bursting heart' until we have heard Miss Monflathers:

[1] Six years earlier, Young Boz the reporter had been light-hearted and sensible enough to make fun of this style, as in his parody of Friedrich Wilhelm Carové's *The Story Without a Beginning*, in the *Morning Chronicle*, 18 December 1834: see W. J. Carlton, *Dickensian*, 1951, XLVII, 67–70. Carové's story had strongly impressed Dickens and was certainly the inspiration, later, of his 'A Child's Dream of a Star' (1850). Carové's writing, with its allegorical form, romantic fancies about Nature, and passages about 'the child', the birds and the flowers, is similar to—and probably influenced—such passages in the *Old Curiosity Shop*. It was ridiculous enough for it to be surprising that Dickens had not continued to see through it; and remarkable as an example of how much of Dickens's adult inspiration came from childhood reading—some, even, of his adult thinking.

> 'Don't you know how naughty it is of you . . . to be a waxwork child, when you might have the proud consciousness of assisting, to the extent of your infant powers, the manufactures of your country; of improving your mind by the constant contemplation of the steam-engine; and of earning a comfortable and independent subsistence of from two-and-ninepence to three shillings a week? Don't you know that the harder you are at work, the happier you are?'

The brief scenes in the Black Country are also a welcome glimpse of the outward world, though even they are in the allegorical manner: on reaching it, the child and the old man land at a dark wharf 'as if raised from the dead and placed there by a miracle'. They meet the old furnace-man, and are led within the factory where 'moving like dreams in the flame and smoke', they see men who labour 'like giants', much like the glimpse the shepherds gave Christian of the by-way to hell. The language can be sharp and spare. Nell knocks at a wayside hovel:

> 'What would you have here?' said a gaunt man opening it.
>
> 'Charity. A morsel of bread.'
>
> 'Do you see that?' returned the man hoarsely, pointing to a kind of bundle on the ground. 'That's a dead child. . . . Do you think I have charity to bestow, or a morsel of bread to spare?'

Yet there is much more in the *Old Curiosity Shop* than 'allegory' and Little Nell. In the company of Dick Swiveller, Quilp, Mrs. Jarley and Sampson and Sally Brass, the trailing clouds of sentiment are soon blown away. There are a dozen or more characters—including Codlin and Short, the Marchioness, Mr. Chuckster, and Kit Nubbles—who are wonderfully good company. One might, perhaps, except Kit Nubbles, under suspicion of his being too obviously virtuous, even though it is 'especially observed . . . that he was by no means of a sentimental turn'. But no one could ever complain of excess virtue or sentiment in the remarkable Dick Swiveller. He is uniquely plausible, unfailingly high-spirited and delightfully natural; and the transformation of his attachment from Miss Wackles and Little Nell to his devotion to the Marchioness, is a far more satisfactory progress than any other in the book.

The dwarf, Quilp, is one of the 'wild grotesque companions' who were to beset the path of the young heroine. In appearance and behaviour he is as far removed from actual life as possible. He is a little fiend, 'as sharp as a ferret and as cunning as a weasel'. Seated at table, 'he ate hard eggs, shell and all, devoured gigantic prawns with their heads and tails on . . . drank boiling tea without winking, bit his fork and spoon till they bent again, and in short performed so many horrifying and uncommon acts', that even his wife and mother-in-law 'began to doubt if he were really a human creature'. Yet he has all the human vices, and even manages to make them seem rather attractive. His ferocity, malice and tyrannical spitefulness have a zest and liveliness about them that secure him one disciple (young Tom Scott) and, so his wife assures us, gives him the same power as Richard III of being able to compel even the best-looking woman to accept his love. He is sadistic, lecherous, dirty, a jibing mocker of all innocently paternal Nelly-worshippers; and he represents the unrestrainedly evil side of human nature, quite as powerfully as the dark dwarfed figure to be released by the extraordinary potions of Dr. Henry Jekyll.

The Marchioness is the most attractive character: with the exception of David Copperfield and Pip, she is the only natural child in Dickens's works. For, though we are assured that she grew up to be 'good-looking' and 'clever', she is never more than a child in the course of the story. In spite of her ill-treatment as the servant of the shady solicitor, Sampson Brass, there is no forced pathos even in the grim scene in which Sampson's sister, Sally, issues her with her dinner of 'about two square inches of cold mutton' and some 'cold potatoes, looking as eatable as Stonehenge'. Her resourceful devotion to Dick Swiveller, who is the only person ever to have shown her any kindness, is more touching than Nell's to her grandfather, and her pawning his clothes to buy him medicine, when he is lying ill, is a great deal more practical than wandering round the countryside hand-in-hand:

> 'I suppose,' said Dick, as she closed the door slowly, and peeped into the room again, to make sure that he was comfortable, 'I suppose there's nothing left—not so much as a waistcoat even?'
>
> 'No, nothing.'
>
> 'It's embarrassing,' said Mr. Swiveller, 'in case of fire—even an umbrella would be something—but you did quite right, dear Marchioness. I should have died without you!'

It is an unattractive thought that, in order to point some particular moral, Dickens appears to have been bent on making her the illegitimate daughter of Sally Brass and Quilp. A long passage in which Miss Brass revealed the fact, was even written and printed before Dickens cut it out in the proofs. The brother and sister come to a bad end, and are last seen as two wretched shadows gliding out at night from the worst haunts of the London underworld, like other terrible spectres seen in its streets, who seem 'the embodied spirits of Disease, and Vice and Famine'. It has sometimes been thought too harsh a fate for two characters so amusing, but it is the shadow of the allegory again, which they had elsewhere helped to hold at bay with a band of characters as varied and entertaining as in any of Dickens's other shorter novels.

At the close of *The Old Curiosity Shop*, Master Humphrey's club was briefly revived, in order to allow him to abstract another manuscript from the clock-case and fall to the weekly readings once again. The new story was *Barnaby Rudge, A Tale of the Riots of 'Eighty*, one which Dickens had had in mind for the past five years. A start on it had actually been made in January 1840; a renewed beginning was made a year later; and its serialization began in February and continued until 27 November 1842.

Barnaby Rudge illustrates one of the difficulties of criticizing Dickens's lesser works, for by what standard is it to be judged? If it is set on the small shelf-full of the greatest novels of the world, its faults are seen to be glaring, its characterization thin, and its plot improbable; put it with Dickens's own works, and it is among the least important; but place it among the English novels of the decade immediately preceding it, and it is obviously outstanding. In fact, none of Dickens's earlier works should be judged without reference to other novels that were being written at the time. Without this it is hard, for example, to understand how the author of the high-spirited *Pickwick* and *Nickleby* could bear to produce the watered-down romance of the first part of *Barnaby Rudge*. It was because he was writing in the tradition of Scott, Bulwer Lytton, and Ainsworth. There was no stimulus to write at full stretch for a public that was delighted with *Eugene Aram* and *Jack Sheppard*. Even Scott was a poor inspiration; he was too slow and pedestrian, and though he was still revered most readers found him rather dull. For, as Trollope said, 'who can imagine . . . *Waverley* coming out in shilling numbers?'

The first half of *Barnaby* is in the old tradition. It is a plain historical novel about comic innkeepers, mysterious strangers, an unsolved murder, and a missing steward. It begins in the traditional manner, 'In the year 1775, there stood upon the borders of Epping Forest . . . a house of public entertainment called the Maypole.' A strange horseman then leaves the inn and goes galloping through the night, to be stopped by 'a red-faced, sturdy yeoman . . . bluff, hale and hearty'. This is Gabriel Varden, the locksmith who, rather like Simon Glover in *The Fair Maid of Perth*, has both a handsome daughter and an apprentice with ideas above his station.

There are faint traces of Scott all through the book. Barnaby Rudge, the simple-minded hero, is like both Davie Gellatley of *Waverley* and Madge Wildfire of *The Heart of Midlothian*; and it has even been suggested that, merely as a joke, Dickens introduced a somewhat thirsty character named Stagg into the story in order to echo the famous line in *The Lady of the Lake*, 'The stag at eve had drunk his fill'. This is too good *not* to be true; and, certainly, it is in keeping with the rest of these half-purposeful reminders of Sir Walter Scott. For they are present not because Dickens was borrowing from his predecessors, but because he was deliberately challenging the greatest of them on his own ground. He was out to write a historical novel that would surpass those of the author of *Waverley*; and, in leading up to the Gordon Riots and the attack on Newgate in the second half of the book, he meant to show that he could go far beyond what Scott had more moderately attempted in his description of the Porteous riots and the storming of the Tolbooth, at the beginning of *The Heart of Midlothian.*

The whole of the first part of the book was nothing but a preparation for the description of the famous riots. This was how Dickens regarded it himself. After the difficulties of starting were over, he began to look forward to the more exciting scenes to come in 'the thick of the story', and he told correspondents he had 'great designs in store'. After correcting the proof of chapter fifty-three, with its description of Lord George Gordon's secretary Gashford watching the rioters pass bent on loot and destruction, he wrote to Forster, 'I thought there was a good glimpse of a crowd from a window, eh?' And a week later he declared, 'I am warming up very much about *Barnaby*. Oh! If I only had him, from this time to the end, in monthly numbers. *N'importe!* I hope the interest will be pretty strong—and in every number, stronger.'

Whether, in writing of Dickens himself, we should make anything or not of his tremendous zest in describing scenes of uprising and revolt, it is difficult to say. He undoubtedly enjoyed writing them, and seemed to feel himself personally involved. As he went on, he wrote, 'I have just burst into Newgate, and am going in the next number, to tear the prisoners out by the hair of their heads'; and, soon after, 'I have let all the prisoners out of Newgate, burnt down Lord Mansfield's house, and played the very devil. Another number will finish the fires, and help us on towards the end. I feel quite smoky when I am at work.' In a sense, he was a rebel at heart, and even had some sympathy with a few of the rioters. But his interest in such scenes was a horrified fascination; he was repelled even more than he was attracted. His sketch of Dennis the hangman helps to show the divided nature of his sympathies, and how far he recognized it himself.

What many biographers who have tried to analyse Dickens have failed to allow for is that, far more than most of his contemporaries, he was aware of his own nature as well as those of his characters and readers. There would have been no need to explain to Dickens how the hangman has such a revolting attractiveness: he even wrote a special article on the subject, a few years later, when he read the letters applying for the post of hangman when there was an official vacancy ('The Finishing Schoolmaster', *Household Words*, 17 May 1851). He understood the strange attraction of violence: how 'sober workmen going home from their day's labour' became 'rioters in an instant', and how drink and violence made men 'fiends', 'wolves' and 'wild animals'. No one knew better how, as he said himself, the 'appetite and love for the marvellous and terrible' are 'among the natural characteristics of mankind' (chapter liv). The madness of Barnaby, the derangement of Lord George, the outrages of the mob which includes ordinary men who seem at first to be steadily pursuing a purpose, are all on the shadow-line between sanity and insanity. Dickens's attitude to the riots, as George Orwell pointed out, is largely clear from the fact that his first idea was to make its ringleaders three lunatics who had escaped from an asylum.

At the same time there is a dithyrambic delight about some of the writing which describes the wanton fury of the rioters not only in their attack on Newgate but simply in their wild pleasure in destruction:

> If Bedlam gates had been flung open wide, there would not have issued forth such maniacs as the frenzy of that night had made. There were men there, who danced and

> trampled on the beds of flowers as though they trod down human enemies, and wrenched them from their stalks, like savages who twisted human necks. There were men who cast their lighted torches in the air, and suffered them to fall upon their heads and faces. . . . There were men who rushed up to the fire, and paddled in it with their hands as if in water; and others who were restrained by force from plunging in, to gratify their deadly longing. On the skull of one drunken lad—not twenty by his looks—who lay upon the ground with a bottle to his mouth, the lead from the roof came streaming down in a shower of liquid fire, white hot; melting his head like wax. . . .

Yet Dickens had a serious purpose in writing such descriptions as well as an enjoyment in feeling his power. The whole novel was intended to be an attack on the old social order, on the weak hesitancy of the authorities, on the incompetent cruelty of the Law, and the hypocrisy of the upper classes who refused to accept the responsibilities of their position. The idea that Dickens had any sentimental regard for the past is completely wrong. As Humphry House pointed out, among the dummy book-backs with which he later decorated his study, was a set called, 'The Wisdom of Our Ancestors—I. Ignorance. II. Superstition. III. The Block. IV. The Stake. V. The Rack. VI. Dirt. VII. Disease.'

Strongly as Dickens believed in authority and hated disorder, he was often exasperatedly rebellious. *Barnaby Rudge* spoke to his own times in urging that society itself was responsible for its ills; and wherever he may have derived this idea (from Bulwer Lytton, Carlyle, or from his own observation) it is strongly though fitfully at work throughout the tale. It is as true of *Barnaby Rudge* as of his next novel, *Martin Chuzzlewit* (see 'Preface' to the 'cheap edition', 1849) that it preaches 'As we sow, we reap'. The vices of society are charged on men of the class of Sir John Chesters, on whom falls the curse of his unacknowledged son, Hugh, at the foot of the gallows, 'the black tree of which [he] is the ripened fruit'. It was with public neglect of the uncared-for children of its cities that Dickens was to declare that 'from every seed of evil . . . a field of ruin is grown. . . . There is no people on earth it would not put to shame.' It was just at this time (31 January 1841) that he was writing to his fellow-novelist, Mrs. Gore, of the children of the city streets, 'I have seen in different towns in England, and do see in London whenever I walk alone into its byeways at night, as I often do, such miseries and horrors among these little creatures —such an impossibility of their ever growing up to be good and happy—that those aristocratic dolls do turn me sick. . . .' For, at this time, to be both radical and middle-class were not thought to be necessarily contradictory.

Nevertheless, he felt that his purpose was sometimes misunderstood, and even while the story was in progress he had to write to explain it to at least two of his readers who had objected. To one, he declared that it was, in part, a protest against the way in which the rich expected the poor to be better than they, and to another that it was his intention 'to pursue cruelty and oppression . . . so long as I have energy of thought and the power of giving it utterance'. He felt that such misunderstandings were due to the difficulties of writing in weekly instalments; and he was so troubled by them that before the story was finished he wrote an Address to his readers explaining that, with his next tale, he meant to go back to 'our old and well-tried plan' of monthly publication.

This was, perhaps, a pity, because though he found it irksome to have to keep strictly to the story, Dickens was learning how to develop a plot. He still had to succeed. Forster put his finger on the main weakness of the novel when he complained that 'the interest with which the tale begins, has ceased to be its interest before the close'. The whole story of the mystery of Mr. Reuben Haredale's murder comes to seem almost irrelevant by the end. There is hardly even any attempt to maintain the suspense, and Edgar Allan Poe rather contemptuously claimed to have foretold the outcome by the end of the fifth chapter. Undoubtedly he was right in saying that the 'dark hints of some uncertain evil' in the first part of the book were bound to be a disappointment as soon as they were explained.

Yet, reviewing in the *Saturday Post*, Poe was quite willing to give high praise to Dickens's power of creating atmosphere, even though he thought he was guided 'less by artistical knowledge and reflection than by that intuitive feeling for the forcible and true which is the *sixth sense* of the man of genius'. He was particularly impressed by Barnaby's conversation and the introduction of Grip. (Poe's 'Raven' owes something to *Barnaby*.) One might add that *Barnaby Rudge* is not unlike Dickens's other historical novel, *A Tale of Two Cities*, in using melodrama to image forces that he would have found it hard to analyse. From recognizing man's love of the 'marvellous and terrible', Dickens was learning to use it to show conflicts within man and society; and already, especially at chapter-endings, he was developing the device of employing symbols to keep his intentions before the reader. The benighted idiot, less intelligent than the raven, his horror of blood, the hangman's heavy ironies, the 'redness' that Gashford burns to see 'blazing in the sky', all serve (as they are repeated) to deepen the effect and help to carry it through to the end.

While he had been in the middle of *Barnaby Rudge*, Dickens and his wife had been on holiday in Scotland, where he had made a great impression at a public banquet which was given him in Edinburgh. As the novel drew to a close, he began to have greater ambitions for travel; and a few weeks before the end he announced in an address to his readers, 'Taking advantage of the respite which the close of this work will afford me, I have decided, in January next, to pay a visit to America.'

Chapter Six

AMERICA—1842: *MARTIN CHUZZLEWIT*

ONCE he had decided to go to America, Dickens lost no time in preparing to leave. Catherine Dickens was persuaded to accompany him, arrangements were made for the children, who were to stay behind, and berths were booked on the steamship *Britannia* which was to leave Liverpool early in January 1842. Even a serious illness could not quench Dickens's enthusiasm. America, he wrote, he had already visited in his 'day-dreams many times', he 'yearned to know' its people, and far from feeling any distaste at its republicanism (like most British travellers) he had every sympathy with its revolutionary origins provoked by the 'obstinacy of that swine-headed anointed of the Lord—his Majesty King George the Third'.

He and Mrs. Dickens were seen off by Forster. They suffered a terrible crossing, in the course of which they gave themselves up for lost and 'waited quietly for the worst'. Several years later Thackeray was sceptical enough to ask one of the ship's officers whether Dickens's published account was exaggerated, only to be assured that the storm was the worst the speaker had ever known. All through their travels Catherine Dickens loyally endured all kinds of hardships without complaining, leaving her husband to take the limelight and thinking chiefly of the children who had been left behind. She wrote to her sister:

You cannot imagine what a dreadful Voyage we had. We were 18 days in our passage and experienced all the horror of a storm at Sea. . . . I was nearly distracted with terror and don't know what I should have done, had it not been for the great kindness and composure of my dear Charles. It was awful. . . . And you may imagine our relief and happiness when towards morning it gradually lulled and although the ship was heaving terribly all day owing to the heaving swell which followed—all further danger from the wind was over.

We met with another danger two or three nights after that. Owing to our unskilful Pilot we ran aground which caused great consternation as we were surrounded by rocks. . . . We were told, after the danger was past, that the sailors had taken off their jackets and shoes ready to swim ashore.

It was with relief that they saw Boston Harbour, where they were met by a dozen newspaper reporters who 'came leaping on board at peril of their lives'. Dickens at once felt an instinctive revulsion. 'If you could have seen how I wrung their wrists!' he wrote.

All other first impressions, however, were favourable. The hotel was 'excellent', and 'good nature, universal'. There were letters of welcome from the authorities of almost every State; deputations from the Far West; and invitations to all kinds of entertainments, balls, and dinners. 'There was never king or emperor', he wrote, 'so cheered or followed by crowds.' He worked hard at getting to know the country, its people and institutions; and then, a week after their arrival, he and Catherine attended a banquet which was the climax of their reception at Boston. 'It was a most superb affair', Dickens told Forster, 'and the speaking *admirable*. Indeed, the general talent for public speaking here is . . . most striking.' Even so, he made his own mark in a speech in which he told his audience how he had 'dreamed by day and night for years of setting foot upon this shore', and how even if he had wandered there 'unknowing and unknown', he would have come, 'with all my sympathies clustering richly round this land and people', and 'with all my energies as fully bent on judging for myself, and speaking out, and telling in my sphere the truth, as I do now when you rain down welcomes on my head'.

From Boston they went on to Hartford, where he enjoyed a visit to a lunatic asylum and they were serenaded by a college choir. But the harmony between Dickens and his hosts was soon to be broken. Towards the end of his speech at Boston, he had made a passing reference to the subject of international copyright, and at a public dinner at Hartford he committed the same offence. Once the meal was over, speech followed speech as toasts were given to 'A Common Language and Literature', 'The Great Republic of Letters', and 'Literature—that Neutral Ground on which Men of Every Clime meet in Peaceful Homage to the Intellect'; and, as he sat listening, Dickens could not help thinking that though they shared a common literature, America contributed little towards it financially, and that it was likely to be neutral ground only as long as certain delicate topics were avoided.

Now, Dickens's strength (and weakness) as a traveller in America, was that he tended to judge everything in terms of right and wrong. He was like one of his own young heroes, he would not 'stand by' and see injustice done. So, when he rose to reply, after graciously thanking his listeners, he said that though it is always difficult to judge an author's 'personal character from his writings', he thought that 'at least a reader will rise from the perusal of a book with some defined and tangible idea of the writer's moral creed and broad purposes'. He went on: 'Gentlemen, my moral creed . . . is very easily summed up. . . . I take it that we are born and that we hold our sympathies, hopes and energies in trust for the many, and not for the few. That we cannot hold in too strong a light of disgust and contempt . . . all meanness, falsehood, cruelty and oppression of every grade and kind. Above all, that nothing is high, because it is in a high place; and that nothing is low because it is in a low one.' After returning further compliments to his hosts, he then came to the point by saying: 'Gentlemen, as I have no secrets from you, in the spirit of the confidence you have engendered between us . . . I would beg leave to whisper in your ear two words, *International Copyright*.'

He reminded his hearers that books by British authors were reprinted in America without any benefit to the writers, and that most of them could ill afford to be deprived of such reward; that American authors suffered even more, since their publishers saw little point in paying them when they could print English works for nothing; and that, as a speaker at Boston had observed, if there had been an international copyright agreement in existence, 'Scott might not have sunk beneath the mighty pressure on his brain.' Like Captain Marryat and Harriet Martineau, who had preceded him, Dickens was determined not to appear to acquiesce in the American piracies; and although he did not directly connect his remarks on his 'moral creed' with the need for international copyright, he left no doubt that he looked on the question as a moral one. Like Carlyle, though he did not then say so, he thought that the matter had been decided long ago by the commandment, 'Thou shalt not steal.'

No worse time could have been chosen for raising the

question—not that either British or American authors had ever allowed it to drop; still, it was unwise to mention it in public. During the past few years 'mammoth' newspapers had arisen, in which all the most popular new works were published for the price of a few cents. Almost all American writers agreed with Dickens and were in favour of a copyright agreement; but in attacking 'piracy' Dickens was attacking the press, and the American press was liable to hit back by any means, fair or foul. No time was lost. *The Hartford Daily Times*, which carried a report of the speech, ominously remarked of international copyright, 'It happens that we want no advice upon this subject, and it will be better for Mr. Dickens, if he refrains from introducing the matter.'

Dickens was not to be dissuaded. He kept to an energetic programme of visiting all kinds of public institutions, from schools to prisons, and when he arrived at New York, he and Mrs. Dickens attended a tremendous reception, known as the 'Boz Ball'. But when arrangements were made for another banquet in his honour he warned the committee that he would feel bound to speak on the subject of international copyright, and that (as he told Forster) 'nothing should deter me . . . that the shame was theirs . . . and that as I would not spare them when I got home, I would not be silent here'.

The dinner itself was a great occasion. In the chair was Washington Irving, the essayist whom Dickens admired almost as much as Oliver Goldsmith, and who had a great admiration for Dickens in return. It was Irving who had written to Dickens, after reading *The Old Curiosity Shop*, and helped to persuade him to come to America. Mrs. Dickens, and a number of ladies, were admitted to hear the speakers and though the chairman was inaudible, Dickens rose to the occasion splendidly. He intended it to be his last public speech in the United States, 'for remembering the short time I have before me in this land of mighty interest . . . I have felt it almost a duty to decline the honours which my generous friends elsewhere would heap upon me, and henceforth to pass through the country more quietly'. He expressed his gratitude for their welcome, 'with a full heart', and declared that he would always bear 'a deeper sense' of their 'kind, affectionate and noble greeting', than it was 'possible to convey'.

Very moderately, he then went on to speak of the copyright question, asserting his right, 'for the last time . . . to appeal to you . . . on a question of universal literary interest in both countries.—And, gentlemen,' he went on, 'I claim this justice: that I have made the appeal as one who has a most righteous claim to speak and to be heard; and that I have done so in a frank, and courteous, and good-humoured spirit of deference to those who frankly, courteously, and good humouredly differed from me in any or every respect.' That was all. The rest of the speech was taken up with graceful tribute to the chairman, who later responded by proposing the toast of International Copyright. Indeed, Irving himself recognized that it would be of great benefit to American authors, and headed two petitions in its favour which were presented to Congress.

In order to understand Dickens's purpose in persisting in his attempt to bring the matter forward, it must not be forgotten that he was now looked upon as the foremost *professional* author of his country. From the first he had set himself to do all he could to raise the standard of his profession. *Pickwick* had been dedicated to T. J.

Talfourd as the author of a Copyright Bill; and *Nicholas Nickleby* contained an attack on dramatic pirates, and several shrewd asides on the dignity of the profession. Though Dickens himself was involved, it was largely as a spokesman for others; and when he wrote to Forster asking him to organize support from 'the principal English authors who signed the international copyright petition', they came forward without hesitation. Before he left America he was able to publish a statement proving that he had not spoken for himself alone.

The rest of his time in New York was passed more quietly before, a week later, Dickens and his wife continued their travels. They went on to Philadelphia and to Washington; to Richmond, to Pittsburg, to Cincinnati, and down the Ohio as far as St. Louis. Where the Ohio joins the Mississippi, they passed the city of Cairo, immortalized in *Martin Chuzzlewit* as Eden, which 'the waters of the Deluge might have left . . . but a week before, so choked with slime and matted growth was the hideous swamp which bore that name'. All through his journey, with the exception of a dinner at Richmond, Dickens kept to his declaration that he would keep away from further public speaking and receptions.

As he journeyed on, his opinion of America began to change. He was at first disillusioned by what he heard about Washington, and the process was carried still further when he reached it. Some of his most outspoken letters were written to Macready, who he knew was strongly pro-American—just as he had himself been before he came. 'It is no use,' he declared, 'I am disappointed. This is not the republic I came to see; this is not the republic of my imagination.' He wrote to him again:

I have not changed—I cannot change, my dear Macready—my secret opinion of this country. I have said to Forster that I believe the heaviest blow ever dealt at Liberty's Head, will be dealt by this nation in the ultimate failure of its example to the Earth. See what is passing now—Look at the exhausted Treasury; the paralyzed Government; the uncouth representatives of a free people; the desperate contests between the North and the South; the iron curb and brazen muzzle fastened on every man who speaks his mind, even in that Republican Hall, to which Republican men are sent by a Republican people to speak Republican Truths—the stabbings and the shootings, and coarse and brutal threatenings exchanged between Senators under the very Senate's roof—the intrusion of the most pitiful, mean, malicious, creeping crawling party spirit, into all transactions of life . . . the silly, drivelling, slanderous, wicked, monstrous, Party Press. . . .

P.S. I need not say that I have many pleasant things to say of America. God forbid it should be otherwise. I speak to you as I would to myself. I am a Lover of Freedom, disappointed.—That's all.

Much of his visit Dickens greatly enjoyed, and he made numerous friends among the people wherever he went. Many of them stood by him even when he published *American Notes* and *Martin Chuzzlewit*, and some of them remained his friends for the rest of his life. But the whole visit was being poisoned by the attacks in the press. A few days after his speech in New York, he wrote privately to the Mayor of Boston to say that the attacks in the newspapers caused him 'agony such as I have never experienced since my birth'. He still kept this from his wife, but, as he warned Macready after he had got home, 'if you knew but one hundredth part of the malignity, the monstrous falsehood, the beastly attacks made even upon Catherine, which were published all over America, even while I was there, on my mere confession that the country had disappointed me—confessions wrung from me in private society before I had written a word', he would not question his opinion. Already, Dickens told the Mayor, scores of newspapers had attacked him 'in such terms of vagabond scurrility as they would denounce no murderer with'.

It is clear that, though he probably exaggerated, Dickens was bitterly hurt by the attacks that were made upon him, and that (although they have not yet been examined very closely) some of them were unforgivable. More than most men, at this time of his life, Dickens was dependent on establishing a friendly relation with his public. He had come to America with 'all his sympathies clustering richly round its lands and people', and now he found this affectionate friendship blasted by men he could only regard as his enemies. The American press was often outspoken, personal, vindictive and irresponsible; and Dickens was caught, for example, between the spicy vulgarities of the *New York Herald* and the moral warfare of the *Washington Globe*, which wrote that:

> If to delineate the human character in its lowest state of ignorance, vice and degradation . . . is to be a Democratic writer, then most assuredly Mr. Dickens is one. He has exhibited human nature in its naked, ragged, deformity, reeking with vice and pollution. . . . Such a school of literature can only aid the course and progress of vice. . . .

It seems evident, too, that Dickens was driven to keep within rather a limited circle of friends and supporters, and that in his outspoken hatred of slavery he put another barrier between himself and public opinion. He had meant to keep silent about it, but, when questioned directly, he did not think it right to conceal his opinions.

They continued their tour by stage-coach, steamer,

and railway. They saw much more of the people when they were away from the cities—too much sometimes—but found them 'by nature, frank, brave, cordial, hospitable and affectionate'. Yet Dickens much preferred 'the educated American . . . cultivation and refinement seem but to enhance their warmth of heart and ardent enthusiasm'. Nevertheless, it was with great relief that they at last passed over into Canada, at the Niagara Falls, where he 'was taken dreadfully loyal after dinner, and drank the Queen's health in a bumper'. They spent just a month in Canada, where Dickens took a leading part in some amateur theatricals at Montreal, returned to New York on 6 June, and six days later sailed for England.

Once home, after enthusiastically celebrating with his friends, he quickly settled to writing a book on his travels. He had always intended to do this, to defray expenses, and his letters to Forster had been written as a sort of journal to work from when he returned. Before he got back, Forster had even been giving readings from them to select friends; Bulwer Lytton enjoyed them, and wrote of a passage now presumably lost 'I have been haunted by visions of the "Piazza" commemorated by Dickens. How Swift would have smiled and revelled!'; and Crabb Robinson (Wordsworth's and Blake's friend) noted, 'I went after breakfast . . . to Forster's to hear him read . . . some of Dickens's letters from America. Better letters I never heard. . . . The descriptions most animated, satire and sublime painting admirably intermixed. I was gratified by finding that he had not been deceived by the gross flattery of the people. He confirms my dislike. . . . Their want of honesty is not so flagrant as their grossness of manners, but it is as certain.'

Once he had accumulated his letters home, however,

Dickens took care to leave out all personal references in his account, all satire, in fact almost everything that made his reports to Forster so entertaining to read. In later years, before they were destroyed, Forster went to the length of having a lock fitted to the letters after they were bound. The actual *American Notes* are pleasantly innocuous; it is the sort of work anyone might have written. Dickens even took the trouble to write a preface, which he later suppressed, in which he explained that his book was 'not statistical . . . comprehends no small talk . . . has not a grain of political ingredient . . . neither does it contain . . . any lengthened or minute account of my personal reception in the United States. . . . This book is simply what it claims to be—a record of the impressions I received from day to day, during my hasty travels in America.' It remains the best American travel-book of the period there is, but it is first in a rather feeble class.

Even before he began writing, he set in train an attempt to organize English authors and publishers to co-operate with American writers in a demand for a copyright agreement. He explained, in a circular letter, that the opposition came only from 'the editors and proprietors of newspapers almost exclusively devoted to the republication of popular English works', who were 'for the most part, men of very low attainments, and of more than indifferent reputation'. A deputation was sent to Gladstone, at the Board of Trade, but, as far as America was concerned, the agreement would have had to be a political measure, and it was in no party's interest to support it. Dickens engaged in one more attempt to push the matter, more diplomatically, in 1852, but it was not for another fifty years that anything effective was done.

Meanwhile there was no lull in the newspaper war. Letters criticizing America were forged and printed over Dickens's name, and letters criticizing Dickens, supposedly signed by prominent men such as Daniel O'Connell, were added to them. The scandal of the American press was neither of Dickens's making nor magnified by his imagination. O'Connell joined him in referring to 'the vileness of a great portion of the newspaper press in the United States', and Forster stoked up the fires with two long anonymous articles in the *Foreign Quarterly*, which their opponents did not hesitate to attribute to Dickens. It is to the credit of most Americans that they do not seem to have let the controversy affect their judgement. They themselves disliked many of the things at which Dickens protested. It is rather remarkable that one of the examples selected by Forster to show the American fear of their own press was the recent notorious *Somers* case, of the execution of a midshipman by his pious commander, which gave Melville the idea for Captain Vere and *Billy Budd*. Yet it was left to Dickens to speak out at the time, and it was he who chiefly suffered the consequences.

To Longfellow, who had promised him a return visit, Dickens wrote sending the copyright circular and accounting for one of the more notorious forgeries:

> You know what the American Press is, and will be, I dare say, as little surprised at this outrage as I was. Still it exasperates me (I am of rather a fierce turn at times) very much; and I walked about for a week or two, with a vague desire to take somebody by the throat and shake him. . . .
>
> I have decided . . . to publish my American Visit. By the time you come to me, I hope I shall have finished writing it. I have spoken very honestly and fairly; and I know that those in America for whom I care will like me the better for the book. A great many people, I dare say, will like me infinitely

the worse, and make a Devil of me straightaway. [28 September, 1842.]

Then, as soon as he had finished *American Notes*, Dickens went on an uproarious holiday in Cornwall with Forster, Maclise, and Clarkson Stanfield. 'I never laughed in my life as I did on this journey', he told a friend; 'seriously, I do not believe there ever was such a trip.' Even so, it was undertaken partly because he thought of opening a new story with a scene on 'the dreariest and most desolate portion' of the Cornish coast. For some reason the idea was abandoned while they were on holiday, perhaps because he found it too remote from the bustling scenes of life that usually moved his pen. Once back, he set to work and wrote to Forster, 'Behold finally, the title of the new book . . . "The Life and Adventures of Martin Chuzzlewig, his family, friends, and enemies".'

As he had promised in the Address to his readers towards the end of *Barnaby Rudge*, the new novel was to be in monthly numbers. Dickens had then complained that weekly serialization was 'most anxious, perplexing, and difficult', but in spite of the change he still found it hard to make a start. In mid-November he wrote to a friend, half-jokingly and half in earnest: 'Your most kind note found me in the agonies of contriving and plotting a new book; in which stage . . . I am accustomed to walk up and down the house, smiting my head dejectedly; and to be so horribly cross and surly, that the boldest fly at my approach. At such times, even the Postman knocks at my door with a mild feebleness, and my publishers always come two together.' It was always an anxious period, and it was with a 'Thank God!' that, three weeks later, he told Forster that the first number was nearly finished.

It was on sale early in the new year, while Dickens

went on 'hammering away' at the number to follow. But it was not long before he learnt that the book was badly received. It was selling less than any of his previous novels, at a time when success was needed more than ever. There were several reasons for this. The public was beginning to take him for granted, the new book was quite unsuitable for the Victorian family, and once a serial had made a bad start it was difficult for it to recover. Things went so far that one of the partners of Chapman and Hall said that they would probably have to cut Dickens's payments by fifty pounds a month. At this, Dickens declared that he would part with them once the novel was finished, and even try to do without a publisher for the future. 'You know, as well as I,' he wrote to Forster, 'that I think *Chuzzlewit* . . . immeasurably the best of my stories.' In the long run his confidence was justified, and it became his best seller next to *Pickwick* and *David Copperfield*. For the moment he was 'so irritated, so rubbed in the tenderest part of my eye-lids with bay-salt', that he hardly felt able to write at all.

Martin Chuzzlewit, nevertheless, has certain weaknesses. The first chapter, which traces the history of the Chuzzlewits, is an absurd rigmarole after the manner of Henry Fielding in *Jonathan Wild*. It also seems to include some forgotten topical satire which missed its aim. Its main fault, after that, is the plot. In construction it is undoubtedly the weakest of Dickens's works, and the worse for an ambition to weave a mystery round the curmudgeonly old Martin Chuzzlewit, who is transformed into a universal benefactor by the final number. Its closing scene, in which all the characters are re-united, is a triumph of theatrical conventionality which would have shamed Vincent Crummles.

It is not even as well planned as *Nickleby* and it has the disadvantage that, being intended as a satire on ordinary life, it needs to be more realistic. It is true that, after he had finished, Dickens said that he had tried 'to resist the temptation of the current Monthly Number, and to keep a steadier eye on the general purpose and design' (*Preface*), but this is by no means clear from the story. It is true, too, that the manuscript shows that by the end of the third number he had already decided on 'Old Martin's plot to degrade and punish Pecksniff in the end'. Yet it is not well worked-out. The situation in which a father (Anthony Chuzzlewit) who so loves his son that he forgives him even when he knows that the son is plotting his murder, was taken from Le Sage's *Gil Blas*; and it should be remembered that, as much as *Pickwick* and more than his other first five novels, *Chuzzlewit* was still written in the tradition of the glorious shelf-full of eighteenth-century novels that Dickens had first read in childhood.

As much as any of his books, too, it is written with a moral purpose. It may be unnecessary to labour this point, but it is impossible to understand Dickens without it, and no one can question that this was his purpose in *Martin Chuzzlewit*. Sara Coleridge noted how, 'besides all the fun', it contained 'very marked and available morals'. Dickens explained, himself, that he 'set out . . . with the intention of exhibiting, in various aspects, the commonest of all the vices'. Forster confirms it: 'The notion of . . . Pecksniff', he says, 'was really the origin of the book; the design being to show, more or less by every person introduced, the number and variety of humours and vices that have their root in selfishness.' More than in any other of Dickens's novels, he bursts through in appeal to the readers, 'Oh, moralists', and

'Oh! ye Pharisees of the nineteenth hundredth year of Christian Knowledge', and 'Oh late-remembered, much-forgotten, mouthing, braggart duty . . . when will mankind begin to know thee!' It was as if he felt sickened by the skill with which he described Pecksniff, and had to expel a gust of righteous indignation.

The best things in the novel, in fact, were not planned but grew and flourished naturally. Mrs. Gamp and Pecksniff, especially, developed in a manner Dickens himself had not foreseen. 'As to the way in which these characters have opened out,' he wrote of them, 'that is to me one of the most surprising processes of the mind in this sort of invention. Given what one knows, what one does not know springs up; and I am as absolutely certain of its being true, as I am of the law of gravitation—if such a thing be possible, more so.' Such, says Forster revealingly, 'was the very process of creation', with 'all his important characters'. Both Mrs. Gamp and Pecksniff were founded on real people, and, given what he knew of them, Dickens felt that almost by a natural law he could show what they would say or do in any possible circumstances.

Pecksniff, himself, was unquestionably drawn from a miscellaneous writer and editor, S. C. Hall—'Shirt-collar Hall', Douglas Jerrold used to call him—and, to leave no doubt, he was introduced in the novel as: 'A most exemplary man. . . . His very throat was moral. You saw a good deal of it. You looked over a very low fence of white cravat . . . and there it lay, a valley between two jutting heights of collar, serene and whiskerless before you.' Whether Hall ever specifically did anything to earn Dickens's disapproval is unknown. He certainly had a reputation rather like Pecksniff's, and for Dickens's taste he may even have had too great a fondness for Americans. Writing to Wilkie Collins about a Fourth of July dinner in London to celebrate American Independence, Dickens still found Hall loathsome enough, even thirteen years later, for his bile to 'begin to shake and swell, like Green's balloon with the gas turned on. . . . Being on the Salt Sea you probably did not see a speech of Samivel Carter Hall's. . . . The snivelling insolence of it, the concentrated essence of Snobbery in it, and the Philogullododgeitiveness where it was steeped, have so affected me that I have flown to Cockle for succour.'

So naturally do some parts of the novel seem to grow rather than develop according to plan, that but for Forster's express authority one would have thought Dickens had meant to show that selfishness and low cunning have their place on both sides of the Atlantic. According to Forster, however, Dickens's resolve to send Martin to America was 'adopted as suddenly' as his hero's decision, in the belief that it would increase the book's popularity. Once there, the moral theme flourishes once more: 'Mr. Pecksniff's house was more than a thousand miles away; and again this happy chronicle has Liberty and Moral Sensibility for its high companions.' If hypocrisy was the English vice, as the French critic Taine declared, then it had soon become naturalized in the United States. Indeed, 'if native statesmen, orators, and pamphleteers, are to be believed', said Dickens, 'that peculiarly transatlantic article, a moral sense', had been quite monopolized by America. The satire of the New York Norrises is based on the fact that they are just like their counterparts in England and that, as the 'good' American Mr. Bevan remarks, 'they are made of pretty much the same stuff as other folks, if they would but own it, and not set up on false pretences'.

No justice can be done to the satire of the rest of the American characters in a few short sentences. Unfair as it may have been, there is such a relish and zest about the way in which Dickens lays on the lash, that it can hardly be matched anywhere else in his work. Washington Irving, who had wept on parting from Dickens, refused to meet him when he was next in England. The poet Bryant's resentment lasted until Dickens's second visit to America (in 1867) when he would neither call on him nor go to one of his Readings. It was not that they objected to his satire of men like Hannibal Chollop, Jefferson Brick, and Elijah Pogram, but that they were unwilling to forgive such insults to their country as the searing attack on 'that Republic, but yesterday let loose upon her noble course, and . . . to-day so maimed and lame, so full of sores and ulcers . . . that her best friends turn from the loathsome creature with disgust'. Nor was it that they found the book unjust, but simply that (as Theodore Roosevelt said) it left a wrong impression—the people described were not truly representative. According to Forster, 'as time moved on a little, the laughter on their side of the Atlantic became quite as great as our amusement on this side'. A doubtful proposition, but at least one can agree with him that in eventually taking it in good part the Americans proved themselves 'a good humoured and placable people'.

Perhaps more significant was the reception of *American Notes* and *Martin Chuzzlewit* in England. The novel was not merely less popular than Dickens's earlier works, but some of the reviewers were in wait ready to trounce him for a radicalism that had previously gone almost unscathed. One of the *Blackwood's* proprietors wrote exultantly of their review, 'It will annoy Mr. Dickens and his clique very much.' Dickens was denounced for his youth, his 'slipshod style', his 'political allusions', and generally for not being born a gentleman. 'Three such reviews', wrote Samuel Warren (the *Blackwood's* reviewer) privately, 'as *Maginn* [i.e. *Fraser's*], the *Edinburgh*, & the *Quarterly* must do Dickens tremendous mischief. He has none to thank, however, but himself for this.' There was a reaction against him. In America and England, Dickens had protested strongly at what he thought was wrong; and to understand his life, if not his work, one must appreciate that his power was explosive partly because it was pent up; if it expressed some of his inner conflicts, it was directed outwards; that it was aimed, and his targets were often well-selected and able to retaliate.

Dickens himself never lost faith in his genius. 'I *know*', he wrote, 'that I could sustain my place . . . . though fifty writers started up tomorrow.' He exulted in a new power to suggest character, if not to show it in its full complexity. From this time forward he had the ability to show *repressed* feelings which may give a grotesque or humorous oddity, or an impression of malignant power. In characters such as Rosa Dartle and Miss Wade, in later novels, the principle was sometimes carried to extremes. A first sketch for Rosa is the scorned Charity Pecksniff, with her thwarted hatred of Jonas. Mrs. Gamp shows a loathsome desire to 'lay-out' one of her patients, a handsome young man, as a corpse. In *Martin Chuzzlewit* Dickens is always showing this new skill, whether in his insight into Jonas's sensations of guilt when he thinks of the body in the wood, or in the words of Pecksniff himself, on the night of the dinner-party at Todgers's, after he has been removed from the room and reappears to address his friends from the landing:

> 'This is very soothing,' said Mr. Pecksniff, after a pause. 'Extremely so. Cool and refreshing; particularly to the legs! The legs of the human subject, my friends, are a beautiful production. Compare them with wooden legs, and observe the difference between the anatomy of nature and the anatomy of art. Do you know,' said Mr. Pecksniff, leaning over the banisters, with an odd recollection of his familiar manner among new pupils at home, 'that I should very much like to see Mrs. Todgers's notion of a wooden leg, if perfectly agreeable to herself!'

It was Carlyle who had said that 'in every man there is a madman', and having discovered this for himself, Dickens went on to show it in his works.

Chapter Seven

CHRISTMAS BOOKS AND *DOMBEY AND SON*

When *Martin Chuzzlewit* was published, in July 1844, it was dedicated 'To Miss Burdett Coutts . . . With the True and Earnest Regard of the Author'. Miss Burdett Coutts was one of the daughters of Sir Francis Burdett, who had inherited the great wealth of her grandfather, the banker, only a few years before. At this time she was aged thirty and had known Dickens for about five years. She was a strange woman. During the first part of her life she was a devoted philanthropist, using her fortune for all kinds of good works, personal charity, Church endowments, and far-reaching social experiments; and once she and Dickens came together he helped her to administer her charities, and suggested all kinds of practical schemes to be carried out. Yet, although she ultimately came to be a woman of strong resolution and acquired a great reputation as a philanthropist, she was extremely reserved and cautiously dependent on others. Her judgement and ability have been overpraised. She owed her eminence to her long life (1814–1906), a sense of duty, and her great inherited wealth.

Yet she was also a good friend, an agreeable companion, and a woman of ready sympathy. She was tall and shy, and seems to have been too unsure of herself, in her position as an heiress, ever to trust to any friendships except with eminent men who were safely married. It was her tragedy that, when she was sixty-seven, she suddenly married one of her secretaries, aged twenty-eight, lost over half her fortune, and was unhappy and disappointed for the rest of her life.

This, however, was yet to come, and has no bearing on her friendship with Dickens, except to account for the way in which as soon as they came to know each other they happily settled down to working in partnership in all kinds of schemes to help the poor in London. She found in him the same affectionate loyalty she sought in her friendship with the Duke of Wellington. Her association with Dickens was a romantic one only in the sense that a great heiress and a great author devotedly worked together, for nearly twenty years, for the good of others.

The first occasion on which they joined forces in anything but private charity, was in their support for the first of the Ragged Schools. This was an educational movement which was started to help the poorest and dirtiest children of the London streets, whom no other school would receive. Dickens's attention had been attracted by an advertisement in the press. He visited the school, which was in the squalid district he had chosen for Fagin's headquarters, and then wrote Miss Burdett Coutts 'a sledge-hammer account', in which he told her of its plight. Another description of the same establishment can be found in a startling letter Dickens sent to the *Daily News* in 1846, in which he wrote of its pupils as 'young thieves and beggars—with nothing natural to youth about them: with nothing frank, ingenuous, or pleasant in their faces; low-browed, vicious, cunning, wicked; abandoned of all help but this; speeding downward to destruction; and UNUTTERABLY IGNORANT'.

Aware that Miss Coutts had just given two hundred

pounds to a Church subscription list, Dickens persuaded her to pay for a bathing-place and to offer other forms of practical assistance. He wanted this to be combined with the stipulation that there should be no narrow-minded or merely religious teaching in its classes, and, confident that Miss Coutts would do what he recommended, he wrote enthusiastically to Forster, 'She is a most excellent creature . . . and I have the most perfect affection and respect for her.'

Although he was already aware of the need for such work, the sight of the Ragged Schools seems to have given a stimulus to another book he had just started 'in the odd moments of leisure left him by *Chuzzlewit*'. Again, it was something completely new, nothing less than *A Christmas Carol*. It was meant to be in the fashion of the old nursery tales; and, once he had started, so Dickens wrote, he 'excited himself in the most extraordinary manner' in its composition, and 'walked the black streets of London' thinking of it, 'fifteen and twenty miles many a night when all the sober folks had gone to bed'.

To some modern tastes, Scrooge has begun to cloy; but this ought not to prevent us from appreciating the ingenuity of the *Carol*'s construction, and the unflagging vitality of its writing. The later Christmas books, with the exception of *The Chimes*, show every sign of having been written to order, but *A Christmas Carol* is spontaneous. It is not all about mistletoe, good cheer, and Christmas pudding. The young thieves and beggars Dickens saw in Field Lane, reappear just as the Ghost of Christmas Present is about to depart:

> From the foldings of its robe, it brought forth two children: wretched, abject, frightful, hideous, meagre, ragged. . . . Scrooge started back appalled.

'Spirit! are they yours?' Scrooge could say no more.

'They are Man's,' said the Spirit, looking down upon them. 'And they cling to me appealing from their fathers. This boy is Ignorance. This girl is Want. Beware them both.' . . .

'Have they no refuge or resource?' cried Scrooge.

'Are there no prisons?' said the Spirit, turning on him . . . with his own words. 'Are there no workhouses?'

The bell struck twelve.

Scrooge looked about him for the Ghost, and saw it not.

Even in *A Christmas Carol* Dickens expresses much more than what Professor Louis Cazamian calls a mere 'philosophie de la Noël'. It is true that the main emphasis is on pious benevolence; but the *Carol* is not just an appeal for a change of heart, for the warning to beware Want and Ignorance, the children of men, is hardly less memorable than Tiny Tim's 'God bless Us, Every One!'

It caused a sensation at the time. Lord Jeffrey considered that it had 'done more good' than could be 'traced to all the pulpits and confessionals in Christendom' during the past year. Thackeray declared that it was 'a national benefit', and Dickens told Macready that he thought it had been 'the most prodigious success' he had ever achieved. Unfortunately, it was financially disappointing. For, still struggling to be independent of publishers, he had persuaded Chapman and Hall merely to bring it out on commission, hoping to reap the full profits himself. But it was too expensively produced, and, after their differences over *Martin Chuzzlewit*, Dickens felt it would be better to find a new publisher. His next book was issued by Bradbury and Evans, with whom he remained until after 1858, when he returned to Chapman and Hall.

He was unsettled altogether, for he now decided to act on a plan he had had for some years, and to live abroad for a while. He was still not happy about publication in monthly parts, and there were times when he was almost appalled at the amount he was writing. He had tried to escape by going to America; he had started the *Clock* to avoid writing fiction; he had even unsuccessfully applied to a member of the government to see if he could be made a London magistrate, like Henry Fielding; and he was now determined to give himself a year off by going to Italy. He had Sir Walter Scott's fate always in mind: he could not help thinking of what he would have given 'to have gone abroad, of his own free will, a young man, instead of creeping there, a driveller in his miserable decay'.

Forster's mild protests were swept aside, and, in a few months' time, Dickens gathered up his family, packed it into an enormous 'old shabby devil of a coach', and set off for Italy. At Lyons they travelled down the Rhône, and at Marseilles they embarked for Genoa. On arrival they settled into the Villa di Bella Vista, a 'lonely, rusty, stagnant staggerer of a domain'. It was summer. The Alps ranged in the distance, the sea was a vivid Prussian blue, and the vineyards below were 'green, green, green'. It suited Dickens, and he wrote home gaily: 'The day gets brighter, brighter, brighter till it's night. The summer gets hotter, hotter, hotter till it explodes. The fruit gets riper, riper, riper till it tumbles down and rots.' He entered into the spirit of Italy, and wrote a series of letters home to Forster, which he intended to use for a book on the same plan as *American Notes*.

After a month or two they moved into another stately home, the Palazzo Peschiere, where Dickens set to work on his second Christmas book. He had, perhaps, been disappointed that his readers had taken to heart only the more comforting passages of his message in the *Carol*, and this time he meant to write something that would 'shame the cruel and canting'. At first, he found it difficult to settle to work. He longed for the familiar streets of London, and wrote that he had never so staggered 'upon the threshold' of a book before. The maddening clash of steeple bells set his brain reeling. Then, suddenly, Forster received a note which said simply, 'We have heard THE CHIMES at midnight, Master Shallow!' and he knew that his friend had found a title.

It was just at this time, while he was unsettled by the difficulties of his work, when convent bells were sounding through the night, and he was sleeping in a strange room where mass had often been performed, that Dickens had an extraordinary recurrence of his dreams of Mary Hogarth. It was not so surprising, perhaps, that it should have happened to him then, but the letter in which he describes it shows that it seemed to him as startling as a vision, 'as real, animated, and full of passion as Macready . . . in the last scene of *Macbeth*'. Mary's spirit seemed to appear before him, 'in blue drapery', like the Madonna, 'in a picture by Raphael':

> It was so full of compassion and sorrow for me . . . that it cut me to the heart. . . . I said, in an agony of entreaty lest it should leave me, 'What is the True religion?' As it paused a moment without replying, I said . . . in such an agony of haste, lest it should go away!—'You think, as I do, that the Form of religion does not so greatly matter, if we try to do good?—or,' I said . . . 'perhaps the Roman Catholic is the best?' . . . 'For *you*,' said the Spirit, full of such heavenly tenderness for me, that I felt as if my heart

would break, 'for *you*, it is the best!' Then I awoke, with the tears running down my face, and myself in exactly the condition of the dream.

The chief importance of the incident, perhaps, lies in what it reveals of the depth of Dickens's feelings. So natural in all other ways, he was unlike almost anyone else in his intensity. Forster, indeed, says that he had recently suffered from doubts and difficulties about religion, and that this was the first consideration 'that would have risen' in connection with it, 'in any mind to which his was intimately known'. This is important, though not revealed anywhere else in his letters, works, or recorded conversations with his friends. It certainly did not indicate any strong leaning to Roman Catholicism, of which he strongly disapproved. It was probably influenced by the very natural association between the name, Mary, and the Virgin; and it is strange to notice, what seems to have caught no one's attention before, that on the head of Little Nell's deathbed, also associated with Mary Hogarth, Dickens's artist had pictured the Virgin and Child.

There were no further developments. The incident was soon past, and Dickens turned his attention to the supernatural machinery of *The Chimes*. Perhaps, however, his predilection for getting over the difficulties of construction in his stories in such a way, is partly to be explained by this extraordinary power of seeing imaginary figures as if they were real, and of endowing inanimate objects with some of his own vitality. In outline, his new story was no more than an account of an old ticket-porter, Trotty Veck, who has a horrifying vision of his daughter's future, from which he prays to the Spirits of the Bells to save her. In some ways, though it is not among his best works, it brings us closer to

Dickens than anything else he wrote. Forster says that 'the intensity of it seemed always best to represent to himself what he hoped to be longest remembered for', and that to the last it had 'a cherished corner' in his heart.

For this reason *The Chimes* will always appeal to those who know Dickens well, though it can never be fully appreciated except by those who understand something of the circumstances in which it was written. It grew out of his deeper thinking about the causes of social injustice and enmity between rich and poor, and was written as an appeal to break down the barriers of prejudice that existed between classes, and to affirm man's common humanity. It was largely provoked by what Dickens read in the newspapers, both at home and abroad, and in particular by a statement of Sir Peter Laurie's, a magistrate (pilloried as Alderman Cute), who threatened to 'put down' would-be suicides by severe punishment, if any more were brought before him.

The final and most pathetic scene, in which Trotty imagines that his daughter is about to leap into the river with her child in her arms, rather than bring her up to a life of shame, was suggested by an actual incident which gave Thomas Hood the impulse to write 'The Bridge of Sighs'. After desperate suffering, a woman called Mary Furley had jumped into the Thames, with her two children under her arms. She, and one child, had been saved: the other was drowned. For this, she was tried for murder, and sentenced to death with some relish by a Judge who added various remarks about her 'premeditated cruelty', and the certainty of her execution. Of course, she was reprieved; but the report of her trial made a great stir at the time, though it has now been completely forgotten.

Such characters and scenes as these were particularly topical. Others were the rick-burner, Will Fern, the political economist, Mr. Filer, and the pompous and patronizing Tory philanthropist, Sir Joseph Bowley, who was framed with Lord Shaftesbury in mind. With the passing of time its fire has dimmed, but composing it left Dickens 'hot and giddy', with large eyes, lank hair and a swollen face. 'I wouldn't write it twice for something', he told Forster. By the time he had finished, he was feverish with work and passion, but intensely proud of what he had done.

Now nothing would suit him but to return to London. There was *The Chimes* to be seen through the press, and even more he wanted to observe its effect on his readers. He dashed off to see more of Italy, and then turned his face towards England, where he arrived at the end of November. A few days later Forster assembled an audience for him which included Carlyle, Maclise, Jerrold, and several other well-known men, and Dickens read them *The Chimes*. 'If you had seen Macready,' he wrote to his wife, 'undisguisedly sobbing and crying on the sofa as I read, you would have felt, as I did, what a thing it is to have power.' Maclise also wrote to Catherine Dickens: 'You will never be able to conceive the effect. . . . We should borrow the high language of the minor theatre and even then not do the effect justice—shrieks of laughter—there were indeed—and floods of tears as a relief to them—I do not think there was ever such a triumphant hour for Charles.'

Dickens then returned to Genoa in time to spend Christmas with his family, and the whole caravan was got on the move again for Rome. While there he continued to send descriptions home to Forster, which were later published in the *Daily News* as 'Travelling Sketches—

Written on the Road'. They were published in volume form during the following year as *Pictures from Italy*, with illustrations by Samuel Palmer. 'It is a great pleasure to me,' he wrote to Forster, 'to find that you are pleased with these shadows in water.' They made a pleasant little book, but had no permanent value.

By the end of May 1845 they were home again, and once again Dickens engaged in a whirl of activities that have little to do with his career as an author. He took to amateur theatricals, and produced Ben Jonson's *Every Man in His Humour*, and began thinking of his next book for Christmas, *The Cricket on the Hearth*. There were two more Christmas books after this, *The Battle of Life* (1846) and *The Haunted Man* (1848), before Dickens saw they were becoming a habit and that he was repeating himself. They were experimentally useful by encouraging him in greater compression through contrivances such as the use of key-phrases ('Lord, keep my Memory Green') and rather obvious allegory. Yet they were forced and marred by being written with one eye on their adaptation for the stage. His novels were less obviously affected by his love of drama than sometimes supposed; but these later Christmas books were ruined by his exaggerated concern for their welfare in the theatre. They did not bring out his best; for one should recognize that Dickens may show at least as much 'control' and 'organization' in a few paragraphs introducing a character as in many of his only too apparent thematic and constructive devices.

Far more important, for the time being, was an invitation to take part in the foundation of a new national daily paper. Dickens had been hankering to do something like this ever since he was established as a novelist. He still wanted a post with a regular salary, and he would dearly have loved to be able to use the Press as an agency to agitate for all kinds of liberal reforms which he could deal with in the novels only indirectly. In 1842 he had offered to take command of the old whig *Courier*, which was about to cease publication, and nail 'the true colours to the mast'; but the proprietors had preferred to see it merge with the *Globe*. Now he had a chance to be editor of a Liberal newspaper, at the height of the battle for Free Trade and the repeal of the Corn-laws, could staff it as he wished, and largely draw up its policy himself. In spite of the misgiving of his friends, he threw himself into the business heart and soul, in partnership with Bradbury and Evans and certain railway capitalists, who also wanted to influence public opinion.

Just what went wrong it is difficult to say. The first number of the *Daily News* was published on 21 January 1846. By 30 January, Dickens was talking of handing in his resignation, and by 9 February it had been accepted. Though some time afterwards (in the preface to *Pictures from Italy*) he referred to the whole affair as 'a brief mistake', he had worked tremendously hard to set the paper going. It seems that he did not get on well with the other directors, that he disliked the irregular hours and routine drudgery, feared the influence of its financial backers, and realized that he was not the man for the job. It is unfair to blame either Dickens or his partners. His place was taken by John Forster, and after further difficulties the paper was safely launched.

As soon as he knew he was free, Dickens took up the idea of a new book in shilling numbers. At the same time he decided to live abroad for a year, where he might concentrate on writing and forget the frenzies of the *Daily News*. He fixed on Lausanne as a suitable place, and, by June, had started travelling there with his wife, six children, and Georgina Hogarth. They rented a little house called Rosemont, which had 'roses enough to smother the whole establishment of the *Daily News*', and soon made friends with a pleasant circle of English residents. Then, at last, he started the new book, and wrote to tell Forster, on 28 June: 'BEGAN DOMBEY!—I performed this feat yesterday . . . and it is a plunge straight over head and ears into the story.'

Dombey and Son, however, was perhaps as closely thought-out in advance as any of Dickens's books, and much more intensely than those which had preceded it. Of all Dickens's novels it most easily allows us to see how the story and structure were planned and grew. The idea of the book had originated early in the year, and since then Dickens had been carefully brooding over it, and thinking out its design. Just before they took the house, he had decided that it would be better to spend the winter in Paris, by which time—so he told Forster on 22 June—he would have written four numbers and have reached 'the very point in the story when the life and crowd of that extraordinary place will come vividly to my assistance in writing'. This clearly suggests that, even before he had set pen to paper, he had thought out the number-division of at least the first part of the book.

Many years later, an interesting account of Dickens's usual method of going to work was given by one of his publishers, Frederic Chapman. In an interview with a reporter from the *Daily Chronicle* (25 June 1892) he laid stress on Dickens's care and sense of responsibility for what he wrote. He first commented on his way with manuscript and proofs, and how 'up to the very moment of the appearance of the book', Dickens took an extremely active part in correcting and altering it; and then explained that when Dickens intended to begin a book he started by 'getting hold of a central idea', which he then 'revolved in his mind until he had thought the matter thoroughly out'. Finally he 'made what I might call a programme of his story with the characters', and 'upon this skeleton story he set to work and gave it literary sinew, blood and life'.

Broadly speaking, Chapman's account was accurate, and in emphasizing that in all Dickens's later works, at least, there is a 'central idea' which was carefully thought out and kept in mind while the plot was developed, he makes an important point that is often overlooked. It is the fact that there was a design or 'central idea' in all his works after *Martin Chuzzlewit*, that makes all the difference between the later novels and the earlier.

As well as this, in writing *Dombey and Son*, Dickens for the first time drew up in detail a series of what are known as his 'part-' or 'number-plans'. These are undoubtedly what Chapman was referring to when he spoke of his 'programme' or 'skeleton story'. They have all been preserved, and all have the same arrangement. Dickens used to take a separate sheet of paper for every monthly number, and then fold it in two. On the right-hand side he would write down what he thought were the necessary chapter-divisions; and, on the left, he used to jot down notes on the possible development of the story. He then usually filled in entries on the right-hand side, so that he could see what was to be done in each chapter of the number in hand. Chapman was wrong only in suggesting that the whole 'skeleton' was completed in advance: it was built up number by number, and the complete design depended entirely on the 'central idea', which existed only in Dickens's mind. But though the over-all plan was never formally set down on paper, there is ample evidence that it was well thought out in advance.

In the case of *Dombey* there can be no doubt about it, for not only can one see that the story follows a plan, if one traces it carefully, but Dickens wrote a letter to Forster explaining his intentions when he sent him the manuscript of the first number. From the opening chapter Forster was able to learn that Dombey was a wealthy London merchant, who believed that 'the earth was made for Dombey and Son to trade in, and the sun and moon to give them light'; and from the very first page he found that the story began with the birth of 'Son'. Before Dickens left England he had already told him that part of the 'central idea' of the new story was that it 'should do with Pride what its predecessor (*Martin Chuzzlewit*) had done with Selfishness'; and in the letters he now went on to explain his intentions:

> I design to show Mr. D. with that one idea of the Son taking firmer and firmer possession of him, and swelling and bloating his pride to a prodigious extent. As the boy begins to grow up, I shall show him quite impatient for his getting on, and urging his masters to set him great tasks, and the like. But the natural affection of the boy will turn towards his despised sister; and I purpose showing her learning all sorts of things, of her own application and determination, to assist him in his lessons: and helping him always. When the boy is about ten years old (in the fourth number), he will be taken ill, and will die; and when he is ill, and when he is dying, I mean to make him turn always for refuge to the sister still, and keep the stern affection of the father at a distance. So Mr. Dombey—for all his greatness, and for all his devotion to the child—will find himself at arms' length from him even then; and will see that his love and confidence are all bestowed upon his sister, whom Mr. Dombey has used—and so has the boy himself, too,

for that matter—as a mere convenience and handle to him. The death of the boy is a death-blow, of course, to all his father's schemes and cherished hopes; and 'Dombey and Son,' as Miss Tox will say at the end of the number, 'is a Daughter after all.'

The letter goes on at much greater length, and the full text (or as much as has been preserved) can be read in Forster's biography. Dickens explained that he meant the daughter's love for her father to grow; and 'so I mean to carry the story on, through all the branches, and off-shoots and meanderings that come up; and through the decay and downfall of the house, and the bankruptcy of Dombey . . . when his only staff and treasure, and his unknown Good Genius always, will be this rejected daughter, who will come out better than any son at last, and whose love for him, when discovered . . . will be his bitterest reproach'.

Of course, there were still many uncertainties: Dickens was not yet sure, for example, what to make of Walter Gay—a promising young fellow who enters the firm—and wondered whether he might not 'show him gradually and naturally trailing away . . . into negligence, idleness, dissipation, dishonesty, and ruin'. Nor had he even yet thought of Dombey's second marriage, his contempt for his wife, and her flight from him across France with his manager, James Carker. But though much still remained to be developed, the way ahead was clear.

Writing, however, he had come to find difficult. He had expected to go slowly at first, and after a while he felt it an effort. It was not 'invention' that was the hindrance, for he even had to restrain himself from launching into extravagances; 'but the difficulty of going at what I call a rapid pace', he told Forster, 'is prodigious'. It was all the more serious because he had undertaken to produce a new Christmas book, as well as to begin *Dombey*, and as the months drew on he found that the exertion of doing both at the same time was agonizing. Nine years before, he had been able to keep two novels going at once; but he was no longer so confident and he was aiming still higher. He confided to one of his friends from Lausanne, that he did not much care for *Pickwick*, just as a few years later he rather sadly wrote, 'the world would not take a Pickwick from me now'. He had a reputation to lose, and though he was pleased with *Dombey*, neither he nor his critics were satisfied with his latest Christmas book *The Battle of Life*.

In Paris he got on much better. At Lausanne he had missed the 'magic lantern' of London, the life and variety of its streets at night, which he felt seemed to revive his imagination and 'supply something' to his 'brain'. Before leaving for France he had learnt of the prodigious success of the first number of *Dombey*, and now he was able to do as he had planned, and tell of the death of Paul. In fact, it came a little later in the story than he had foreseen; but, at last, early in January 1847, he was able to write to Miss Coutts: 'Between ourselves —Paul is dead. He died on Friday night about 10 o'clock, and as I had no hope of getting to sleep afterwards, I went out, and walked about Paris until breakfast-time next morning.'

When the number was published it made a tremendous impression. Today, the pathos seems so forced that we fail to notice that there was something new about the way it was managed. In the number-plan Dickens had noted: 'Paul's illness only expressed in the child's own feelings. News of Paul's illness. No. Not otherwise described.' It was hardly too *sentimental*: an objection made at the time was that it was rather over-calculated —and certainly the repetition, from the end of the first chapter, of the image of dying as setting out on a 'dark and unknown sea', was carefully planned.

Lord Jeffrey, who had been so overcome by the *Old Curiosity Shop*, was caught unprepared. He had written enthusiastically to Dickens after reading the third number, when he said, 'I am quite in the dark as to what you mean to make of Paul, but shall watch his development with interest.' Two months later he wrote: 'Oh, my dear, dear Dickens! What a No. 5 you have given us! I have so cried and sobbed over it last night, and again this morning. . . . Since the divine Nelly was found dead on her humble couch, beneath the snow and ivy, there has been nothing like the actual dying of that sweet Paul.' Thackeray, too, was carried away by it. He threw the new number down, exclaiming, 'There's no writing against such power as this—one has no chance!'

But the next difficulty was one that Jeffrey pointed out, for 'after reaching this climax in the fifth number', he wrote, 'what are you to do with the fifteen that are to follow?' Dickens realized the danger, and put down an emphatic note on his plan: 'Great point of the No. to throw the interest of Paul *at once on Florence*.' The very fact that the memorial in the church is at first to be inscribed 'beloved and only child', reminds us, as the sculptor reminds Mr. Dombey, that he still has a daughter. However, there was much else to be done. A few chapters later there are 'New Faces', and we are introduced to Mrs. Skewton and her daughter Edith, the future second Mrs. Dombey.

A new impetus was now given to the tale; and in spite

of delays and difficulties brought on by the arrival of Dickens's fifth son (and seventh child), he turned to the novel again with his old enthusiasm, writing to his friend Macready of 'sitting in my smallest of temporary dens, with *one half of the current number yet to write*—with my thoughts so shaken by yesterday, that I cannot fall to work—and yet with such an infinite relish for the story I am mining out, that I don't care twopence for being behindhand, and hope to make a dash, a plunge and a finish, with what the people who entice you to play on the racecourses call, "A firm heart and a bold resolution, them as don't play can't win, and luck attend the Royal Sportsman!" '

Edith and her mother were new figures to set off against Florence, for just as her brother had helped to bring out her glowing love and affection so her new step-mother's degradation was to contrast with her freshness and innocence. Before he had begun to write about them, Dickens had jotted down a sketch of the new characters in his notes: 'The mother and daughter. The mother, and her cant about "heart", and nature—Daughter who has been put through her paces, before countless marrying men, like a horse for sale—Proud and weary of her degradation, but going on, for it's too late now, to try to turn back.' Mr. Dombey marries her from pride, because she has rank and beauty that can be bought and paid for, and because she may yet provide him with a son. He tries to humble her, but she runs away with his manager, Mr. Carker, whom she hates, and succeeds in humiliating both husband and lover. For a second time all Dombey's hopes are destroyed, the House of Dombey is brought to its downfall, and only then are father and daughter united as Dickens intended.

No one can say that the character-portrayal of Edith

is entirely satisfactory. Dickens was handling what was then an intensely difficult subject. It was not simply that he had to be careful about what he wrote because his novels were read aloud in the family circle; but that, as the French critic Taine discovered, even men, among themselves, invariably spoke of adultery as a crime. Yet Edith was meant to be regarded with some sympathy, and to accomplish this she is deliberately conventionalized, made more 'distant' from the reader, and shown as a sort of tragedy queen. Today, even sympathetic critics such as H. W. Garrod speak of the women in *Dombey* as 'impossible'. But this is rather harsh, and it even seems quite likely that Dickens intended them as an answer to those who said he could not describe women, just as the story of the novel was meant to prove that he could design a plot.

Certainly a definite theme seems to be introduced when Polly Toodle is described, in the first number, as 'a good plain sample of a nature that is ever in the mass, better, truer, higher, nobler, quicker to feel, and much more constant to retain, all tenderness and pity, self-denial and devotion, than the nature of men'. This is brought out even more strongly in Florence. Mr. Toots constantly exhibits Susan Nipper to us as an 'extraordinary woman'. Women play the more active part in the story, from the kitchen 'chorus', up through Mrs. Chick and Miss Tox, to the high drama of Edith's flight with Carker. They play the main part and, on the whole, support it fairly creditably. Yet even so, they are always described from the outside, as if they were a separate species. Edith Dombey may resent being 'put through her paces', but this is how Dickens always treats her himself. 'Beautiful and stately', 'dumb and motionless', so she appears to the last. Yet to the end, women have the predominant part. Even Mrs. MacStinger 'comes over' Captain Bunsby. Susan produces another daughter, 'a female stranger . . . and I'm glad of it'; and 'Dombey and Son is a Daughter after all'. At the very close the last scene is not, as Dickens had intended, an echo of Paul's death and 'what the wild waves were saying', but an account of old Dombey's devotion to his little granddaughter, for 'no one, except Florence, knows the measure of the white-haired gentleman's affection for the girl'.

An outstanding theme is undoubtedly the attack on the importance attached to money. Dombey, himself, uses money to cut himself off from all human ties except pride in his son. He tells Polly Toodle, when he engages her as a nurse, 'When you go away from here, you will have concluded what is a mere matter of bargain and sale, hiring and letting.' He loses one wife with the thought that there is 'something gone . . . well worth the having', and rashly invests in another. He regards his riches as everything, until they have melted away, and he recalls Paul's question, 'Papa! what's money . . . I mean, what's money after all?'

To some extent it is just the old Dickensian moral that no one who is interested in making money merely for its own sake is to be regarded favourably; it is partly the teaching that a rich man cannot easily enter the Kingdom of Heaven; and it is also part of what Edmund Wilson calls Dickens's growing 'indictment against a specific society: the self-important and moralizing middle-class who had been making such rapid progress in England and coming down like a damper on the bright fires of English life'. When helping with negotiations for the financial backing of the *Daily News*, Dickens had come in contact with successful business-men and company promoters for the first time. John Chapman, who was alleged to be the 'original' of Dombey, had introduced him to George Hudson, the fraudulent 'Railway King'—rather to Dickens's disapproval. It was a world of 'new men', which he both disliked and despised.

There has been an attempt to link Dickens's disapproval of such developments in society with his supposed regret for the past and his description of the railway in *Dombey*. The railway has been said to be 'seen only as destructive' and ruthless, with 'no suggestion of hope' or social progress. But this is extremely questionable. Although Carker is killed by an express, his end is deserved. To Toodle, as a stoker, it is something familiar after which to name his eldest child, 'Biler'. To Dickens, about this time, a railway journey was always 'wonderfully suggestive' and it was when travelling by train that he had the idea for his 'A Child's Dream of a Star'. Although the railway journey in chapter xx seems a symbol of Death to Mr. Dombey, this is only at a time when he feels that everything he meets is 'setting up a claim to his dead boy'. Death is in his thoughts, not ours. For when it forces its way in through the wretched suburbs of the town, and Mr. Dombey looks out through his carriage window, 'it is never in his thoughts that the monster who has brought him there' has merely 'let the light of day in on these things: not made or caused them'.

Even so, the firm of Dombey and Son is a disappointment if we expect the novel to provide a picture of what it was like to be a merchant-prince of the mid-nineteenth century. Although everyone who reads Dickens must be agreed by now that a childhood recollection of his novels is hopelessly inadequate for a mature understanding of his genius, the book is not only 'suitable for children' but almost its whole sentiment is curiously childish. Much is once more made of fairy-tale associations, and these are rather overworked. Again, it is one thing to have the setting for Florence's home vividly fancied from the child's point of view when she is left its lonely mistress (chapter xxiii): the mansion in which 'dust accumulated, nobody knew whence nor how, where spiders, moths, and grubs were heard of every day', and 'an exploratory blackbeetle now and then was found immovable upon the stairs, or in an upper room, as wondering how he got there'. It is quite another thing when this shades into a labouring appeal to feel with her 'true young heart' whatever is 'solemn . . . dim . . . murmuring . . . faint . . . far-off . . . soothing . . . wild, weak, childish . . . half-formed' or 'cruel'. It would be wrong to fail to discriminate between different levels in Dickens's writing, even though there is nothing to be gained from dwelling on the novel's weaknesses which are a certain childishness, a fairy-tale whimsicality, the obvious absurdities of Edith's pride, and the way in which the writer's skill is abused whenever he turns aside from life to a false drama which he has confused with the world of the stage and his own Christmas books.

No doubt largely because of the sentiment of Dombey and daughter it is an easy book to pillory; yet it may also be seen as marked by a 'bold, rapid and highly simplifying art'. It is the novel selected by Dr. F. R. Leavis to show that the poetic power he sees in *Hard Times* is apparent throughout Dickens's work. In 'Dombey and Son' (*Sewanee Review*, LXX, 1962) he finds proof of a 'poetic conception of his art' and an 'inexhaustibly wonderful poetic life' in Dickens's prose. For, everywhere, he goes on, 'in description and narrative and dramatic presentation and speech, we have exemplified that vitality of language which invites us to enforce from Dickens the truth of the proposition that in the Victorian age the poetic strength of the English language goes into the novel, and that the great novelists are the successors of Shakespeare'. Dickens has his own tradition, one may say, which came not only through the English novel and the dramatists of the seventeenth and eighteenth centuries, but more directly through the impress of the language and imagination of Shakespeare—his sanity and the abundance of his characters—both on Dickens himself and on the culture of his readers.

It was exceptional for Dickens to traffic with his critics: the only other known occasion was when E. S. Dallas reviewed *Our Mutual Friend*. But after he had finished *Dombey*, Dickens wrote to the editor of the *Sun* to ask him to convey his 'warmest acknowledgements and thanks' to the writer who had reviewed the last number. 'The sympathy expressed in it', he went on, 'is particularly welcome and gratifying.' He followed this with a short note to the writer of the notice (who was Charles Kent, the editor himself), in which he remarked that 'he had never addressed a similar communication to anybody except on one occasion'. Yet, if we turn back to the review to see what moved him, it is to find what appears little more than a conventional though warmly enthusiastic tribute. By far the most part is in praise of the novel's 'many strange, original, life-like, and admirable characters. . . . For it is not the least important or the least remarkable among the numerous peculiarities of Mr. Dickens as a novelist . . . that he imparts to a fictitious being an absolute and visible individuality. The actors in his tales are no mere pasteboard fantoccini, moved by the threads of an ingenious plot . . . they are as actual as flesh and blood, as true as humanity.' It also recognizes the vividness of his occasional scenes, instancing the auction at Dombey's house in chapter lix. It is clear that Dickens was still delighted at recognition of the lively actuality of his characters and the personal contact they seemed to give his readers with their author. 'An old friend has left us, the voice of a dear favourite is silent': these are the terms in which Kent wrote of him, and which Dickens welcomed; and this is at least partly how he hoped to be read. Dickens's authoritative command of his readers does largely depend on his 'voice': a poetic power over words which enables him to conjure into life the world and people of his imagination.

The conclusion of *Dombey* also brought him a letter from his old father-in-law, George Hogarth, whose review of *Sketches by Boz* had once pleased him so much. Dickens replied to say that he was 'quite as sensitive to applause' which he knew to be sincere, as he had been a dozen years before. He affirmed 'a great faith in Dombey, and a strong belief that it will be remembered and read years hence', and invited Hogarth to 'a "Dombey dinner"', which was to be held 'to celebrate the completion of the story'.

Chapter Eight

ACTOR, EDITOR, AND AUTHOR: *DAVID COPPERFIELD*

THE *Dombey* dinner was held on 11 April 1848, and Dickens then set himself to organize another amateur production of Jonson's *Every Man in His Humour*. Its purpose was to raise money for Sheridan Knowles the dramatist, and to install him as curator at Shakespeare's house at Stratford. Dickens had already thrown himself into acting, producing, and managing several times before, and between 1847 and 1857 his amateur company appeared over thirty times in the provinces and about as many in London. He was obsessed with the Theatre. Ostensibly, the purpose of his productions was usually to raise money for distressed authors, or for a society with the same object that he and Lytton started in 1850, called the Guild of Literature and Art; yet he had a portable theatre built at his new home, Tavistock House (where he moved in 1851), and to the last he was interested in dramatics, for dramatics' sake.

It was not simply that he liked acting. He enjoyed producing and managing quite as much as performing; he revelled in directing others, taking all the responsibility, in seeing to every detail of arduous and complicated tours, as well as rehearsing each play with professional thoroughness. He was never able to relax without something to do; his only relief was to lose himself in work. He seemed to want to escape both from his life at home and the imaginative world of his books into one which consisted of nothing but almost meaningless detail. It was just because acting and managing made no demands on his creative resources, that he was able to expend such vast energy upon them and still remain fresher than anyone else at the end.

Even the themes of the plays he undertook were only loosely adapted to his personality or inner demands. Many of his parts were farcical. Others were of characters who renounced the women they loved, or who had a murder on their conscience. Dickens could slip them on and off without disturbing his inner nature. Of course he showed some emotion when he was playing these parts: he would not have been a true Victorian or true to himself if he had not; but such performances usually left him undisturbed. He treated them like his charitable work for Miss Burdett Coutts, as a wilderness of immediate practical demands into which he could retire to forget more pressing responsibilities. He enjoyed acting, and yet to the end it was the managerial side of the theatre that he really aspired to. Just before he died he asked a friend what he thought one of his 'most cherished day-dreams' was, and immediately gave the answer himself, 'To settle down for the remainder of my life within easy distance of a great theatre, in the *direction* of which I should hold supreme authority.'

Another project which now took up a tremendous amount of his time, was a reformatory home for prostitutes which he had started for Miss Coutts. The idea of the home was to take off the streets any women who sincerely wished to escape from such a life, clean up their manners and morals, and ship them off to the colonies. From 1847 to 1858, Dickens acted as chairman of an administrative committee, and undertook almost entirely the business of supervising it. He took most of the decisions on who was to be admitted; constantly advised the resident superintendent on discipline, training, and day-to-day management; and eventually went into all the necessary arrangements for sending them overseas.

He was obviously interested in the psychology of the women he had to deal with, but it is equally clear that he enjoyed nothing so much as deciding on every detail connected with the place, from what was to be done about the drains to dealing with the girl who was found in the front parlour with a policeman at four o'clock in the morning. Even allowing for the fact that all his letters about the home were written to a Victorian maiden lady, they are extremely unrevealing. Dickens had, in actual life, none of the sentiment for 'fallen women' that he showed in his books, or that men like Wilkie Collins admitted openly. The home was run in a manner that the citizens of Coketown would have called 'eminently practical'.—'The motto of the place', Dickens wrote, was ' "Don't talk about it—do it." ' With the exception of what he wrote about Little Emily and Martha in his next novel, *David Copperfield*, he made practically no use of what he learnt there, and even Little Emily was untypical of the women in the home. One of his cardinal principles in encouraging their reform was that they should be allowed to look forward to marriage after they had emigrated; but at the end of *Copperfield* Dickens was careful to leave Emily a wilting spinster, 'A slight figure, kiender worn; soft sorrowful blue eyes; a delicate face; a pritty head, leaning a little down . . . That's Em'ly.' The interesting thing about Dickens's connection with the home is that it tells us nothing about him, except that he had tremendous practical ability and a passionate love for administration.

The most important undertaking that was still in his

mind was the establishment of a weekly magazine. Even before the *Daily News* interlude, he had thought of starting one to be called *The Cricket*; while he was writing *Dombey*, he was inclined 'to the notion of a kind of *Spectator* (Addison's)'; and by the summer of 1849 he wrote 'I think I have, without a doubt, *got* the Periodical notion.' By winter he was making plans to start it in the spring.

In deciding on its form, Dickens relied greatly on Forster and put up all kinds of ideas to him, only to see his friend knock them down. Forster was rightly afraid that Dickens wanted to make the magazine so personal that it would then be difficult to get other writers to contribute and to keep it going. On the other hand, he fully agreed that it must be something more than the usual run of literary weeklies, which were little more than collections of dull reviews. Eventually, they decided on a weekly miscellany, which was to consist of stories and articles 'in the liveliest form that could be given to them'. Above all, it should appeal to the imagination: but by method of treatment rather than choice of subject. It was to sell for twopence, and was to be printed by Bradbury and Evans. Ownership was to remain in Dickens's hands. W. H. Wills, an old *Daily News* associate, was to be appointed assistant-editor. It was to be entitled *Household Words*, and the first number was to be published on 30 March 1850.

There was no better organizer than Dickens for starting a magazine, and this time he had begun on the right lines and was completely in charge. He began to recruit contributors, starting with Mrs. Gaskell, who had come to the fore, in 1847, with her novel *Mary Barton*. Dickens wrote to her to say that there was 'no living English writer' he would 'desire to enlist in preference to' its author. To Mary Howitt, a miscellaneous writer, he explained that he was 'particularly anxious to deal with . . . all social evils, and all home affections'. In 'A Preliminary Word' to the first number, he explained again that it was the purpose of the new work 'to bring into innumerable homes, from the stirring world about us, the knowledge of many social wonders, good and evil'.

The first two volumes of *Household Words*, especially, were used to preach social reform, largely in the sphere of public health. The imitator of Addison devoted much of his time to writing articles about the sewerage-system of London, which was then of great topical interest. *Household Words*, indeed, is extremely unlike the sort of magazine Dickens had once had in mind, which he had meant to call *The Cricket*, or *The Robin*. Even W. H. Wills, who was efficient but whom Dickens privately thought very dull, appealed to his chief in vain for something comic; and it was only because he felt 'an uneasy sense of . . . a want of something tender' in the second number that Dickens bestirred himself to write 'A Child's Dream of a Star'. Yet the event showed that he had correctly foreseen the public demand. After only a fortnight, he was able to write to Miss Burdett Coutts, 'Household Words I hope . . . will become a good property. It is exceedingly well liked, and "goes", in the trade phrase, admirably.' The work of starting it, he admitted, was 'something ponderous, but to establish it firmly would be to gain such a great point for the future (I mean my future) that I think nothing of that'.

Meanwhile, he had also been engaged in writing *David Copperfield*. He had started thinking about it, according to Forster, as far back as 'the later part' of 1848; and then, after a burst of work before Christmas, he had decided on a holiday before he began the new novel. Accordingly, he had set off with John Leech and Mark Lemon for Norfolk. They first visited Norwich, explored the scene of a recent multiple murder, and then went on to Great Yarmouth by coach. Dickens was captivated by the old town. He was delighted with its smell of pitch and oakum and tar, and the way in which 'the town and tide' were 'mixed up like toast and water'. Although he had not yet thought of a plot for his new book, he was determined to work into it a description of his latest discovery. His visit, he wrote to Forster, 'was the success of the trip . . . Yarmouth . . . is the strangest place in the world . . . I shall certainly try my hand at it'.

Yet he still did not know exactly how. Later the same month, he christened his sixth son, Henry Fielding Dickens, 'in a kind of homage to the style of the work he was now so bent on beginning', and had an idea for the character of Mr. Wickfield. In February he began the search for a title. He was evidently thinking deeply about the new book, and wrote that his mind 'was running like a high sea'. He fixed the title and started writing just in time for publication on 1 May. Though the novel is remarkable for showing a further advance in the way it was planned, Dickens never had more than one number in hand once serialization was under way. And when once he even overheard a lady in a shop ask for the next number of *David Copperfield* before a word of it had been written, he felt 'a vivid sense of mingled enjoyment and dismay'.

He began with difficulty. 'My hand is out', he wrote to Forster; 'today and yesterday I have done nothing. Though I know what I want to do, I am lumbering on like a stage waggon, and . . . the long Copperfieldian perspective looks snowy and thick.' Yet he did what was needed. In the very first number, three of the main themes of the novel are provided for and we are introduced to the Peggottys, the Murdstones, and Miss Betsey Trotwood, who do not merely represent three sets of characters to be developed according to the author's whim, but whose part in the perspective was already sketched out.

By the time he was writing the second number he had a remarkable idea. For the past two years he had had by him the fragment of autobiography which recounted the story of his childhood. At his wife's suggestion it had been given up, and in any case what it told was too painful to confess. But now that he was writing in the first person, for the first time, he saw a great opportunity to make use of it. Into the second number went the account of his childhood reading; into the third went some of his recollections of Wellington House Academy; and into the fourth were inserted, almost unaltered, the account of his time in the blacking-factory (changed to Murdstone and Grinby's) and the desolate life he had led for a while in London. 'I really think I have done it ingeniously', he wrote to Forster, 'and with a very complicated interweaving of truth and fiction.' Mr. Micawber was introduced into the same number, and throughout the whole novel the seeds of his recollections blossomed in the most out-of-the-way corners and crevices and in a manner that was detectable even by some of his readers at the time.

David Copperfield occupies a special place in Dickens's works. Just as it stands in a central position in the succession of his novels, with seven before and seven coming after, so it unites the ease of his youth with the greater sense of design of his maturity. For the nineteen-number novel, with sixty or more chapters, an autobiographical narrative offered several advantages. It developed naturally in several stages, and, as the story stretched over a greater period of time than the other novels, it was less crowded and easier to follow. Moreover, Dickens had grasped that characters might be shown who developed at the same time; and although it is still very tentative and experimental in this, David and Uriah develop, and so do Dora and Traddles, while others at least have the semblance of doing so.

Yet this is not to say that E. M. Forster's distinction between 'flat' and 'round' characters can easily be illustrated from the novel. Rather too much has been made of a loose and simple definition. Analysis was not what Dickens was after, nor any of the other novelists of that time. He merely wanted to show characters as vividly as possible in their appearance and speech. If he praised another novelist, in his letters, he singled out the qualities of force, originality, and skill of expression. At this time, he was like Trollope (writing twenty years later) who held that it was the main business of the novelist to make his characters 'speaking, moving, human creatures'. They would have utterly rejected Henry James's dictum that 'a character is interesting as it comes out, and by the process and duration of that emergence'. It was not their way. The statement is not even true, and never can be true of comedy. As Arnold Bennett records in his *Journals* he and T. S. Eliot agreed, Dickens's way was to 'conventionalize' a character, and make it 'form part of the pattern, or lay the design of a book'. Every novelist, he rightly explained, has to select, and though Dickens may have oversimplified sometimes, he always ensured that his characters made 'an impression' and that this impression was part of a design.

His method was now first to find a theme, his characters and setting next, and only lastly a plot which would unite them all. This was one of the reasons why he used to describe himself as in agonies of thought about his books for months before he began to write. It was, at least partly, why he felt he must decide on a title before he even wrote a word. John Forster, with whom it was all carefully discussed, even held that in *David Copperfield* 'more than in any other of Dickens's novels . . . the incidents arise easily, and to the very end connect themselves naturally and unobtrusively with the characters of which they are a part'. He explained that there is a main theme running through it: 'a unity of drift or purpose is apparent always, and the tone is uniformly right. By the course of events we learn the value of self-denial and patience, quiet endurance of unavoidable ills, strenuous efforts against ills remediable; and everything in the fortunes of the actors warns us, to strengthen our generous emotions and to guard the purities of the home.' So astoundingly varied are the characters, so abundant the humour, and so artfully meandering the course of events, that what Forster said about the drift and purpose has usually been overlooked. It is largely owing to John Butt that we now realize that the novel has a central theme and unity. Something of this can be seen in the great chapter, 'Tempest', in which Dickens's opening words, as David, can be shown to be completely justified: 'I now approach an event in my life, so indelible, so awful, so bound by an infinite variety of ties to all that has preceded it in these pages, that, from the beginning of my narrative, I have seen it growing larger and larger as I advanced, like a great tower in a plain, and throwing its forecast shadow even on the incidents of my childish days.'

Much of it had been foreshadowed as early as the third chapter, in a passage Dickens had the foresight to add in proof after his draft of the opening number was complete. How much of it was actually designed can be judged only after a careful comparison of Dickens's part-plan with a close reading of the book, and what it cost him to write can be seen in a letter to Forster: 'I have been tremendously at work these two days, eight hours at a stretch yesterday, and six and a half today, with the Ham and Steerforth chapter, which has completely knocked me over.' Two days later he added, to another correspondent, that he was 'in a tremendous paroxysm', and that the chapter was still 'on the Anvil'. Emily's seduction, or 'fall', had been planned from the first number when she told David she wanted to be a lady and ran out along the baulk of timber overhanging the water. Steerforth's death was foreseen; and Ham's, not certainly, but it was implicit in the irony of Emily's fear for Peggotty and Ham when out at sea, 'I wake when it blows . . . and believe I hear 'em crying out for help. That's why I should like so much to be a lady.' The chapter describing the tempest concludes with an old fisherman approaching David:

> I asked him, terror-stricken . . . 'Has a body come ashore?'
>
> He said, 'Yes.'
>
> 'Do I know it?' I asked then.
>
> He answered nothing.
>
> But he led me to the shore. And on that part of it where she and I had looked for shells, two children—on that part of it where some lighter fragments of the old boat . . . had been scattered by the wind—among the ruins of the home he had wronged, I saw him lying with his head upon his arm, as I had often seen him lie at school.

It was just as he had seen him lie on his first night at Salem House, when Steerforth had yawningly asked:

> 'You haven't got a sister, have you?'
> 'No,' I answered.
> 'That's a pity,' said Steerforth. 'If you had had one, I should think she would have been a pretty, timid, little bright-eyed sort of girl. I should have liked to know her. Good-night, young Copperfield.'

It was just as he had seen him when he stayed with his friend for the first, and last, time; and, looking into his room as he was about to catch the early coach for Yarmouth, had found him, 'fast asleep, lying easily, with his head upon his arm, as I had often seen him lie at school'.

The tale of Little Emily is a definite strand running through *David Copperfield*; but Dickens was not deceiving himself when he told a friend that he had 'constructed the whole with immense pains', and that it was 'so woven and blended together' that it was extremely difficult to abstract her story for telling in the Public Readings. David, Steerforth, and Emily are all children who have grown up without a father. It was Mrs. Steerforth's boast that her son had never been denied anything, and David himself goes on to say that as he grew up he found that he too had 'an undisciplined heart', which had to learn the lesson that there are times when it must subdue itself to others.

As John Forster says, 'everything in the fortunes of the actors' shows us that a true marriage, and loyalty to the 'purities of the home' are the underlying subject of the book. This is brought out very strongly in the story of David, Dora, and Agnes; but it is also the only good reason for the tale of the Strongs and Maldons; it links up with Steerforth and Emily, and even with the lesser characters, such as Aunt Betsey and her mysterious husband; Peggotty and Barkis; the Traddleses and the Micawbers. It is not too much to say that when Miss Trotwood calls David's mother, 'a very Baby', in the first chapter, and she confesses that she 'was but a childish widow, and would be a childish mother if she lived', Dickens had already thought of David's 'child-wife' Dora.

It is unfortunate that it is the story of Dr. Strong and his wife, and the suspected seducer, Jack Maldon, which is left to underline this main theme. It is a disappointing episode. The marriage of the young girl to the old Doctor is rather distasteful. Dickens's heart does not seem to have been in it; and it would never have been necessary but for the unavoidable length of the book. It hardly even seems to have any relevance until it suddenly comes to a climax in an intense and over-dramatic scene in which Annie Strong explains, in front of everyone, that although she had been so young when she was married, she is proud of her husband and respects him. She says that it is true that, when she had been even younger, she had liked her cousin (Jack Maldon), and might have even come to love him, 'and might have married him and been most wretched', for '*There can be no disparity in marriage like unsuitability of mind and purpose.*'—'I pondered on those words', says David, 'as if they had some particular interest or some strange application that I could not divine. There can be no disparity in marriage like unsuitability of mind and purpose.' Annie went on, 'If I were to be thankful to my husband for no more, I should be thankful to him for having saved me from the first mistaken impulse of my undisciplined heart.'

It is easy to see why David finds these words so impressive, and why they are repeated as a refrain. As he leaves the Strongs, with his aunt, Dickens makes him repeat them again, and ends the chapter with a fanciful symbol recalling the state of his own marriage to Dora, 'Little Blossom': 'My mind was still running on some of the expressions used. "There can be no disparity in marriage like unsuitability of mind and purpose." "The first mistaken impulse of an undisciplined heart". . . . But we were at home; and the trodden leaves were lying underfoot, and the autumn winds were blowing,'

In the next chapter about Dora, when David makes his last attempt to 'form her mind', he says, 'these words of Mrs. Strong were constantly recurring to me, at this time; were almost always present to my mind. . . . For I knew now that my own heart was undisciplined when it first loved Dora.'

Every character in the story has a place somewhere in the design, and this was so new for Dickens at the time that one of his friends (H. F. Chorley) reviewing the first number in *The Athenaeum*, even thought that Aunt Betsey had been drawn 'in pure waste', and that with the end of the first chapter she had vanished for good. But those days were over. Far from casually introducing a character that would never come to anything, Dickens tended to have the fault of resuscitating some of them when their parts were over. Mr. Murdstone re-appears —perhaps defensibly—preparing to marry another heiress; but Littimer and Heep in jail are just another device to fill out a novel of unwieldy length. They spoil the design by a typical Victorian excess.

Nevertheless, although Dickens sometimes added to his intentions, they were usually clear-cut and definite. In *The Real David Copperfield* Robert Graves quite wrongly assures us that Dickens seldom 'looked more than a couple of months ahead for the development of his plot', and from what some critics have to say one would imagine that Dickens was always prepared to alter course at a moment's notice. What really happened when a crisis arose can be seen from an exchange of letters between Dickens and a neighbour of his who discovered that he had taken her as the 'original' of his portrait of the volatile dwarf, Miss Mowcher. She could see how Miss Mowcher, as Steerforth's friend, was to be made a sort of procuress for Little Em'ly, and was deeply hurt at having her deformity held up to ridicule. She wrote Dickens a despairing appeal that was genuinely pathetic; but far from being remorsefully anxious to make amends, he rather unwillingly agreed to change the development, and explained that it would take him several months. In time he managed to do all she wished, but only at the cost of painfully modifying his intentions.

Yet, however one looks at Miss Mowcher, she still remains one of Dickens's greatest comic characters. The richness and variety of the comedy in *David Copperfield* ought not to be taken for granted. The serious nature of the design is something relatively new, and its analysis is so much easier than an appreciation of its comedy that it is bound to be given disproportionate attention. But Mr. Micawber and Miss Mowcher do more than leave a mere 'impression'. They start up to life before our eyes, and one would no more expect their characters gradually to 'emerge' or 'come out' in a few scenes than one would if they were real people. They deserve our wonder. They are in Dickens's great tradition, and together they reduce the distinction between 'flat' and 'round' characters to something like absurdity.

What is a rounded character? Just one which is constructed round more than one idea or quality: 'for when there is more than one factor in them', E. M. Forster says, 'we get the beginning of the curve. The really flat characters can be summed up in one sentence such as "I never will desert Mr. Micawber." ' It is true that Mrs. Micawber was probably never meant to be anything more than a sketch—though in fact her chief catch-phrase is not the one about deserting her husband. She is a mere pendant to Micawber. But E. M. Forster gives us the impression that Dickens never created any but flat characters, which by some unfair sleight of hand he managed to 'bounce' us into accepting as round. Nothing is explained. He admits that somehow Dickens succeeds in giving a 'wonderful feeling of human depth', But it is all accounted for as an illusion. 'It is a conjuring trick', he says. 'Part of the genius of Dickens is that he does use types and caricatures . . . and yet achieves effects that are not mechanical and a vision of humanity that is not shallow. Those who dislike Dickens have an excellent case. He ought to be bad. He is actually one of our big writers.' His only attempt to account for this is to say that writers like Dickens and Wells are 'very clear at transmitting force'. How they do so is not explained. If this means that their own personalities and styles were so forceful that almost every sentence they wrote was shaped with life and vigour, then the whole subject is dropped just as we are coming to the point.

Dickens's success with his comic characters is because they live entirely in their dialogue. Even Mrs. Micawber seems vividly alive because she is of the same stamp as Mrs. Nickleby and Mrs. Gamp. They all live in their speech. Every natural turn of phrase is caught up, turned and arranged in a glorious succession of sparkling inanities and wit, nonsense and telling shrewdness, and phrases that we at once recognize as our native speech transformed into dialogue past man's 'tongue to conceive or his heart to report'. The definition of a 'round' character is that it is capable of giving us 'a happy surprise'. Yet there is no need to confine this to psychological development. Characters such as Mrs. Micawber and her husband, Miss Mowcher and Mrs. Crupp are capable of giving 'a happy surprise' every time they open their mouths. Short samples of quotation are useless: they miss imparting the wonderful sense of creativeness that can only be given by pages at a time. But Miss Mowcher's first appearance, Mrs. Crupp's services at the dinner-party, and Micawber everywhere, are among the greatest things in the book.

The purely comic characters are supported by comic grotesques and others who are only gently humorous or odd. Those such as Mr. Murdstone, Mr. Creakle, and Uriah Heep are entirely villainous, but are made bearable because there is usually a touch of humour in them. Physically they are invariably repulsive, but there is almost always something amusing about what they have to say. Mr. Creakle introduces himself, 'I'll tell you what I am . . . I'm a Tartar.' Uriah recounts his loathsome family history, 'Father got the monitor medal by being umble. So did I. . . . "Be umble Uriah", says father to me, "and you'll get on."' Mr. Murdstone begins a problem of arithmetic, 'if I go into a cheesemonger's shop and buy five thousand double Gloucester cheeses at fourpence-halfpenny each, present payment . . .' Even so, they are exceptional. The oddities of many of the characters in *David Copperfield* are subdued. Mr. Chillip, Mr. Omer, and Mr. Spenlow are delightfully observed and described, but could find a place anywhere in fiction or ordinary life. It is not only their peculiarities that impress us. They are described as people David knew and remembered, and as he might have recalled them. It is another of the advantages of the autobiographical narrative that it sometimes restrained Dickens's natural exuberance.

The weakest parts of the novel are the serious characters, who are often shadowy and conventional. They have nothing much to say. In spite of Dickens's belief that Little Emily would be remembered, which is true, she is barely present in the novel, hardly ever says anything, and does nothing but run away. There is just a space all round her. Daniel Peggotty and Ham strike the right attitudes, but they have nothing but grand commonplaces to utter. Dickens skirts round the theme with great skill, but it is no more than a great display of misplaced talent. Hetty Sorrel is much overrated in *Adam Bede*, but Emily is less than a shadow beside her. The Strongs are almost ludicrous in comparison with Dorothea and Casaubon in *Middlemarch*. Although it may be unfair to contrast the central figures of one novel with minor characters from another, it helps to emphasize that there are parts of *David Copperfield* that will not stand being taken too seriously. Dora is not to be dismissed in the same way: Dickens had the advantage of writing about a real situation there, not only in the sense that it was close to his personal experience, but that it is one of universal possibility. That 'there are faults in the book', as John Forster says, 'is certain', yet none 'incompatible with the most masterly qualities'.

As the central novel of Dickens's development, and as one fictionally and actually autobiographical, *David Copperfield* was especially close to the novelist. He was clear of this himself when he wrote, in the preface to the first edition, 'I do not find it easy to get sufficiently far away from this Book' and that 'no one can ever believe in this Narrative, in the reading, more than I have believed it in the writing.' Seven years later, too, he was to confess, 'Of all my books I like this the best.'

Dark shadows lie across the story, but its general impression is of light and fulfilment. On Dickens's own admission (in one of his speeches) his golden childhood memories of Chatham were intertwined with the Yarmouth scenes, of which he writes in the novel:

> I don't know why one slight set of impressions should be more particularly associated with a place than another, though I believe this obtains with most people, in reference especially to the associations of their childhood. I never hear the name, or read the name, of Yarmouth, but I am reminded of a certain Sunday morning on the beach, the bells ringing for church, little Em'ly leaning on my shoulder, Ham lazily dropping stones into the water, and the sun, away at sea, just breaking through the heavy mist, and showing us the ships, like their own shadows.

No one can forget David's agony as a child, his loneliness and desperation, but he is never defeated or overwhelmed by his secretly unhappy life. Even when dividing his time between Murdstone and Grinby's and the debtors' prison, he enlivens the Orfling with his fancies as they watch the rising sun gilding the Thames, and he makes stories for himself, as he says, 'out of the streets, and out of men and women'. And even as his thoughts go back 'to that slow agony' of his childhood, he writes almost with pride, 'When I tread the old ground, I do not wonder that I seem to see and pity, going on before me, an innocent romantic boy, making his imaginative world out of such strange experiences and sordid things.' For the long Copperfieldian perspective is made to lead to fulfilment. As David and Agnes learn of each other's love they thank God, and 'long miles of road then' open out before his mind, and, he says he recognizes 'toiling on . . . a ragged way-worn boy forsaken and neglected, who should come to call the heart even now beating against mine, his own'.

We are brought at last to see Agnes, like so many of the less convincing characters, as standing for more than herself. Dickens presents her as a symbol of how love can lead a man's life to be fulfilled and given higher purpose. For, as they are at last united, 'clasped in my embrace,' David writes, 'I held the source of every worthy aspiration I had ever had; the centre of myself, the circle of my life, my own, my wife; my love of whom was founded on a rock.' As Hillis Miller explains:

> David's relation to Agnes is a late example of that transposition of religious language into the realm of romantic love which began with the poems of courtly love, and which finds its most elaborate Victorian expression in *Wuthering Heights*. David has that relation to Agnes which a devout Christian has to God, the creator of his selfhood, without whom he would be nothing.

Thus, when the story comes to an end, David prays that she may be beside him at his death, so that 'when realities are melting from me like the shadows which I now dismiss,' he may 'still find thee near me, pointing upward!' And so already—if only sketchily worked out—Dickens associated his (and David's) 'unhappy want of something' in life, as more than a lost love, but the need for the 'religious dimension'.

The reviews written at this time are disappointing. They are all chiefly concerned with the book's moral teaching. *David Copperfield* and Thackeray's *Pendennis* were published simultaneously, by the same firm, and in comparing them most of the reviews had nothing more valuable to say than to praise Dickens because he was optimistic, and to blame Thackeray because he was not. *The Times* thought that 'rising from Mr. Dickens's work you forget that there is evil in the world and remember only the good. Rising from Mr. Thackeray's, you are doubtful of yourself and everybody at large.'

After reading his rival's book, Thackeray generously asked, 'Who can rival this great genius?' Dickens himself dismissed it as his 'favourite child', and it at once became the most popular of his works. It has never lost its universal appeal: readers return to it again with the delight of discovery. It won Dickens as many new readers as *Pickwick*, among them many who had felt that they were too fastidious to enjoy anyone so popular. Contributing to the *Nineteenth Century*, many years later, Matthew Arnold wrote:

> There is a book familiar to us all . . . I mean *David Copperfield*. Much as I have published, I do not think it has ever happened to me before to comment in print upon any production of Charles Dickens. What a pleasure to have the opportunity of praising a work so sound, a work so rich in merit. . . . 'Do not read your fellow-strivers . . .,' says Goethe. . . . But to contemporary work so good as *David Copperfield* we are in danger perhaps of not paying respect enough, of reading it (for who could help reading it!) too hastily. . . . What treasures of gaiety, invention, life, are in that book! What alertness and resource! what a soul of good nature and kindness governing the whole!

Chapter Nine

BLEAK HOUSE AND *HARD TIMES*

EARLY in 1851 Dickens began his dramatic activities for the Guild of Literature and Art, and prepared his company for a performance before Queen Victoria in May. In March, however, John Dickens had been seriously ill, and on the last day of the month Dickens wrote to Forster, 'My poor father died this morning.' He had come to have a tolerant affection for him, and though there was a touch of Prince Hall to Falstaff about his sorrow—'I could have better spared a better man'—in years to come he was to admit that the longer he lived the more he learnt to respect him.

Mrs. Dickens was also ill, but, leaving her under the care of the doctors at Malvern, where they were staying, Dickens came up to London to speak at a dinner in aid of the General Theatrical Fund. This was a benevolent society which he worked hard to assist throughout his life. Great efforts had been made to release him from his promise to preside, but the need was urgent, and no one else so suitable could be found at short notice. Before he left for the hall, he spent some time happily playing with his baby daughter, Dora. While he was in the course of his main speech, Forster was called from the room to receive the news that the child had suddenly and inexplicably died. Returning to the hall, he proposed the toast of the chairman, saying that 'in whatever direction Mr. Dickens pursued his literary path, his practical philanthropy was ever palpable'. Someone called out 'Humbug!' but Forster staunchly kept on, and when the dinner was over, broke the sad news to his friend. The Royal performance was postponed, but was given a few weeks later on 16 May.

Throughout the summer, Dickens spent his time partly on tour with the amateur players, and partly with his family at Broadstairs. He also arranged to move from Devonshire Terrace to a larger house in Tavistock Square. He was 'wild to begin a new book', and after they had settled in by the end of November, the work was advertised, the title was fixed, and by 7 December he was able to report, 'I have only the last short chapter to do to complete No. 1.' *Bleak House*, as the new book was called, went well, and when publication day came early in March it proved to be a great success. The sales began 'blazing away merrily', and by the time it came to an end eighteen months later he was able to write to a friend, 'it beat dear old Copperfield by a round ten thousand or more. I have never had so many readers.'

Bleak House defies summary, though again it shows a great advance in construction. It begins as an autobiographical novel, being the story of a young woman teacher, Esther Summerson, who is rather like Jane Eyre. To enlarge its scope, however, the narration alternates between the conventional third person and Esther. Dangerous as this is, it is kept fully under control.

Esther's own story is merely melodramatic: the further advance in structure shown by *Bleak House* is that the novel is made to open out like a painted fan until we see the whole of contemporary society from the inhabitants of an aristocratic country house to the denizens of the London rookeries. Yet everything radiates out from, and converges on, the High Court of Chancery, where the interminable case of Jarndyce *v.* Jarndyce has been proceeding for the past forty years.

In its style and characterization it is among Dickens's best. There is tremendous zest in the satire of the Law and of life at Chesney Wold. His fancy has full rein, not only in the well-remembered set-pieces like the description of the fog at the beginning, of life in Tom-all-alone's, or of Mr. Chadband discoursing upon 'Terewth'. Details of every scene, and every character, are selected so that they stand out in high relief. Old Krook comes forward 'with his head sunk sideways between his shoulders, and his breath issuing in visible smoke from his mouth, as if he were on fire within. His throat, chin and eyebrows were so frosted with white hairs, that he looked from his breast upward, like some old root in a fall of snow.' We are introduced to the formidable church social-worker, Mrs. Pardiggle, a woman 'with spectacles, a prominent nose, and a loud voice, who had the effect of wanting a great deal of room'. Mr. Vholes, Richard Carstone's 'legal adviser', appears as 'a sallow man with pinched lips that looked as if they were cold, a red eruption here and there upon his face, tall and thin, about fifty years of age, high-shouldered and stooping. Dressed in black, black-gloved and buttoned to the chin.' And old Mr. Turveydrop, fashioned after the example of the late Prince Regent, makes his bow, 'A fat old gentleman with a false complexion, false teeth, false whiskers, and wig . . . who was pinched in, and swelled out, and got up, and strapped down, as much as he could possibly bear.' So they are described on their first appearance.

The writing itself is more fanciful than ever, and sometimes almost 'metaphysical' in its conceits. 'I have purposely dwelt on the romantic side of familiar things', wrote Dickens in his preface; and, although this was said as an afterthought at the end of his defence of the possibility of Spontaneous Combustion as described in the case of Mr. Krook, it is a welcome sign that he had come to recognize that he was never intended to be a realist. Though, like other novelists of his time, Dickens never published any considerations about his art, he knew well enough what he was doing. When someone criticized him for overloading his narrative with imaginative fancies, he wrote an important explanation of his principles to Forster:

> It does not seem to me to be enough to say of any description that it is the exact truth. The exact truth must be there; but the merit or art in the narrator, is the manner of stating the truth. As to which thing in literature, it always seems to me that there is a world to be done. And in these times, when the tendency is to be frightfully literal and catalogue-like . . . I have an idea (really founded on a love of what I profess), that the very holding of a popular literature through a kind of popular dark age, may depend on such a fanciful treatment.

When Lord Lytton evidently offered the same sort of criticism, Dickens was prepared to admit that he sometimes so delighted in an unusual idea 'that I dare say I pet it as if it were a spoilt child'; and he added that he did not deny the charge, or question what Lytton said, 'otherwise than upon this ground—that I work slowly and with great care, and never give way to invention recklessly, but constantly restrain it; and that I think it is my infirmity to fancy or perceive relations in things which are not apparent generally'. It was George Henry Lewes who had attacked Dickens for the absurdity of Krook's Spontaneous Combustion, and it was George Eliot who followed her husband's precepts in the long dissertation she inserted in *Adam Bede*, in which she attacked novelists who cannot 'write the exact truth'. After Dickens's death, Lewes went even further and criticized him for the same faults, more systematically, in an article in the *Fortnightly Review*, to which it was left to Forster to reply.

Part of the reply can be found in Forster's analysis of *Bleak House*, and part has been left for elaboration more recently. As Jack Lindsay says, with Dickens the development is often not in the characters themselves but in the book as a whole. In *Bleak House*, explains Forster, 'the characters multiply as the tale advances, but in each the drift is the same'. Forster was even afraid that the book 'suffered by the very completeness with which the Chancery moral is worked out . . . too little relieved, and all pervading'. Yet this is part of its claim to greatness. It is not simply that everyone in the story is somehow connected with the great Chancery case of Jarndyce *v*. Jarndyce, but that the whole book is a unified study of society. The Court of Chancery is representative not only of corruption and social decay, but is itself symbolized by the junk-shop kept by Krook, known as the 'Lord Chancellor', and his savage cat expressive of 'strict statutes and most biting laws'. His tenant, poor mad Miss Flite, has her place in the scheme, and his own death symbolizes the end 'of all authorities in all places under all names soever, where false pretences are made and where injustice is done'.

In this lies part of Dickens's greatness as a satirist; and part is to be found in the relish with which he exposes political corruption at Chesney Wold and lightens it with humour. Sir Leicester Dedlock's conversations with his cousin Volumnia about the General Election, and his horror that his housekeeper's son (a successful industrialist) has been invited to go into Parliament, are as effective as the satire of Chancery. Lord Boodle's after-dinner conversation with Sir Leicester is the old inimitable Dickens again:

> 'Supposing the present Government to be overthrown, the limited choice of the Crown, in the formation of the new Ministry, would lie between Lord Doodle and Sir Thomas Coodle. . . . Then, giving the Home Department and the Leadership of the House to Joodle, and the Exchequer to Koodle, the Colonies to Loodle, and the Foreign Office to Moodle, what are you to do with Noodle? . . . What follows? That the country is shipwrecked, lost and gone to pieces . . . because you can't provide for Noodle!'

This is tremendously good fun. But, unfortunately, some critics have attempted to take it perfectly seriously. We even have Bernard Shaw declaring that Dickens's 'penetration of our party system with its Coodle, Doodle, Foodle, etc., has never been surpassed for *accuracy*'. So much has sometimes been made of Dickens as a critic of society that this can hardly be allowed to pass. It has been built into a conception of Dickens as a profound social prophet, attacking 'the forces of greed and privilege spinning their labyrinthine web of corruption . . . modern England . . . the world of an acquisitive society'. If one merely substitutes the names of the ministers of the day who held the actual offices coveted for Noodle & Co. (Palmerston, Gladstone, Sir George Grey, and Lord John Russell) one can see that it is better to enjoy it as a burlesque than to pretend it is a serious and accurate analysis of the party system.

The great point about Dickens's 'anatomy of society' is that it is practically a post-mortem. Whether he is describing Chancery, Tom-all-alone's or Chesney Wold, it is in terms of something ruinous and in decay. Hablot K. Browne's final illustration of 'The Mausoleum at Chesney Wold' in the last number, marks the end of the era of Whig landed proprietors, just as the introduction of Mr. Rouncewell on the political scene marked the beginning of what Dickens hoped were better things. Mr. Rouncewell, the enlightened industrialist, is an embarrassment to those who see Dickens as a proto-Marxist. But he was not a mere oversight. A few months after the book was finished Dickens publicly expressed his belief 'in the fusion of different classes, without confusion; in the bringing together of employers and employed; in the creating of a better common understanding among those whose interests are identical . . . and who can never be in unnatural antagonism without deplorable results'. Dickens certainly had faith in the new forces of industry, and to assert that he believed that mid-Victorian England was a society in decay is as absurd as to imagine that it was so in fact!

Just as in *David Copperfield*, some of the characters in *Bleak House* were drawn from people Dickens knew personally. One of them was the likeable Lawrence Boythorn, whom he intended 'as a most exact portrait of Walter Savage Landor'. The other was the better-known character of the brilliant but selfish Harold Skimpole, who was taken from Leigh Hunt. What impelled Dickens to do it, it is hard to say. Hunt had the half suspicion that it was because he had shown no interest in the Guild. But it is more likely that certain recognizable 'originals' somehow stimulated Dickens's creative power so much that he felt unable to resist them.

Whatever is written in excuse of Dickens's motives and Hunt's somewhat damaged reputation only makes it clearer that the resemblance was extraordinary. Dickens altered Skimpole's Christian name (which had at first been 'Leonard'), changed him from thin to fat, and ordered his illustrator to make him 'singularly unlike the great original', but the likeness always remained. Dickens boasted of it. After Forster and another friend had warned him of it and he had 'toned' down Skimpole, he broke out in a letter to the Hon. Mrs. Richard Watson: 'I suppose that he is the most exact portrait that was ever painted in words! The likeness is astonishing. I don't think it could possibly be more like himself. . . . There is not an atom of exaggeration or suppression. It is an absolute reproduction of a real man.'

The most striking similarity lay in the wonderful way in which Dickens caught Hunt's tone and style. It was too close even to be called a parody, but it was this that made Skimpole instantaneously recognizable and ever-delightful. Of course it is also true that Skimpole's dishonesty was closely based on Dickens's knowledge of Hunt's notorious vagueness in financial matters, and at least one of Hunt's former friends declared that Skimpole was an 'exact moral photograph', and that he had been 'daguerrotyped to the life'. Fortunately Dickens was a good enough fiction-writer to be able to appease Hunt afterwards by a convincing denial; but what remains most astonishing is the superb artistry and cleverness of his performance.

For much of the art of the novel and the pleasure it gives lie on the surface: in the dialogue, the manipulation of the characters, and in the assured and flexible tones of the writer whose triumph in presenting his novels (and himself through his novels) was of course quite as much one of art as of character. It is true that, to his public and to himself, his personality and his work were always closely related, and that by the majority of his readers they have often been identified and confused. It was even a natural consequence of his way of writing and his conception of himself as an entertainer that it should result in a cult of his personality. Yet none of this was inconsistent with the highest achievements and his giving a wonderfully controlled and brilliantly sustained performance. To ask for a novel by Dickens without the sense of his presence would be to ask for something *less*. This presence of the writer is not simply in the scenes directly taken from life as in *David Copperfield*, in the fictional autobiographies of Esther Summerson and Pip, or in the very occasional passages in which the novelist speaks out directly, but in almost every turn of phrase, every conception, and in the world he creates. For, as a novelist, Dickens is always what he once planned to be if he could speak to his readers through his own periodical, 'a sort of previously unthought of Power', an 'inseparable companion', always present in his work; and this power is to be found not only in the obviously forceful passages, but in the continued vitality of his language and the sense it gives of someone continuously and consciously presenting his scenes.

In *Bleak House* one might instance the opening chapter, almost all those which are set in Chancery and Cook's Court, the displays of Skimpole, or the smooth surface of Tulkinghorn which drives Dickens to writing about him instead of simply presenting what he says. With these are the passages in the novel which show melodrama at its highest, which reveal his mastery as a writer without inwardly involving us in the fortunes of the characters. Chapter xlviii, 'Closing-In', for example, presents a marvellous succession of scenes, from Lincolnshire to London, from the world of fashion and the dismal grandeur of the Dedlock's town mansion, to the departure of Tulkinghorn through 'the wilderness of London', to his chambers in Lincolns Inn Fields. For:

> In these fields of Mr. Tulkinghorn's inhabiting, where the shepherds play on Chancery pipes that have no stop, and keep their sheep in the fold by hook and by crook until they have shorn them exceeding close, every noise is merged, this moonlight night, into a distant ringing hum, as if the city were a vast glass, vibrating.
>
> What's that? Who fired a gun or pistol? Where was it? . . .

All such scenes show Dickens's verbal resourcefulness; they may shade into melodrama, and even into staginess, bathos and near dullness when the serious characters have to carry the story forward without inward life of their own. Yet even the flattest scenes have the resource of purpose and precision.

At the same time, to maintain that much of the art of a novel such as *Bleak House* is on the surface is not to be blind to what Edmund Wilson calls 'the symbolism of more complicated reference'. This goes beyond what we have already seen, the way in which Krook expressly 'symbolizes' the Lord Chancellor; his shop, the system of law; his tenants, its victims; his death, the consequences. The symbols here each stand for something; they are no more nor less than what the nineteenth-century novelists often spoke of as 'allegory'. Throughout everything Dickens writes he shows that this was one of his most constant modes of thought; and however complex the correspondences may be, there is still usually an articulated skeleton of meaning: Chancery stands for the whole condition of England, or all authorities whatsoever; it corresponds to muddle and confusion between classes, in government, in social conditions, and then in religion and in the human condition itself. Much of this is obvious;

for whenever the victims of Chancery die, for example, Nemo, Jo, Gridley, Richard, Mr. Tulkinghorn and Lady Dedlock, the wider implications are clearly stated or implied. We are turned, from time to time, in other directions than the criticism of society; Jo on the street corner, looking up at the great cross of St. Paul's, may possibly be thinking 'that sacred emblem to be . . . the crowning confusion of the great confused city'; and there is Miss Flite with her caged birds, 'Hope, Joy, Youth, Peace, Rest, Life, Dust, Ashes, Waste, Want, Ruin, Despair, Madness, Death, Cunning, Folly, Words, Wigs, Rags, Sheepskin, Plunder, Precedent, Jargon, Gammon, and Spinach!' And besides this, there is the way in which the novel stands for the whole world of Dickens's imagination, his way of looking at life, including its ambiguities and contradictory elements, his uniquely personal feelings; and to come at this one must accept that the novel also stands by and for itself.

Yet it can never stand entirely by and for itself. Addressed to its own times, it cannot escape its context which is part of its language. Attempts to accept the novels as self-contained or autonomous, moreover, lead to the difficulty for most readers that in opening interpretation to almost all possibilities, many are lost. It takes the patience and scrupulousness of Hillis Miller, in his chapter on *Bleak House*, to show the 'special quality of Dickens's imagination', and how he seeks to 'get behind the surface by describing all of it bit by bit'. For the novels are so extraordinarily full of possibilities and meanings, and these all lie within such dense and imaginative verbally-realized life, that to broaden freedom of interpretation can be self-defeating. Anyone can seize on a train of images or themes, and trace them rapidly through the novel; and a dozen critics could pin down a score of themes, all justified by the text. To go further and to rearrange themes or patterns which would have been foreign to Dickens's purpose, which go against the grain of his culture, and even to argue that as the novel has a meaning of its own any contradictions have an especially important part, may result from an attempt to read Dickens as if he were Kafka. Indeed, he was very like him—so far as a man can be who would have rejected his attitude to life, and whose art depends so largely on the control of a rich and sensitive response to life and people and all they do and say. But the life of the novels is so abundant that denied the reader's attention to narrative and the sense of an urgently intent author addressing the reader—which are their first and fundamental principles—they constantly tend to diffusion and chaos.

For the value, in itself, of finding new themes is limited. It is too easy. Very simply, for example, one might choose as a single theme once again 'the need for Love': one which is centred in Esther, branching out in her relations with her 'darling' Ada, with the deprived Jellyby children, with everyone at Greenleaf, Miss Flite, the brickmakers' women, the Coavinses, and—obviously—with Jarndyce and Allan Woodcourt. There is clear textual justification for linking whole groups of satellite characters with the same theme. Underpinning the whole plot structure and motivating its events, moreover, is the love of Esther's mother and Captain Hawdon which still proves so strong, after his death, that (as Edmund Wilson says) it pulls the world of the novel apart. In a real sense this is one of the major themes. And one could easily flutter through the pages of the novel to find a dozen more.

Yet such dissection may lead to seeing much less than

the whole. These themes do not simply help to offer something for everyone: they are made sufficiently part of each other in the story to unite to give an overwhelming impression of life; and nothing less than to give such a total impression, apparently all-embracing, expressed with personal intensity, and told as a narrative, was the challenge that Dickens now constantly met and overcame with each of his novels.

In spite of its popularity with the general reader, *Bleak House* was not well received by the reviewers. The conservative were upset by its social criticism, the younger reviewers appear to have felt that if they praised it there was nothing new to be said, and Dickens's advance in his technique as a novelist was something that evaded them all. *The Spectator* asserted that it suffered from 'an absolute want of construction'. It is ironic that many of the critics of Dickens's day denied that he had any skill in constructing a novel, while many of our own have attributed his increased confidence in handling his plots to Wilkie Collins. T. S. Eliot has even implied that this can be seen as early as *Bleak House*, before Collins had written anything but *Rambles Beyond Railways*, *Antonina*, and *Basil*. In fact, however much Dickens enjoyed the company of his new friend, whom he had first met when selecting the cast for the Royal performance of *Not So Bad As We Seem*, he learned virtually nothing from him as a novelist until he came to write *Edwin Drood*. As can be seen from some of Collins's prefaces, they disagreed fundamentally about the main problems of evolving a plot; and Dickens privately expressed his opinion of the construction of *The Moonstone* as 'wearisome beyond endurance'.

T. S. Eliot's best comment on Dickens is in a lecture on Yeats, in which he pays tribute to the way in which he pre-eminently displayed 'the special character of the artist as artist—that is, the force of character by which . . . having exhausted his first inspiration', he was able 'to proceed to such a masterpiece as *Bleak House*'.

The book was finished in September 1853, while Dickens was on holiday at Boulogne. After a short break, he then started out on a two-months' tour of Switzerland and Italy with Collins and another friend, before he returned to London and resumed writing for *Household Words*.

Earlier in the year he, and other members of the Guild, had attended a great banquet to Literature and Art, which was held in Birmingham. There, he had been presented with a silver salver and a diamond ring, and had spoken on the place of Literature in the nineteenth century. He had explained that he gloried in writing for a wider public than the authors of old, and that the people had set writers free 'from the shame of the purchased dedication' and 'from the scurrilous and dirty work of Grub Street'. In return, he maintained that 'Literature cannot be too faithful to the people', and 'cannot too ardently advocate the cause of their advancement'.

While he was at dinner, he learnt that there was a movement afoot to start a new Literary and Scientific centre—the Birmingham and Midland Institute. He was greatly interested in the idea and, on the way to the station, offered to give a public reading of *A Christmas Carol* in order to help the funds. 'There would be some novelty in the thing', he explained, 'as I have never done it in public, though I have in private, and (if I may say so) with great effect on the hearers.' His offer was eagerly accepted, and he undertook to read in the Town Hall for three nights just after Christmas.

The readings were an enormous success, and both

Dickens and his audience enjoyed every moment. His hearers were extremely responsive, and, after a moment's doubt as to 'whether it was quite practicable to conceal the requisite effort', he soon found himself at ease, 'and that we were all going on together . . . as if we were sitting round the fire'. When he came to the part where the Ghost of Christmas Present introduced Scrooge to the two children, a reporter observed that he read with particular emphasis. 'This passage', he wrote, 'was magnificently given, and brought down a burst of applause that clearly indicated in what direction the sympathy of the audience lay.'

Incidents like this help to show how close the connection was between Dickens's works and the events and interests of contemporary life. The week before, the same hall had been used for a national conference on reformatory schools. Indeed, as the reporter of the *Birmingham Mercury* said, Dickens had won 'the admiration and affection of a large proportion of the British people', because they recognized in him 'a household teacher—a fireside expositor of the great social and educational questions about which the legislature is AT LAST beginning to trouble itself'.

Among other new subjects to which Dickens now turned his attention was the question of the relations between Capital and Labour. While he had been on holiday in Italy, the previous year, his attention had been caught by reports of a great strike by the weavers of Preston; so, at the end of January, when it was in its twenty-fourth week, he visited the town to see things for himself. He was thinking of writing an article about the strike for *Household Words* and he already had an idea in mind for a new novel which would deal with life in the industrial north. As a writer he was disappointed in what he saw at Preston; but as one who sympathized with the workers he was greatly impressed by the quiet and orderly way in which the strike had been conducted. He refused to admit that either side had a monopoly of justice, and his published conclusions have a strangely modern ring in their demand for 'authorized mediation'. For, 'masters right, or men right', he wrote, 'there is certain ruin to both in the continuance or frequent revival of this breach'.

His progress with the novel went on steadily. It was started in January in London and finished at Boulogne in July. It had begun largely because the circulation of *Household Words* had been falling, and his partners had felt that only a serial story by Dickens could pull it round. When it was published, in April, the sales doubled in the first ten weeks, and kept climbing steadily until its close. It was another triumph, which Dickens felt was crowned by its dedication to Carlyle.

Yet though it sent up the circulation of *Household Words*, it was rather poorly received by the reviewers. Macaulay disliked it for its 'sullen socialism'; and Ruskin and Shaw enjoyed it because they misread it in the same way as Macaulay. Henri Taine liked it, and John Forster was diffident; and until Dr. F. R. Leavis promoted it to somewhere near the top of Dickens's novels it has been overlooked and undervalued. It is too stiff and mannered to be popular; yet it was the first of Dickens's later novels to have the advantage of being written for weekly publication. 'The difficulty of the space', he wrote, 'is CRUSHING'; but it compelled him to write with economy, and forced him to fit the story into a compact structure.

In comparison with the other novels its subject, thought, and style require more attention than it deserves simply as a work of fiction. In discussing them we can hardly avoid referring to Dr. F. R. Leavis's 'Analytic Note' in his *The Great Tradition* (1950). A weakness of this note at the time it was written was that Leavis did not seem to see that his remarks on *Hard Times* were capable of a much wider application to Dickens's works. Its strength is in his interpretation of the novel as what Henry James called a 'moral fable'—that is, a fictional story with a clear intellectual purpose. Leavis's recognition that Dickens's writing shows 'a full critical vision, a stamina, a flexibility combined with consistency, and a depth that he seems to have had little credit for', was just though rather belated. He also surprisingly paid tribute to 'the astonishing and irresistible richness of life that characterizes the book everywhere', and termed the author 'poet dramatist'.

Dickens's main intention, as Leavis says, was 'to comment on certain key characteristics of Victorian civilization'. He was concerned about the difference (as he expresses it in the first chapter) between Fact and Fancy. The purpose of the novel was to emphasize, with all his power and skill, that this was not just a rhetorical antithesis: that mere fact, or logic, that leaves half of our lives out of account—any method of ruling conduct or affairs that lacks sympathy, love, and understanding between human beings—is, in the end, not merely sterile, but bitterly destructive of all the moral virtues, beauty, and everything that is best; that a sound life cannot exist without happiness; and that the proper education of children must take into account their moral development, which it should foster through their fancy and love of life. The government of a country, he maintained, cannot safely be left to be administered from self-interest, nor trusted to a single class certain to look after itself first and last. He held that the relations between Capital and Labour, or (as he preferred to call them) between Masters and Men, can never be properly managed or understood if it is assumed that they must be in a perpetual state of conflict, or that the men must inevitably be subject to the paternal rule of the masters. Above all, he believed that the relations between men and women; between father and children, mother and child, or brother and sister; between friends, or any persons in almost any permanent association, must originate and be rooted in liking, affection, or love.

The novel was thus a protest not merely against certain characteristics of *Victorian* society, but against certain tendencies to be found in any industrial civilization. It was a protest against all repression of the human spirit by the letter of the classroom, the constitution, the law, and the so-called principles of political economy. Dickens's purpose was not just to strike at everyday, run-of-the-mill, mid-nineteenth-century 'utilitarianism' —and especially not at anything so abstract as the Utilitarian philosophy as expounded by Bentham and Mill. It was aimed at all kinds of social abuses which he thought ran counter to human life and happiness because they were framed according to supposed 'facts' while they ignored obvious human needs. That is why even the sawdust ring of the circus was preferable to the cinders of Coketown or the dust and ashes of the political arena. The novel has such a broad purpose even though it included references to some of Dickens's living contemporaries which most of them were unable to recognize, and satire of specific abuses which was too pointed to be understood by the general reader; and it is only by understanding this broader purpose (which is not so obvious that it can be taken for granted) that one can see how it unifies Dickens's remarks on Stephen Blackpool's marriage, the aesthetic theories of the 'third gentleman' in the second chapter, the problems of Trade Unionism, Louisa's marriage to Bounderby, and her brother's theft from the Bank. Dickens once said that the ideas in the book took him 'by the throat' and forced him to write. A careful reading shows that he succeeded in giving them a unified purpose, and that *Hard Times* has coherence and power which deserve great respect even though it is not as entertaining as most of the other novels.

Unfortunately, its purpose has often been misunderstood. Because it was partly about the differences between a mill-owner and his men, it has been thought that Dickens wrote it in order to take sides; and because both Mr. Bounderby, the mill-owner, and Slackbridge, the trade union agitator, are described as utterly worthless, he has alternately been claimed as a kind of socialist and hailed as faithful to capitalism after all. In fact Dickens was not so simple-minded. He was very like many people today. He thought it just that there should be the right to strike, but almost always wrong to use it. He disliked extremists on both sides. He hated employers like Bounderby, and he distrusted trade union organizers such as Slackbridge. He was in favour of all attempts to encourage better industrial relations and for conciliation on both sides; and he considered that the Government should take action by setting up an independent body to arbitrate between them. Addressing an audience of working men in industrial Birmingham at the reading of the *Christmas Carol*, a month before he started *Hard Times*, he had referred perfectly happily to the value of education 'in the bringing together of employers and employed; in the creating of a better understanding of those whose interests are identical'.

Yet Lionel Stevenson, writing on 'Dickens's Dark Novels' (*Sewanee Review*, li, 1943) has thought that Dickens watched 'the beginnings of a sounder structure of Trade Unions, initiated . . . in 1851, by . . . the Amalgamated Society of Engineers', with interested approval. It was nothing of the kind. When the men of this well-organized new union struck, next year, he wrote to a friend with intense disapproval of their official leaders:

> As to the Engineers . . . I believe the difficulty in the way of compromise, from the very beginning, is not so much with the masters as with the men. Honorable, generous, and spirited themselves, they have fallen into an unlucky way of trusting their affairs to contentious men, who work them up into a state of conglomeration and irritation, and are the greatest Pests that their own employers [i.e. the working men] can encounter upon earth. I am much mistaken if this be not the case.

This is only a detail in regard to the novel, but it is central to an understanding of what Dickens thought of his own times and how he commented on them in the novels. It also bears more directly on *Hard Times* than at first appears because a careful study of actual affairs at the time, of what Dickens wrote in the novel, what he said in his letters, and what he wrote in *Household Words*, shows that the conditions described in *Hard Times* are much closer to the engineering strike of 1852 than to the dispute at Preston. For, at this time, although the Preston spinners and weavers struck for more than six months, they acted altogether without a 'union'; their leaders were not permanent organizers but local workmen; and whereas the fundamental issue at stake in Manchester had been the principle of the 'closed shop' (whether union men would agree to non-union men's working alongside them) and was a tactical struggle for power, at Preston it was a straight fight about pay. The story of Stephen Blackpool, in the novel, the weaver who is sent to Coventry because he so strangely refuses to join his union, is well enough in sentiment, but false in fact, false to the context of the novel, and false in character. It arises from Dickens's confusion of two different communities. The whole novel, in fact, tends to be weakest just where certain writers would like to see it come out strongest—as a study of industrial capitalism.

He was neither an apologist for industrial capitalism, nor a critic. Still less should one be tempted to conclude that Dickens was even a minor prophet in the line of Ruskin and William Morris. In spite of the praise Ruskin deservedly gave the novel for its teaching on general education and political economy in *Unto This Last*, he rightly ignored its other implications which would have deeply disturbed him. For although Shaw wrote, in an important introduction to the novel, that 'Dickens's occasional indignation' had 'spread and deepened into a passionate revolt against the whole industrial order of the modern world' (Waverley Dickens, 1911), this is certainly wrong if we take it to mean that Dickens protested against the arrival of the machine and somehow foresaw where it would lead. For there are other unperceived topicalities (mainly chapter ii) which show that Dickens meant to satirize certain recent and most enlightened attempts to improve industrial design in his own worst Bounderby manner; and although he dropped these satirical intentions as he went on, they are still a clue to a tendency within the novel.[1] Dickens is essentially varied

[1] See John Holloway, '*Hard Times*: A History and a Criticism', in *Dickens and the Twentieth Century*, ed. J. Gross and G. Pearson, 1962; and my own 'Dickens and the Department of Practical Art', *MLR*, XLVIII, 1953.

and paradoxical. Ruskin summed him up acutely, on writing to Charles Eliot Norton, immediately after Dickens's death, to say that he 'was a pure modernist—a leader of the steam-whistle party *par excellence*. . . . His hero is essentially the ironmaster.'

Indeed, altogether too much can be made of the industrial scenes in the novel, in comparison with the domestic life of the Gradgrinds and Mr. Sleary's circus. Unfortunately Dickens himself was responsible for calling attention to them when he began to write. He chose as part of his subject a dispute in the cotton industry just when the Preston strike was in everyone's mind. He was publicly said to have visited the north to verify his impressions. He published the article on Preston in *Household Words* a few weeks before the first instalment of the novel, and made it clear to attentive readers that the agitator, Slackbridge, was partly drawn from one of the local leaders at Preston; and, on top of everything else, even before *Hard Times* had finished its run in *Household Words*, he advertised as its successor a novel by Mrs. Gaskell called *North and South*, which also turned out to be based on the Preston dispute. His subsequent denial that there was any necessary connection between Coketown and Preston made no difference therefore. The *Westminster Review* declared that: 'when it was announced . . . that Mr. Dickens was about to write a tale called *Hard Times*, the general attention was instantly arrested. It was imagined the main topic of the story would be drawn from the fearful struggle being enacted in the north.' In fact, it went on, his readers had been disappointed. The purpose of the book seemed to be to show that if a child were brought up in a circus it would be a prodigy of virtue, while if it were sent to a model school it might grow up to rob a bank or make a prostituted marriage. Such misunderstandings were a natural consequence of reading the story with nothing but topical events in mind; but although this was not the fault of the novel, it was partly the fault of the novelist.

Wrong as the reviewers of the time were, present-day critics who still try to see it mainly as an expression of 'Dickens violent hostility to industrial capitalism and its entire scheme of life', are even more misleading. It is abundantly clear, in many ways, that Dickens was genuinely more sympathetic to workers—even when on strike—than most men of his class in his time or ours. Yet he was not interested in condemning capitalism. A few years later, for example, he was prepared to accept the presentation of a gold watch, at Coventry, without protesting at a speaker who praised his works because they did not include 'a single word that tended to irritate one class against another' and because they had the practical effect of helping to prevent industrial disputes! Obviously enough, Dickens did not deserve this: but a serious study of such issues was not at the heart of his examination of society, superficially topical as he made it in *Hard Times*.

For the book is typical of many of Dickens's novels in that it was so curiously topical; and an essential element in any complete understanding of Dickens must be the way in which he wrote for men of his time. Yet the further this is pursued the clearer it is that Dickens used topicality as a means of *communicating*—it never gives his true subject. This goes further than even Dickens himself could explain, as he tried to in a letter to an American publisher, written just after he had brought *Hard Times* to a close:

> I think it possible that I may have considered the powers and purposes of fiction a little longer and a little more

> anxiously and attentively than your lady friend. To interest and affect the general mind in behalf of anything that is clearly wrong—to stimulate and rouse the public soul to a compassionate or indignant feeling that it *must not be*—without obtruding any pet theory of cause or cure, and so throwing off allies as they spring up—I believe to be one of Fiction's highest uses. And this is the use to which I try to turn it.

In effect, though, through fiction he aroused the public, and by using public issues he helped both to awaken his creative force and to hold his readers' attention. (Not unreasonably, he did not care to make precise distinctions.) It was a circular approach. He used events men knew of to help to speak to them more directly, and then he tried to write simple truths about their relations one with another. For, certainly, *Hard Times for These Times* should be interpreted as a *moral* fable, in the everyday sense. It may even be called 'a morality drama', which is Edgar Johnson's term. And, like the Christmas books and the other novels serialized in *Household Words* and *All the Year Round*, it is based on Christian morality.

When Sissy, the adopted circus-girl, chats with Louisa, the clever daughter of the 'eminently practical' Mr. Gradgrind, she reports her disappointingly slow progress at school, and tells how 'after eight weeks of induction into the elements of Political Economy, she had only yesterday been set right by a prattler three feet high, for returning to the question, "What is the first principle of this science?" the absurd answer, "To do unto others as I would that they should do unto me".'

Or, again, she tells Louisa how the schoolmaster had set her some problems:

> 'Then Mr. M'Choakumchild said he would try me once more. And he said . . . that in a given time a hundred thousand persons went to sea on long voyages, and only five

hundred of them were drowned or burnt to death. What is the percentage? And I said, Miss,' here Sissy fairly sobbed as confessing . . . to her greatest error; 'I said that it was nothing.'

'Nothing, Sissy?'

'Nothing, Miss—to the relations and friends of the people who were killed. I shall never learn.'

In many ways, even, the story is to be read less as a fable than as a parable, or a tract for the times. If it is not read thus, Stephen's fall down Old Hell Shaft, at the end of the book, and the star he thought he could see as he lay there dying, is as trite and tasteless a piece of false piety as an author has ever committed:

'I ha' fell into a pit that ha' been wi' th' Fire-damp crueller than battle. I ha' read on't in the public petition, as onny one may read, fro' the men that works in pits, in which they ha' pray'n an pray'n the lawmakers for Christ's sake not to let their work be murder to 'em. . . . But look up yonder, Rachel! Look above!'

Following his eyes, she saw that he was gazing at a star.

'It ha' shined upon me,' he said reverently, 'in my pain and trouble down below. It ha' shined into my mind. . . . Often as I coom to myseln and found it shinin on me down there in my trouble, I thowt it were the star as guided to Our Saviour's home. I awmust think it be the very star!'

They lifted him up, and he was overjoyed to find that they were about to take him in the direction whither the star seemed to him to lead. . . .

They carried him very gently along the fields, and down the lanes, and over the wide landscape. . . . It was soon a funeral procession. The star had shown him where to find the God of the poor; and through humility, and sorrow, and forgiveness, he had gone to his Redeemer's rest.

Of course Dickens was attacking society, but not—as Shaw would have it—in company with Karl Marx in order to arouse revolution, but in the hope that all who were part of it would act with greater Christian humility and charity.

It is time, in fact, for us to consider Dickens's religion. It is so easy to generalize about his attitude, yet so difficult to pin him down. Biographically speaking, he appears to have been brought up partly as a nonconformist, to have been a unitarian for a while in the early 'forties, and to have become a rather intermittent churchgoer in the last period of his life. He definitely felt a need for religion, although little for worship. He cared nothing for dogma. Theologically speaking, it might be said of him as Shaftesbury said of Palmerston, that he did not 'know the difference between Sydney Smith and Moses'. It may be true that he could 'never be properly described as a religious man', but as George Orwell admits, 'he "*believed*" undoubtedly'. Orwell refers to a letter Dickens wrote to his youngest son, in 1868:

> You will remember that you have never at home been harassed about religious observances, or mere formalities. I have always been anxious not to weary my children with such things, before they are old enough to form opinions respecting them. You will therefore understand the better that I now most solemnly impress upon you the truth and beauty of the Christian Religion, as it came from Christ Himself, and the impossibility of your going far wrong if you humbly but heartily respect it. . . . Never abandon the wholesome practice of saying your own private prayers, night and morning. I have never abandoned it, and I know the comfort of it.

Dickens wrote prayers and a *Life of Our Lord* for his children's use, and though they left out the doctrine of the virgin birth they were pious and sincere. Gladstone rather ludicrously remarked of *Nicholas Nickleby* that there was 'No church in the book, and the motives are not those of religion', but the second part of his statement was certainly wrong. Other critics of the day wrote of him as 'the prophet of an age which loves benevolence without religion' (*Rambler*, 1854) and more recently Professor Louis Cazamian has termed the whole Dickensian ethos a mere 'philosophie de la Noël'.

But though Dickens was unsure, was without a strong personal religious experience, and often suspicious of the well-meaning of the Church, he would not have been the same man or written the same books without a religious faith. To a critic as sensitive to such things as, for example, Humphry House, 'the exaggerated consolation' that Poor Jo, in *Bleak House*, is supposed to derive from the Lord's Prayer, 'not merely degrades the use of it into a kind of private superstition, but also has the mood of somebody in a state of utter emotional collapse . . . mouthing formulae from another scheme of values as if they expressed his own'. Yet this is much too strong. It is true that such a scene may be intellectually contemptible, since it comes from someone who guided himself by nothing more profound than the parable of the Good Samaritan. Yet, unsatisfactory as this may be, Dickens's religious faith was expressed not simply at the level of his readers, but at that of the majority of humanity.

For, although the student of the Victorian period who tries to judge Dickens as if he were an inferior Newman, Arnold or George Eliot, has always started back appalled, in matters of religion Dickens does appear to have essentially expressed the broad general feelings and opinions of his readers. He was neither intellectual nor analytical. But even our present historians have yet 'to put back religion, particularly popular religion, into the picture of nineteenth-century England' (G. Kitson Clark, *The Making of Victorian England*, 1962, p. 24). The historians and critics have concentrated on what has appeared intelligible and rational from their points of view; but, as Professor Kitson Clark writes, in order to understand 'the springs of action it is important to try to understand the emotions, the irrational feelings, the prejudices, the experiences which form men's minds'; and this is exactly what very few writers who have glanced at Dickens's faith have failed to do.

Again, although even as early as the eighteen-fifties the part of the Englishman's nature which had once 'found gratification in religious life', was already 'drifting into political life', as Beatrice Webb found at the beginning of her career, each of these interests was still often interpreted in terms of the other. This was not merely, as House partly suggests in the chapter on 'Religion' in *The Dickens World*, a habit of thought and a manner of speaking; but because Christian values were still widely enough accepted to stand against those of material success. The contrast between them is at the heart of what Dickens wrote. Whether he was declaiming about 'the duties of a Christian government', as in his address 'To Working Men' (1854), or simply stating his faith, as in his Will, wherein he again exhorted his children 'to try to guide themselves by the teaching of the New Testament', his writing always carries conviction. It does so not because its power came from the simple faith of his readers but because he was largely convinced himself.

Chapter Ten

POLITICAL VIEWS AND *LITTLE DORRIT*

DICKENS was now spending more and more of his time in France. For the summer of 1854 he took a villa at Boulogne, and left two of his boys at school there when the rest of the family returned to London. In February 1855 he went to Paris with Wilkie Collins for a fortnight's holiday, and next autumn he brought the whole family over to apartments in the Avenue des Champs Elysées, where they stayed for the next seven months. He seems to have divided his time chiefly between writing and visiting the theatre, and took the opportunity to arrange for Hachette to bring out an authorized translation of his works. He lived even less among literary circles in France than in England, though Paul Féval says of Dickens's reading of contemporary French novelists, that 'he knew us all'. He had a particular admiration for Balzac, though he deplored the unrestrained development of his personality.

It was not the mere gaiety of Paris that attracted him, but its air of efficiency and life. He was simply amused by some of the effects of the luxury of the Second Empire. He admired the French talent for getting things done, and wrote an article for *Household Words* contrasting the brisk administration of Paris with the bumbling ways of the London Court of Common Council. He even felt that the painting of his compatriots lacked 'character and purpose' in comparison with the French, and that there was 'a horrid respectability about the best of them . . . strangely expressive . . . of the state of England'. Dickens himself, indeed, had come to set such a high value on mere efficiency that this was beginning to be reflected in his manner and appearance; for, as a French portrait-painter, Ary Scheffer, despairingly remarked as he was trying to capture his expression, 'At this moment, *mon cher Dickens*, you look more like an energetic Dutch admiral!' There is no disguising the fact that although Dickens disliked Napoleon III personally and detested his anti-liberal policies, the more he thought about politics the less faith he felt in the future of parliamentary government in England.

Unfortunately, he had been thinking about politics more and more. Ever since he had started *Household Words* he had shown an increasing interest in them, and a growing exasperation. This had partly been expressed in his last two novels; and, as he now felt that the government was remaining obstinately obstructive to all sound new measures, he began to grow angry. He even felt almost sympathetic with Chartism, though he had nothing but contempt for 'the stupidest socialist dogma that there is only one class of labourers upon earth'. But he did believe that party government was an utter failure, and that England was governed only by a narrow class. When war was declared on Russia in the spring of 1854 he correctly saw that it would be used as a further pretext for putting off social reform, and once the news began to come in of how disastrously the army had fared in the Crimea, he felt convinced that as well as being corrupt the government was completely incompetent.

He at once wrote a strong appeal 'To Working Men', blaming Parliament, and warning 'the working man . . . that without his own help he will not be helped but will pitilessly be left to struggle . . . with disease and death'. Some of his friends remonstrated with him, but he refused to withdraw. The fact is that Dickens despaired of parliamentary government, and had had no faith in it from the days when he had worked in the gallery. Early in 1854, he had written that 'as to Parliament, it does so little and talks so much that the most interesting ceremony I know of in connection with it was performed . . . by one man, who just cleared it out, locked up the place, and put the keys in his pocket'. This was not just a joke. Eighteen months later he wrote to Forster, 'I really am serious in thinking . . . that representative government is become altogether a failure with us . . . and that the whole thing has broken down since that great seventeenth-century time.' Next month he wrote to another correspondent, 'As to the suffrage, I have lost hope even in the ballot.' It was largely historical sentiment that united Dickens, Carlyle, and Forster in the regret with which they looked back to the days of the Commonwealth; but certainly Dickens, as well as Carlyle, had lost all faith in reform through Parliament.

Nor was this simply due to his impatience during the difficult time of the war in the Crimea. For most of his life Dickens took some pains to avoid making pronouncements on the political scene outside his novels; but less than a year before his death he raised a storm of disapproval when he summed up his political creed in a speech at Birmingham: 'My faith in the people governing', he said, 'is infinitesimal; my faith in the People governed, is, on the whole, illimitable.' In spite of his care, on his next visit, to explain that by 'the people governing', he had merely meant 'the people who govern us', he could hardly have expected his views to be welcomed by anyone who believed in a Parliament. 'The people governing' were the Liberals under Gladstone; two of Dickens's close friends were in the Cabinet; and in the same speech, to John Bright's Birmingham constituents, he went out of his way to compliment their member, who was then at the Board of Trade. It was hardly unreasonable of a local correspondent to complain that what he said was remarkable for 'showing his ambition to be a disciple of Carlyle in his worst phase'. His hearers were entitled to ask what alternative he advocated. As *The Times* remarked, 'sentiments like this might be justifiable in the latitude of St. Petersburg or Pekin, but then they would not be likely to get a hearing there'.

Dickens was greatest as a moralist. As a politician he could be as misguided and unfair as Carlyle. He was by no means completely under the latter's dominance, but he followed his lead in supporting authority when a rising in Jamaica (in 1865) was put down with unnecessary bloodshed and cruelty; and whereas Mill, Darwin, and Huxley demanded an inquiry, Dickens allied himself with Tennyson, Carlyle, and Governor Eyre. The pious philanthropist Honeythunder, in *Edwin Drood*, was probably a satire on those who followed Mill. Again, in his first Christmas number after *Little Dorrit*, called 'The Perils of Certain English Prisoners', the hero is a private in the Marines who expresses a dislike for all natives, and a longing to kick one of 'the Sambos', or 'let fly with his right . . . exactly without knowing why, except that it was the right thing to do'. It is true that this was written at the time of the Indian Mutiny, but it shows him in an unattractive light; and if only slightly influenced by Carlyle, Dickens was largely in agreement with him. However brilliant he was as an entertainer, and however often he has been misrepresented or misunderstood, Dickens's social criticism could be unfair and his political views wrong.

So much needs to be said as an introduction to his activities in 1855. The disastrous fate of the army in the Crimea the previous winter, and strong public criticism led by *The Times*, had resulted in a demand for administrative reform. Dickens lent his support to a society which was formed for this purpose, and gave one of the most brilliant speeches of his career at a meeting it held in June. 'He was gravely in earnest', it was reported, when he denounced the Prime Minister for his heartlessness and flippancy in the face of disaster. 'The first great strong necessity', Dickens wrote after the meeting, 'is . . . to carry the war dead into the Tent of such a creature as this Lord Palmerston, and ring it into his soul . . . that Dandy insolence is gone for ever.' One month later he started *Little Dorrit*.

The new work was his greatest social satire. Yet, at the same time, it had other qualities which deserve our attention. It is certainly one of Dickens's darker novels; many of the characters are unattractive; and it is less lightened by humour than most of his other books. The story is involved and contains far too many mysteries. Dickens had been happy with an autobiographical narrative in *David Copperfield* and *Bleak House*, and now that he returned to a tale in the third person he relapsed into all the old intricacies he had used as long ago as *Oliver Twist*. He even seemed distrustful of his new skill; for though in his story of William Dorrit, the Father of the Marshalsea, he was able to make the narrative grow partly out of the character, Rigaud, Flintwich, and Tattycoram are nothing but dummies from the Dickens waxworks. Each has a dark secret, and near the end of the story everything grew so involved that, for the first time when plotting a novel, Dickens felt it necessary to write a 'Memo for working the story round', to see how the characters were connected and what problems were left to be solved.

Yet in spite of this relapse, much remains. Many of the characters are as full of life as ever. The inhabitants of Bleeding Heart Yard have a new truth to life. Cavaletto is amusing, Pancks in the old style, Casby cleverly done, and his daughter Flora ever memorable. She was Dickens's old admired Maria Beadnell, who, remembering her young lover as she read of David Copperfield's courtship, had written to remind him of the old days. She was married now, she said, and 'toothless, fat, old and ugly'. Dickens was enraptured at the thought of meeting her, and then bitterly shocked when he did so. The woman who had inspired Dora Spenlow had become Flora Finching:

> Flora, always tall, had grown to be very broad too, and short of breath; but that was not much. Flora, whom he had left a lily, had become a peony; but that was not much. Flora, who had seemed enchanting in all she said and thought, was diffuse and silly. That was much. Flora, who had been spoiled and artless long ago, was determined to be spoiled and artless now. That was a fatal blow.

Like his own hero, Arthur Clennam, Dickens's eyes 'no sooner fell upon the subject of his old passion, than it shivered and broke to pieces'. *Little Dorrit* is the work of a man disillusioned by everything he turns to, an iconoclast intent on stripping away all false disguises.

A main strand in the narrative is the story of Little Dorrit herself, the young heroine who has been brought up within a debtor's prison, and who never ceases to love her old humbug of a father. She is only slightly portrayed, as a narrative character, she is rather tiresome, there is such a want of reality in her. The central figure is William Dorrit, who has been in prison so long that he is known not only as her father, but as the Father of the Marshalsea. He was also related to Dickens's father, since he was at least partly based on memories of John Dickens as he had been when shut up in the same prison walls. He is vain, pompous, and above all patronizing. He represents everything that exasperated Dickens in his smug, self-satisfied fellow-countrymen, who were content to be imprisoned within old ways by their government, or shut up in a set of their own stupid conventions, as long as they could preserve an appearance of genteel respectability. According to Gissing, 'the subtlest bit of humour in all Dickens's books' is the scene in which Dorrit entertains an old pensioner from the workhouse, Mr. Nandy. It certainly combines all Dickens's expert observation and mastery of dialogue with his new wry disillusion; and though one may regret the loss of his old optimism, his new outlook gave him a fresh view of things and a further insight into character.

Linked to the Dorrits are the Clennams. Mrs. Clennam represents all that was fierce and hard in repressive religion. She has shut herself up in an old house brooding over old wrongs. Arthur Clennam, her son, eventually marries Little Dorrit. Through Arthur, however, there is a link with the Meagleses, with whose daughter Pet he had been in love before he had noticed Little Dorrit. The Meagles family is linked with a Miss Wade, who tells her own story within the novel, 'The History of a Self Tormentor'. Pet marries a dilettante artist, Henry Gowan, type of all that Dickens detested in members of his own profession, insincere and incapable of taking anything seriously. The Gowans are linked with the Barnacle civil servants and the money-making Merdles; and the Merdles intermarry with the Dorrits. The important thing about the novel is not that Dickens fell down on the plot, but that he discovered how to manipulate a vast range of characters, and to bring them into relation with one another so as to reveal how the greater part of society was a colossal sham.

This was something new: too new for him to have sacrificed the machinery of plot altogether, though it is evident that he had half a mind to do something of the sort when he began. 'It struck me that it would be a new thing', he explained to Forster, 'to show people coming together, in a chance way, as fellow-travellers, and being in the same place, ignorant of one another, as happens in life; and to connect them afterwards, and to make the waiting for that connection a part of the interest.' He was unable to do this, but he was obviously only slightly interested in the mere intrigue, and far more concerned to impose a single atmosphere on the book, and give it unity of mood. This is partly effected by consistency of style, and partly by a succession of inter-relating images. The collapse of Mrs. Clennam's house, the crash of the financial 'house' of Merdle, and the ruin of the rather obviously contrived symbol of William Dorrit's 'castle in the air' are all part of a plan. The imprisonment of Dorrit in the Marshalsea, of society within the bonds of convention, of enterprise under state slackness, of those in quarantine at the beginning of the book, and those in the prison at Marseilles, all likewise have their place in a scheme. Dickens meant it to be so. As fast as the story opened out before him, he succeeded in keeping it together. 'Society, the Circumlocution Office and Mr. Gowan', he wrote to Forster, 'are of course three parts of one idea and design.' It is not one of the most entertaining of Dickens's novels; Thackeray is said to have dismissed it as 'damned stupid'; but if only for the principle of its design *Little Dorrit* would deserve, with *Bleak House*, a respected place in the history of the novel.

Yet the book had another purpose and a tremendous effect. It was an attack on financial corruption, political incompetence, and Society. Into writing the chapters which expose them Dickens put all his skill and power. The chapters 'Containing the Whole Science of Government' and the one in which the swindling financier Merdle gives a grand dinner-party for the Barnacles are among the best things he ever wrote. Mr. Merdle is rather more than the share-pushing cheats of *Nickleby* and *Chuzzlewit*: he is congratulated by a representative from the Treasury as 'one of England's world-famed capitalists and merchant-princes'. Yet his exposure remains something much less than an attack on nineteenth-century capitalism, and it is doubtful whether it was meant to be anything of the kind. Alfred Merdle, like John Sadleir and Leopold Redpath, the real men on whom he was based, was just a large-scale common swindler. His story exposes the Mammon-worship of the public and the Government (the spirit Carlyle attacked in his *Latter-Day Pamphlet* on George Hudson, the Railway King) but it is not an attack on capitalism itself: for that he would have had to satirize some successful swindler.

In fact no one objected to the exposure of Merdle. No one could. What they did resent was the attack on the Civil Service and the Government in the description of the Circumlocution Office. As a satire, this is beyond praise: 'The Circumlocution Office was (as everybody knows without being told) the most important Department under Government. No public business of any kind could possibly be done at any time, without the acquiescence of the Circumlocution Office. Its finger was in the largest public pie, and in the smallest private tart.'

Dickens poured all his contempt for officialdom into the description of Lord Tite Barnacle and his vast family who had all fastened themselves to the national ship. How they administered their departments according to the sublime principle of 'How Not To Do It', is skilfully linked with a description of how the same principle was practised by those who were actually in the Government. 'Public Departments and professional politicians' are mentioned together. The Circumlocution Office is said to have been 'a nursery of statesmen'. There are the Barnacles of the hustings. As a satiric exposure of some of the realities of government at that particular time, it was completely justified. But whether it is right to accept it now as a satisfactory and complete analysis of mid-Victorian society is quite another matter.

That several recent biographers have accepted and praised the truth of its social insight needs no substantiation. The great exception was George Orwell, who saw that Dickens fantastically simplified what he was writing about:

> At the back of his mind there is usually a half-belief that the whole apparatus of government is unnecessary. Parliament is simply Lord Coodle and Sir Thomas Doodle, the Empire is simply Major Bagstock and his Indian servant, the Army is simply Colonel Chowser and Doctor Slammer, the public services are simply Bumble and the Circumlocution Office—and so on and so forth. What he does not see is that Coodle and Doodle . . . *are* performing a function which neither Pickwick or Boffin would ever bother about.

It is essential to read Orwell's essay in full. It must be recognized, too, that Dickens fully believed that conditions were so bad that a revolution might break out in England at any moment. He wrote to Layard, the leader of the administrative reform movement, that he believed the discontent 'to be . . . extremely like the general mind of France before the breaking out of the first Revolution, and in danger of being turned by any one of a thousand accidents . . . into such a devil of a conflagration as never has been beheld since'. He continued to fear this, on and off, for the rest of his life. He was completely mistaken; and he was mistaken because his analysis of society was mistaken. It was not an accident. He was wrong because he left too much out of his consideration.

The counter-attacks made on him at the time by writers in the leading reviews were hopelessly inept. It was almost impossible to answer a work of fiction. One exception, however, was the reply made by Fitzjames Stephen in the *Saturday Review*. Stephen was responsible for a whole series of slashing attacks on Dickens, and most of what he wrote can be dismissed. Even this attack has recently been discounted because it has been said that he had personal reasons for defending the Civil Service. But the main point of Stephen's remarks was not that he wanted to write on behalf of the bureaucracy but of parliamentary government. 'Whatever else our Parliament is', he wrote, 'it is the only popular government in the world which has been able to maintain itself . . . and there is no country in which the great ends of civil society . . . are more fully maintained or in which the private character of public men stands higher. . . . Our statesmen may sometimes provide for their cousins and nephew in the public service, but they do not sell their official secrets, or make fortunes on the Stock Exchange.'

This was a fair reply to Dickens, for though he had also been shocked by the activities on the Bourse, France was still his ideal. In a burst of irritation, he reduced Miss Burdett Coutts's companion, Mrs. Brown, to tears when she once said something slighting about the French. It also needs bearing in mind that Dickens seldom tried to explain what he would put in place of the institutions he attacked. His limitations may have helped to make him more effective as a satirist, but it is time his own presumptions as a social prophet were exposed.

In fact, it is arguable that Dickens's political views were beginning to be affected by his private troubles. His growing radicalism was due not only to his observation of the changing state of the country but also to his own changing attitude to life. He was finding little pleasure in his success, for the greater it was the more difficulty he found in maintaining it. He appeared to know no rest except in action; and as John Forster wrote:

> Not his genius only, but his whole nature, was too exclusively made up of sympathy for, and with, the real, in its most intense form, to be sufficiently provided against failure in the realities around him. There was for him no 'city of the mind' against outward ills, for inner consolation and shelter. It was in and from the actual he still stretched forward to find the freedoms and satisfactions of the ideal, and by his very attempts to escape the world he was driven back into the thick of it.

Yet one of the mysteries of *Little Dorrit* remains, its significance as Dickens's attempt to create a 'city of the mind' as a refuge from all that harassed him. If *Hard Times* represents, as it does, a somewhat superficial linking of

Christian ethics with everyday life and which may be associated with the real world in which Dickens played so active and open a part in journalism, on the stage, in public speaking and private philanthropy, then *Little Dorrit* and *Our Mutual Friend* represent successive stages in an escape from every day reality which was surely connected with his private life. How far this new extension of the Dickens world within the novels is a success is another matter.

In *Little Dorrit* the religious dimension is perceptibly marked out. Although Humphry House remarked that 'religion had no part in the original conception' of Mrs. Clennam, this is completely wrong; her Old Testament ethic is contrasted with the New Testament spirit of Little Dorrit from the first. By the end, Little Dorrit is largely an allegorical representation of divine grace, as 'every morning' she ascends to Clennam's room in prison, 'winged to his heart bringing the heavenly lightness of a new love'. She is also the voice of Nature, and of the happier memories of childhood. As she and Mrs. Clennam pass over London Bridge together, 'great shoots of light' stream 'among the early stars, like signs of the blessed later covenant of peace and hope that changed the crown of thorns into a glory'. And, more significantly, as the sun strikes on the black prison gate which had closed behind her when Clennam had turned her away, we are also told that its 'long bright rays' strike 'aslant across the city . . . bars of the prison of this lower world'. In other words, there are two worlds, in one of which we are shut in, even by the bright rays of the sun. So much is made clear, though for many readers not without the perceptive analyses of Lionel Trilling and Hillis Miller.

Elsewhere, symbolic references are brought into play

about the 'dark road of life' (Book I, chapter xxvi), and the ferry by which Clennam passes across the river on the way to see his earlier love, 'Pet' Meagles. It evidently symbolizes Time, and as Clennam solemnly gazes on the 'real landscape and its shadow in the water', he sees that there 'there was no division; both were so untroubled and clear, and, while so fraught with solemn mystery of life and death, so hopefully reassuring to the gazer's soothed heart, because so tenderly and mercifully beautiful'. The two worlds are one.

Thus the symbolism of imprisonment is obviously one that goes beyond man's relation to society, and that involves the whole condition of life. Structurally, and in detail, it is finely worked out so that it greatly extends the novel's meaning; but the writing is so much less certain and pointed in parts clearly meant to be spiritually affirmative that this side to the novel is sometimes unsatisfying. Yet it would certainly be false to argue that this uneasiness is a part of the ambiguity of the novel that would justify us in ignoring the comparative unsureness of the writing.

For it was written affirmatively, and it introduces us biographically to a new Dickens, and a very different kind of man (editor, actor, reformer, boon companion) from the one he has often been thought. Indeed, his distress at this time, which precedes the break-up of his marriage by several years, shows Dickens's own difficulty in coming to terms with himself. Lionel Trilling finds that Clennam's situation in the novel offers 'an analogy to the familiar elements of a religious crisis', and that the novel is marked by Dickens's personal involvement. With most men one might have expected this to show in the documents of his biography; but hardly anywhere can this be traced except in his letters to Forster, until the complete break that came with the disruption of his marriage.

It would be wrong to ignore that the religious crisis or self-questioning was not part of a very human domestic 'unrest', but just as rash to decide which dominated the other. One may certainly detect stray clues in the terse and generally unrevealing notebook which he began in January 1855 and from which Forster printed extracts in his chapter, 'Hints for Books Written and Unwritten'. They include some of the key images of the novel, including the ferry by the peaceful river. It has some entries that might be read as applying to Dickens himself, 'the man, always, as it were, playing hide and seek with the world, and never finding what Fortune seems to have hidden when he was born'. He writes of 'the man who is incapable of his own happiness. Or who is always in pursuit of happiness. Result, where is happiness to be found then. Surely not everywhere . . .' He was anxious to escape from pre-occupation with himself, and writes with contempt of 'the man whose vista is always stopped up by the image of himself. . . . Would be a good thing for him if he could knock himself down'; for, although this note was later hastily marked 'Done in Podsnap' (of *Our Mutual Friend*) it applies to many characters in *Little Dorrit* as well.

Such is the tone of the early entries, when the 'motes' of *Little Dorrit* were 'floating in the dirty air', and they evidently agree with the well-known but little emphasized letters Dickens had been writing to Forster at about this time. For, as early as *David Copperfield*, Dickens had foreshadowed one of the notebook entries in evidently thinking of himself (like David) as seeking 'realities in unrealities', and complaining of 'the old unhappy loss or want of something'. Then, later, but still as early as 1856, he suddenly wrote to Forster:

> Again I am beset by my former notions of a book whereof the *whole story* shall be on top of the Great St. Bernard. As I accept and reject ideas for *Little Dorrit*, it perpetually comes back to me. Two or three months hence, perhaps you'll find me living with the monks and Dogs a whole winter. . . . I have a *serious* idea that I shall do it, if I live. [Italics added.]

Presumably he was 'serious' even about 'a whole story'. He had proposed living in a Swiss convent two years before, and he also writes of himself in his letters as being driven in his life by an 'irresistible might . . . until the journey is worked out', as if he were one of 'the restless travellers' of *Little Dorrit* on 'the pilgrimage of life'. Forster speaks of his attempt to escape the world as an attempt to get 'the infinite' out of 'the finite'. In writing to another friend (Hon. Mrs. Richard Watson, 7 December 1857) Dickens says, 'Realities and unrealities are always comparing themselves before me, and I don't like Realities except when they are unattainable.' There is, from this time, a great division between the realities and unrealities of Dickens's life, though hard to trace so closely to himself did he usually keep it.

We should understand that Dickens's biography is not a clear, uncluttered story. At this stage in his development, it is only a second-best way of getting to know him, and we must recognize that by now he was infinitely more subtle, reserved and conscious of playing a part than biographers have usually allowed.

His inner concern was sometimes apparent in spite of himself; for like his own characters he had found that the shadow of his past only lengthened the further he left it behind. As he moved up into a different society, he began to show resentment at class divisions and a hidden lack of ease. He did not restrain his increasing impatience with administrative incompetence and constitutional government, and he revealed a disquiet in his retirement to France where he could meet what people he chose on his own terms, and in various bitter disputes in which he became involved with public societies. As early as 1856 he had written to Forster from Paris: 'The old days—the old days. Shall I ever, I wonder, get the frame of my mind back as it used to be then? . . . I find that the skeleton in my domestic closet is becoming a pretty big one.'

Chapter Eleven

SEPARATION—AND *A TALE OF TWO CITIES*

DICKENS's unrest continued to grow, and the 'domestic skeleton' became more difficult to conceal. Eventually, just a year after he had completed *Little Dorrit*, he separated from his wife. When the crisis came, it took place suddenly; but it had been reached only after several years. Yet though the main outline of events is fairly clear, the real feelings of the people concerned and what it was that drove Dickens and his wife apart are still hard to explain.

There are two main reasons for this. The first is that Dickens himself was so extraordinary that it is difficult for the ordinary person to understand the power of the driving-force which took control of him at this time and allowed him neither rest nor relaxation. Even when he was writing a novel, editing a magazine, working for Miss Burdett Coutts, or indulging in amateur theatricals, there were times when he was still so restless that, he wrote, he felt 'as if the scaling of all the Mountains in Switzerland . . . would be but a slight relief'. To tire himself sufficiently to sleep, he took to walking, through the night, from Tavistock Square to a new house he had acquired at Gad's Hill, near Rochester! Anyone can offer to analyse him, but the stress under which he lived is almost impossible for the ordinary person to imagine.

The other reason which makes it difficult to understand what happened is that we know so little about

Mrs. Dickens. She was a good, kind-hearted, middle-aged matron, with a rather reserved manner and fat little wrists over which her bracelets would sometimes come tumbling into the soup at dinner! As the years went by, she seems to have suffered from some kind of nervous illness, but no one who knew her ever had anything to say of her but praise. Yet even that was always rather vague: Hans Andersen thought that she was just like David Copperfield's Agnes, which seems to have been, in some ways, justified.

Dickens's dissatisfaction went back several years, but the immediate trouble began in 1857. During the summer of 1856 Wilkie Collins had written a play called *The Frozen Deep*, which Dickens produced for the 'children's theatre' at Tavistock House. It was performed in January, with Dickens in one of the leading parts and with the usual sensational effect. His friends flocked to see it, and, looking round the audience, Douglas Jerrold observed that there were 'Judges enow to hang us all', while Thackeray declared that 'if that man would now go upon the stage, he would make his £20,000 a year'. The play had an exhilarating effect on Dickens himself. It had a melodramatic plot—the story of the man who saves his rival and dies in the arms of the woman he loves—but it was an exception to Dickens's usual parts in that it stirred him profoundly. He derived a 'strange feeling out of it', he wrote, 'like writing a book in company; a satisfaction of a most singular kind, and which has no exact parallel in my life'.

Six months later, Jerrold suddenly died and, on discovering that the family of his old friend was in difficulties, Dickens set himself to raise a fund for them. One of his main activities was to get the amateur company together again and produce *The Frozen Deep*; and it was arranged that it should be performed before the Queen, and put on in both London and Manchester. For the provincial performances, professional actresses were necessary; and so, on the advice of a friend, Dickens engaged a well-known actress, Mrs. Frances Ternan, and two of her daughters, Maria and Ellen.

The performances were the usual success, and Dickens's letters were full of praise for the elder daughter, Maria; but his attention had really been caught by her fair-haired eighteen-year-old sister, Ellen. It had been an old joke, when it had been a merely amateur company, for the 'Manager', as Dickens was called, to pretend to fall in love with his leading actresses; but all at once he discovered that the joke had become serious. It was just because he was so unaccustomed to such affairs that he was completely helpless: there seemed nothing to be done about it.

He went off on holiday with Collins; they wrote a sketchy little series of articles called *The Lazy Tour of Two Idle Apprentices* and collaborated in 'The Perils of Certain English Prisoners' for the Christmas number of *Household Words*. Yet at the same time (23 October 1857) he was writing to Collins, 'I want to escape from myself. For, when I *do* start up and stare myself seedily in the face, as happens to be the case at present, my blankness is inconceivable—indescribable—my misery amazing. . . . The domestic unhappiness remains so strong upon me that I can't write, and (waking) can't rest, one minute. I have never known a moment's peace or content, since the last night of The Frozen Deep. I do suppose that there never was a man so seized and rended by one spirit.'

About the same time he confided in Forster, who was both kind and outspoken, and who reminded his friend of all that he and Catherine had gone through in their married life. He did not encourage Dickens to make too much of the difficulties of his profession, or to overlook that there was much to be said on the other side. Dickens was more gentle in his reply, and wrote of his wife:

> God knows she would have been a thousand times happier if she had married another kind of man. . . . I am often cut to the heart by thinking what a pity it is, for her own sake, that I ever fell in her way. . . . I claim no immunity from blame. There is plenty of fault on my side, I dare say, in the way of a thousand uncertainties, caprices, and difficulties of disposition; but only one thing will alter that, and that is, the end which alters everything.

His only solution was to cut himself off from Catherine as far as possible and to lose himself again in action. He had a separate bed made for him, sealed up the communicating-door with Mrs. Dickens's bedroom, and arranged to spend as much of his time as possible at Gad's Hill while leaving her at Tavistock House. Unable to settle to writing, he also decided to try what he could do by giving readings from his works in public. He had already often done this for charity, and he now meant to see if it could be done for profit. In spite of opposition from Forster, who argued that it was 'a substitution of lower for higher aims', he went on to give the first of a series of public readings starting on 29 April 1858.

All this while he had apparently seen little of Ellen Ternan, and there is no mention of her in his letters. Yet he seems to have found it impossible to keep away from her altogether, and some time early in May came the dramatic break with his wife.

Exactly how it came about is uncertain, but the story goes that a bracelet which Dickens had ordered for Ellen was delivered to Mrs. Dickens by mistake. She left the house and went to stay with her mother. Mrs. Hogarth and another daughter, Helen, then rallied to her support, and went round madly gossiping about what had happened. Dickens was incensed about outsiders being brought into his affairs, and refused to allow his wife to return.

The Hogarths are another group of people about whom it would be necessary to know more if the affair were to be completely explained. Ever since the visit to America in 1842, another of Catherine's younger sisters, Georgina, had been living with them and helping to look after the children. She was a neat and capable woman, but, since she idolized Dickens and always took his part, her very presence in the household did not make their domestic difficulties any easier from Catherine's point of view. Mrs. Hogarth, on the other hand, seems to have grown to dislike her son-in-law more and more, and to have resented having to be dependent on him for various benefits. She and her daughter Helen now began spreading the story that the break was mainly due to Georgina, and, before they knew what was happening, this had caught on, and all over London people were saying that she was not only the chief cause of the trouble, but that she was expecting a child. All this was false. But it was extremely unpleasant for everyone concerned, and it was obvious that it would cause even more scandal to deny. Dickens was furious, and through the efforts of his lawyers he forced Mrs. Hogarth and her daughter to sign a statement in which they denied that there was any truth at all in the rumours they had helped to put about.

Meanwhile, Dickens had been forcing on the arrangements for a legal separation. Early in May 1858, Catherine agreed that she should henceforth live apart and asked Mark Lemon to act for her in arranging the terms. By the 21st everything was virtually settled, and the deed of separation was finally drawn up and entered into by the end of the month. Dickens wrote to inform Miss Burdett Coutts of his intentions on 9 May, and told his eldest son on 10 May. It was arranged that Mrs. Dickens should receive an allowance of £600 a year, and that the eldest son should live with her. The rest of the children were to go with Dickens, although from time to time they should visit and stay with their mother. Dickens insisted that it was essential for the sake of the whole family, including Mrs. Dickens, Georgina, and the two grown-up daughters, that every effort should be made to keep up appearances.

Largely because of this he refused to back out of the limelight, but gave several important speeches during May and June, as well as continuing with the public readings. He also thought that he ought to make a public statement about what had happened; and, after consulting Forster who advised against it, and the editor of *The Times* who was in favour, he issued a personal address in *Household Words*. He said that he regarded his domestic affairs as private, but that in view of his conspicuous position and his relations with the public, he wished to deny as emphatically as possible the misrepresentations and rumours which had been circulated, not only about him, but about others connected with him. 'I most solemnly declare', he concluded, 'that all the lately whispered rumours touching the trouble at which I have glanced are abominably false. And that whosoever repeats one of them after this denial, will lie as wilfully and foully as it is possible for any false witness to lie before heaven and earth.'

Notwithstanding what has sometimes been said about it, this has a good effect at the time. The only extra trouble it caused was that when Dickens circularized the statement to various newspapers and periodicals with a request for its publication, Mark Lemon and Bradbury and Evans, the publishers, refused to print it in *Punch*. Dickens's relations with Bradbury and Evans had been growing worse for some time, and he now broke them off completely. Mark Lemon, who was the editor, acted with fairness and dignity, but the rest of the *Punch* staff seem to have taken up the affair as a feud. More trouble then arose with the press, when an American reporter got hold of the statement Dickens had forced Mrs. Hogarth to sign, and printed it in company with a letter he had written to his reading-manager. This was a much more outspoken account of the affair, written entirely from Dickens's side, which he had meant only for his manager to show privately to people in theatrical circles when he was making arrangements for the readings. It caused another wave of rumours, which left Dickens with a further 'sense of wrong' and the feeling, as he said, that his heart was 'jagged and rent and out of shape'.

In spite of much that has been written there appears little doubt that, for the time being, Dickens was as innocent in his relations with Ellen Ternan as he said. His air of outrage and martyrdom was largely justified, even though he had behaved in a manner that could not fail to arouse scandal. Yet he went on in exactly the same way. He paid for Ellen's eldest sister, Frances, to go to Italy to have her voice trained, and a year later had her introduced to some of the leading actors in France when she thought of having further training for the stage. While she was away, accompanied by her mother, he kept his eye on Maria and Ellen, who were living in apartments he had recommended for them in Berners Street.

Yet, at this time, his attitude seems to have been purely protective, though in fact we know practically nothing whatsoever of their relations for the next few years. For a while, Ellen went on with her career on the stage. A young musician, a friend of Dickens's eldest son, mentions meeting Dickens at Mrs. Ternan's house in Ampthill Square. Always assuming that Ellen at last became his mistress (and of this there is no reasonable doubt) it was probably not until some time about the mid-sixties. In 1867 he appears to have provided her with a house at Peckham. All this is to anticipate, however, since for the moment Dickens's tension was unrelaxed, and he was still in a state of despair, mysteriously writing to Collins on 6 February 1859, 'Tomorrow . . . when you will receive this is my birthday. I have not had the heart to make any preparations for it—you know why.'

He was, in fact, in an unhappy situation. In spite of all his efforts to explain, he found that Miss Burdett Coutts chiefly sympathized with Mrs. Dickens, and seemed somewhat jealous at Dickens's obvious interest in a younger woman. Rather to his annoyance, she kept offering to be a mediator in order to bring husband and wife together; but she no longer turned to him for advice, and since they gave up all the work they had formerly shared—and which he had so obviously enjoyed—Dickens was left with little to do. He never made another attempt to get together his amateur company, and for a period he even lost his interest in writing.

Thus, for a while, he had nothing to occupy himself with but the public readings and a rather futile quarrel with Thackeray. The only solid work ahead was caused by the breach with Bradbury and Evans, which meant that Dickens decided to discontinue his partnership with them in *Household Words*, and to start a new magazine without them.

It is this which evidently aroused him. He had parted with Bradbury and Evans on extremely bad terms, and as they had decided to go into competition by starting a weekly paper of their own called *Once a Week*, it at once became a point of honour with Dickens to beat his rivals out of the field. He looked about for a new title, and, even after all the recent publicity, was with difficulty restrained from calling it *Household Harmony*! However, he finally decided on *All the Year Round*, and announced that the first number would be on sale on 30 April, containing a new story by himself.

As usual, he found it difficult to begin, but early in March he was able to write to Forster, 'I have got exactly the name for the story that is wanted . . . A TALE OF TWO CITIES.' It was to be a story of the French Revolution, which had first occurred to him about twelve months before; and, having enlisted the aid of Carlyle, who sent him a selection of books, he settled steadily to work. Both the story and the magazine in which it was published made a great impression with the first number, and by the fifth number the circulation of *All the Year Round* was three times greater than that of *Household Words*.

The novel itself, was somewhat experimental, as Dickens still did not feel satisfied at having to write in such small portions as weekly publication required. He tried to make it almost entirely narrative, therefore, and worked closely over the story to see that it ran swiftly, unchecked by the need for appearing week by week, and so arranged that his variety and vivid descriptive power should appear in narrative. As before, he found that 'the small portions' in which he had to write it drove him 'frantic', but he explained to Forster he had set himself the task 'of making a *picturesque* story, rising in every chapter with characters true to nature, but whom the story itself should express, more than they should express themselves, by dialogue'.

It is easy to find improbabilities in the plot—forced into it, partly, by compression—but it has the design Dickens intended: rising from the dramatic scene on the Dover Road at the opening of the story, and leading up to the sensational climax, at which Carlyle declared 'it's wonderful' and Forster turned 'white with admiring approval'. Only Wilkie Collins hinted he could have done it better; and Dickens turned on him promptly with the fair retort that if it had been 'done in your manner . . . it would have been overdone . . . too elaborately trapped, baited and prepared'. The intention of the work was *not* to create a mystery or arouse suspense, but to reveal a developing pattern both in the relations between the characters and a great historical event, and 'to show, by a backward light, what everything has been working to—but only to *suggest* until the fulfilment comes'.

Yet the success of the story depends less on the mere mechanics of the plot than on the way its themes and incidents are fused and concentrated by the choice of graphic symbols. The blood-red wine outside Defarge's shop, the blue flies searching for carrion in the Old Bailey, the spectre-white dust covering the figure hidden under the coach, the golden thread, and the dark storm gathering over Dr. Manette's house which was to burst over Paris, all intensify the effect of the rapidly succeeding scenes. They are given equal importance in the way they are used to emphasize the major theme of inevitability by recalling the past and suggesting the future. 'It is always preparing', Madame Defarge tells her husband. 'It must be so', declares Carton. 'It could not be otherwise', says Darnay; while from the first, before the story opens, there is the ominous knowledge that 'It is likely enough that, rooted in the woods of France and Norway, there were growing trees . . . already marked by the Woodman, Fate, to come down and be sawn into boards, to make a certain moveable framework . . . terrible in history.'

The doctrine of determinism was derived from Carlyle, as were the contrast between sham and reality and the faith that the historical process was ultimately for good. In the preface to the novel Dickens explained that it was intended to be 'a popular and picturesque means of understanding that great time, though no one can hope to add anything to the philosophy of Mr. Carlyle's great book'. And its most insistent theme was the same as that of *The French Revolution*: that certain conditions must always lead to anarchy and anarchy destroys itself: 'There is not in France . . . a blade, a leaf, a root . . . which will grow to maturity under conditions more certain than those that have produced this horror. . . . Sow the same seed of licence and oppression over again, and it will surely yield the same fruit according to its kind.'

Yet in *The French Revolution* the faith in regeneration was almost ironical, while in the novel it was no less strong than the impression of menacing destiny. Even in the darkest scenes there is the steady suggestion of a brighter future in which 'the evil of this time' will be 'gradually making expiation for itself and wearing out'. It is to be found not only in Carton's final vision. Each of the three men grouped about Lucie Manette is 'recalled to life'. Her father regains his, on release from the Bastille; her husband's life is restored by his deliverance from La Force; and Carton finds his by seeking to lose it. As he paces the solemn streets of Paris on the night before he gives himself up in place of Darnay, the words of the service at his father's graveside persistently arise in his mind: 'I am the Resurrection and the Life, saith the Lord: he that believeth in me, though he were dead, yet shall he live'; and as he watches the skies darken before dawn, 'the night' turns pale and dies, 'while it seems as if Creation were delivered over to Death's dominion', until 'a glorious sun rises with the new day' and seems 'to strike those words to his heart'. As he faces death beneath the guillotine they recur again: not simply as a seemly pious ending, but as a vital expression of a Christian ethic, which all along has been contrasted with the savagery of the Revolution from the hint that the spy Barsad was like Judas and the lingering scene about the wayside cross as Monsieur the Marquis passes on to his death at the hands of one of the revolutionary *Jaquerie*.

Such was the purpose Dickens had in mind, and so far it was successfully achieved; but the increased concentration and precision of plot were attained at the cost of exposing serious faults. It has neither the range nor humour of the earlier works. Stryver is a fine bold sketch, and his hesitant decision to honour Lucie with a proposal is magnificently comic with a rightful place in the story. But though Jeremy Cruncher, as a body-snatching 'Resurrectionist' ironically underlines the idea of regeneration, he is no more than a tool in the plot with neither vitality nor wit. For both the serious and the comic figures, Dickens's attempt to have their characters expressed by the story largely meant leaving most of them out.

The relations between Lucie and the men are drastically simplified so that they are threadbare, stiff, and unconvincing. As a story of incident it is tremendous, but it could not avoid dialogue and fails to show the characters in action. The first meeting between Lucie and her father, for example, suggests that it owes less to reality than to Dickens's memory of the recognition scene between Cordelia and Lear which had so impressed him when acted by Macready. As Dr. Manette begins to remember the past he forms 'his speech with his lips' before he voices it:

> But when he did find spoken words for it, they came to him coherently, though slowly.
>
> 'How was this?—*Was it you?*'
>
> Once more, the two spectators started, as he turned upon her with a frightful suddenness. But she sat perfectly still in his grasp, and only said, in a low voice, 'I entreat you, good gentlemen, do not come near us, do not speak, do not move!'
>
> 'Hark!' he exclaimed. 'Whose voice was that?'
>
> His hands released her as he uttered this cry, and went up to his white hair, which they tore in a frenzy.

Its fault is not that it attempts to be dramatic, but that it seems derivative and conventional. Dickens explained in the preface that 'the main idea' of the story came to him when acting in *The Frozen Deep*; his notebook shows that it was partly conceived as 'like a French drama' from the first; and immediately after completing it he is known to have packed off the proofs to France to see if the performance of a stage-version in Paris would be allowed by the Imperial censor. But, if excellent theatre, the dialogue too often has many of the pretentious faults of Victorian drama: just when it ought to convey emotional depth and conflict it begins strumming on stock phrases until released by action. Unlike many of the earlier works, such as *The Chimes*, it has not the excuse of being unabashed melodrama. *A Tale of Two Cities* is an attempt at romantic tragedy, wonderfully told, but failing at complete success.

The association of the novel with *The Frozen Deep*, in which Dickens had appeared with Ellen Ternan, has helped to give point to the belief that it re-enacts the drama of his own dilemma; and there is much to support such a judgement, although nothing to prove it. The important thing is, however, that if this opinion is accepted, it must go with the recognition that he was still justified in asserting that he had been misunderstood. For even though the same spirit of renunciation remarkably reappears in some of the later short stories, such as *George Silverman's Explanation*, it is far too powerfully raised in every scene connected with Lucie Manette for it to have contradicted Dickens's feelings about his own predicament.

Lucie is the central figure of the novel; and while her husband, who has no conflict in his feelings about her, is no more than a shadow, the self-sacrifice shown by Sydney Carton is obvious, and even the story of her father's love for her is one entirely of resignation. In the scene between her husband and father, Dr. Manette also triumphs over his love, like Carton, and agrees to give her up, even though, he says, 'She is everything to me; more to me than suffering; more to me than wrong.'

As an 'imprisoned' figure in the story, one might have expected to find that Dr. Manette was closer to Dickens than anyone else in the novel, and this seems to be borne out by other characteristics. When Manette is in despair, he is like Dickens in feeling a compulsive need for action, for it was equally 'the character of his mind to be always in singular need of occupation'. We know him as a man of 'great firmness of purpose, strength of resolution, and vigour of action'—as a man who is aware of a 'suppression always shut up within him'. Undoubtedly Dickens identified himself with Carton, with Charles Darnay, and perhaps with all the characters in the story, but possibly with none more than with the father—for at this time he still meant to keep to the declaration in the 'Violated Letter', in which he had said of Ellen that she was as 'innocent and pure, and as good as my own dear daughters'.

Part of the interest of the story lies in the way in which Dickens uses so many simple characters to express his own complex sense of life. As everyone recognizes, he divides himself into two between Carton and Darnay. As Carton gazes in the mirror, he sees Darnay as all that he might have been, and, similarly, we are shown Carton as the man who has 'fallen away from' all Darnay is. Yet this would fail of its effect if we did not also feel Dickens's striving to express his sense of the nature of personality through Manette's divided consciousness, though the twin figures of the St. Evrémondes (again divided in the opposition of uncle and nephew), in the powerful human forces released by the long-suppressed Revolution, and in 'the wonders' that he writes 'all of us have . . . hidden in our breasts, only needing circumstances to evoke them'. Such figures and incidents are multiplied and deepen the effect of the story, an aim of which appears to be to express the impression Dickens had of the mystery and purpose of life.

Forster said of Dickens that he liked to dwell on life's

'coincidences, resemblances, and surprises. . . . The world, he would say, was so much smaller than we thought it; we were all so connected by fate without knowing it . . . and tomorrow bore so close a resemblance to nothing half so much as yesterday'; and Dickens's use of Christian symbols throughout the novel is admittedly partly parasitic. They are borrowed for a purpose not purely Christian and to express not the resurrection of Christ nor certainly of the individual, but to communicate a sense of the mystery and wonder of life. For example, when waiting for their execution, we see Carton and the seamstress, 'stand in the fast-thinning throng of victims . . . as if they were alone. Eye to eye, voice to voice, hand to hand, heart to heart, these two children of the Universal Mother, else so wide apart and differing, have come together on the dark highway, to repair home together, and to rest in her bosom.' Then her number is called, and 'the murmuring of many voices, the upturning of many faces, the pressing of so many footsteps on the outskirts of the crowd, so that it swells forward in a mass, like one great heave of water, all flashes away'. She passes to a land where Carton tells her there is 'no Time' and 'no trouble'. The emphasis of the scene is on the mystery of love and sacrifice; but of human love and sacrifice. Carton prophesies of himself that he will survive in the memory of Lucie and her child. The rest is a mystery.

Once again, what is holy in life is shown in terms of romantic love. Carton lays down his life for Lucie rather than Darnay. As he parts from the seamstress, 'she kisses his lips; he kisses hers; they solemnly bless each other'. When Madame Defarge finally faces Miss Pross, hate confronts love, and 'love, always so much stronger than hate', triumphs. Lucie's love overcomes fear of her father when she first meets him; and his restoration begins as they embrace and 'his cool white head' mingles 'with her radiant hair', which warms and lights it 'as though it were the light of Freedom shining on him'. Love, standing for all the forces of life, lasting power and goodness is shown to be as strange and wonderful as the steps which lead Madame Defarge to her fate, as the ways by which the hidden account comes to light of the prisoner of One Hundred and Five, North Tower, as the first meeting of Carton and Darnay or the reunion of Miss Pross and her brother Solomon, and as the essentially 'profound secret and mystery' of 'every human creature . . . to every other' (chapter iii).

For all its weaknesses, the story evokes this sense of wonder and is told with tautness and power. It is not easy to single out its best passages: their effect depends on the atmosphere of the novel, quickly wrought up in Mr. Lorry's nightmare in the Dover coach, and then strongly maintained. Forster had thought it a risk for Dickens to rely 'less upon character than upon incident' and for 'the actors' to be 'expressed by the story more than . . . by dialogue'. Certainly almost everything does come to depend on the story and the manner of telling it. It was a bold experiment, some of the interest of which lies in what it reaches towards rather than what it achieves.

Criticism has sometimes tried to make out that there is a special political significance in the fact that Dickens chose to write about the French Revolution. Yet, although it is true that Dickens actually believed in the possibility of a vast uprising in England, if the state refused to listen to the just demands of 'working men', he kept to the main theme of the story with sound judgement, and without glancing back. He never turns from presenting the Revolution as the inevitable consequence of all that had gone before. The whole novel has too great a general significance for it to be profitable to devote much attention to isolating personal opinions: in brief, it was Carlyle, with the emphasis on the New Testament rather than the Old.

Chapter Twelve

GREAT EXPECTATIONS

At Gad's Hill, Dickens now became a sort of country squire. He cut himself off from London society, made new friends, and settled down to a new life. One day, in September 1860, after he had been reading the biography of some eminent man, he decided to put much of his past on the bonfire; and, enlisting the aid of his children, he gathered together almost all his old papers, and the letters he had received from his friends and the famous, and burnt them in a field at the back of the house. As they went up in flames, Dickens remarked, 'Would to God every letter I have ever written was on that pile.' After that, he destroyed all letters as he received them. He meant his break with the past to be definite.

He had started a new series of papers in *All the Year Round*, called *The Uncommercial Traveller*. Few of his articles were ever mere journalism. If he were not so well known as a novelist, he might have been recognized long ago as a great English essayist. Like his articles in *Household Words*, they are often vivid and powerful. Yet, when the first edition was published in 1861, readers must have been struck by their sombre nature. The first paper was about a terrible shipwreck, several were about the activities of the police, others were on workhouses, sick soldiers, tramps, night walks, and the Paris morgue. The dark side of Dickens's later work is sometimes exaggerated, but here it was almost unrelieved.

It was while he was writing one of his papers for *The Uncommercial Traveller* that he came on the subject for his next novel. Originally meant just for an article, it seemed 'such a fine, new, grotesque idea' that it was promptly reserved for a book. 'It so opens out before me,' Dickens wrote to Forster, 'that I can see the whole of a serial revolving upon it, in a most singular and comic manner.'

He began writing it for publication in monthly numbers, but it so happened that the circulation of *All the Year Round* had begun to sink under the weight of a serial by Charles Lever, and it was decided that Dickens must come to the rescue. He accordingly set to work, and in a short while the tale took shape. With the first three weekly numbers, Dickens managed to get in a boy and a convict, Pip and Magwitch, 'the pivot on which the story will turn', which 'was the grotesque, tragi-comic conception that first encouraged me'. Joe Gargery, the blacksmith, was introduced, with Wopsle and Pumblechook, which he thought made the opening very 'droll'. 'I have put a child and a good-natured foolish man in relations that seem to me very funny.' Altogether, he felt able to assure Forster, 'you will not have to complain of the want of humour as in the Tale of Two Cities'.

It is not surprising that Forster had been disappointed with the comedy in *A Tale of Two Cities*. In reviewing Dickens's last three novels, the critics had almost unanimously complained at his refusal to repeat *Pickwick*, *Nickelby*, and *Chuzzlewit*. Miss Coutts had even been worried that Dickens was beginning to show his unhappiness in his writing, and Dickens had been disturbed. Though he had given up trying to justify his own actions, he was anxious to vindicate his work, and hastily replied: 'As to my art, I have as great a delight in it as the most enthusiastic of my readers; and the sense of my trust and responsibility in that wise, is always upon me when I take pen in hand. If *I* were soured, I should still try to sweeten the lives and fancies of others, but I am not—not at all.'

Fortunately the humour of the novel is one of the happiest things about it. Joe turns out to be more serious than he was at first meant to be, but it is rich with other comic characters, from Wopsle and Pumblechook to Wemmick and 'old Bill Barley, lying on the flat of his back, by the Lord. Lying on his back like a drifting old dead flounder . . . bless your eyes!' What was more, Dickens discovered a secret that he was for ever afterwards trying to impart to his contributors to *All the Year Round*, of using humour 'to enhance and intensify' the serious parts of the novel. The comedy makes the serious elements stand out. It gives relief. The humorous chapters do not simply alternate with serious ones: the strands of comedy and tragedy are closely interwoven, as Dickens had intended from the start. The scene with the boy and the convict in the churchyard is amusing as well as exciting. Even Jaggers can be comic. Pip's first outright lie after his visit to Satis House is irresistibly funny, in spite of the consequence that his concealment of the truth leads to his estrangement from Joe.

It is the fundamental irony of the book that makes this possible from the start: the fact that it was tragicomic in its initial conception. The first three numbers establish this at once. The tone is good-humoured. It seems like Dickens in his old manner, but the approach is altogether new. Once again, the story begins on a Christmas Eve. Yet there is not a flake of snow in sight, not a robin on the bough, nor a turkey on the table. Only the cold mist on the marshes, an escaped convict in a churchyard, a gibbet looming over the flats. There are no carols: Pip says he has gone to hear them, but he lies. Stirring the pudding makes his arm ache. There are no bells, no Christmas games. Just a good dinner broken up by the arrival of a sergeant with a party of soldiers searching for the convict.

Except in the boy and the blacksmith there is no spirit of goodwill or charity, though Mr. Pumblechook passes round a bottle with such a gush of joviality that he appears to forget that he has just made a present of it to Mrs. Joe: 'As I watched them while they all stood clustering about the forge, enjoying themselves so much, I thought what terrible good sauce for a dinner my fugitive friend on the marshes was. They had not enjoyed themselves a quarter so much, before the entertainment was brightened with the excitement he furnished.' Touches like this warn us that as well as having freshness and novelty about it, the book is to be a work of new subtlety and insight into character.

Indeed, as well as being Dickens's best narrative, and a social satire, it is again a Jamesian 'moral fable'; and, once again, this morality depends on the Christian ethic, which is also used with a new discretion. So discreetly is it used, in fact, that it has usually been overlooked, and certain writers have even declared that it is not there at all.

According to Bernard Shaw, for example, 'Pip, like his creator, has no religion. . . . Pip never prays, and church means nothing to him but Mr. Wopsle's orotundity.' But, strictly speaking, this is not true. We are thrice told that he prayed when Orlick had him trapped in the old sluice-house on the marshes, and, all along,

Christian behaviour and worldly behaviour are contrasted, especially directly after Pip comes into his money. When he and Joe go to church, after solemnly burning his indentures, one of the neatest touches is Pip's thought that 'perhaps the clergyman would not have read that about the rich man and the kingdom of Heaven, if he had known all'. By the time of his sister's funeral, Pip is chastened enough to notice 'the worldly-minded Pumblechook . . . [who] even when those noble passages were read which remind humanity how it brought nothing into the world and can take nothing out, and how it fleeth like a shadow and never continueth long in one stay, . . . [coughed] a reservation of the case of a young gentleman, who had come unexpectedly into large property.' Both are contrasted with Joe Gargery, who does not merely represent 'the old Christmas ethic', as Humphry House considered, but is always represented as a Christian. In fact, this is even rather overdone. When, in his old burnt apron, he says good-bye to Pip as he leaves the forge, 'And so God bless you, dear old Pip, old chap, God bless you!' Pip says he thought, 'The fashion of his dress could no more come in its way when he spoke these words, than it would come in its way in Heaven.' And, in his penitence, when he finds that it has been Joe who has been looking after him in his fever, Pip breaks out, 'O God bless him! O God bless this gentle Christian man!' In his simplicity and goodness, and in his love for children, Joe is of the Kingdom of Heaven.

It would be wrong to see this as an accident. The self-seeking of several of the other characters is underlined in the same sort of way. The Pocket family, waiting to inherit from Miss Havisham, discuss Matthew, the only one who spoke out to her with sincerity:

> 'Poor dear soul!' said the lady, with an abruptness of manner quite my sister's. 'Nobody's enemy but his own!'
>
> 'It would be much more commendable to be somebody else's enemy,' said the gentleman; 'far more natural.'
>
> 'Cousin Raymond,' observed another lady, 'we are to love our neighbour.'
>
> 'Sarah Pocket,' returned Cousin Raymond, 'if a man is not his own neighbour, who is?'

'Beggar my Neighbour', the game that Pip and Estella play in front of Miss Havisham in the weird old house has an additional significance.

But this concern with the moral is shown not only in phrases struck off here and there, it is part of the whole meaning of the book. It is the story of several minds which have shut themselves off from ordinary life and everyday affection, turned in upon themselves, and begun to corrupt. Satis House stands for them all. In his last interview with Miss Havisham Pip comes to realize 'that in shutting out the light of day, she had shut out infinitely more; that in seclusion, she had secluded herself from a thousand natural and healing influences; that her mind, brooding solitary, had grown diseased, as all minds do and must and will that reverse the appointed order of their Maker'. In the end, what is natural and good is right after all.

Miss Havisham sets herself to have vengeance on the world, and only brings a new desolation on herself. It is the same with Estella; and even, to a lesser degree, with Orlick, Magwitch, and Jaggers. But, by the end, the emphasis is all on forgiveness. After the scene in which Pip tells Estella and Miss Havisham that he has at last learnt who his benefactor is, Estella always remembers that Pip said 'God bless you and God forgive you.' In the interview just before she meets her death, Miss

Havisham begs Pip to forgive her, while he replies 'I want forgiveness and direction too much to be bitter with you.' As she lies dying, and as he bends over to kiss her, her last words endlessly repeated are, 'Take the pencil and write under my name, "I forgive her".' Throughout the last stage of his expectations, Pip grows more and more to realize how much everyone is in need of forgiveness, until at the very end he begs Joe and Biddy, 'as you have been to church today, and are in charity and love with all mankind', to forget his faults and to forgive him.

The emphasis is all on the Christian virtues of charity and love, and it is a Christian forgiveness that they mean. Even Magwitch is made to take his part, for (right out of character) he rises from his place in court when he is condemned by the Judge, and replies, 'My Lord, I have received my sentence of Death from the Almighty, but I bow to yours.' As the sun strikes through the great windows of the court, and the Judge sentences the thirty-two men and women standing in the dock, it sends 'a broad shaft of light between the two-and-thirty and the Judge, linking both together, and perhaps reminding some among the audience, how both were passing on, with absolute equality, to the greater Judgement that knoweth all things and cannot err'. Again, as Magwitch lies dying, Pip tells him of his daughter and how she is now 'a lady and very beautiful'; and then, thinking of what they have just been reading together, he says, 'I thought of the two men who went up into the Temple to pray, and I knew there were no better words that I could say beside his bed, than "O Lord, be merciful to him, a sinner!"'

This was the same Magwitch who had so horrified Pip and Herbert by carrying about with him a 'greasy little black clasped Testament . . . solely to swear people on in cases of emergency'.

Yet it is still true that the novel is also a searching study of a society in which what Marx called 'the sordid cash nexus is the chief bond between man and man'; and to say that Pip is a snob is not enough. That is Thackeray's country. Pumblechook and Mrs. Pocket are snobs, but Dickens chose to depict the gulf separating the class which works for others from the class which has others working for it. It is a gulf which, as soon as he comes into money, Pip leaps at a bound. Money, he thinks, will do anything. It will make a gentleman of him, it will give him Estella; or at least, if he is too ashamed to re-visit the forge, it will allow him to send Joe 'a penitential codfish and a barrel of oysters'. It enables Miss Havisham to torment her relatives, and to train Estella so that she may have her revenge. Jaggers is for money. Even Wemmick wants portable property. Above all, Magwitch has learnt its power. He throws his greasy bursting wallet on the table:

> 'There's something worth spending in that book, dear boy. It's yourn. . . . I've come to the old country to see my gentleman spend his money *like* a gentleman. That'll be my pleasure. . . . And blast you all!' he wound up, looking round the room and snapping his fingers once with a loud snap, 'blast you every one from the judge in his wig, to the colonist a-stirring up the dust, I'll show you a better gentleman than the whole kit on you put together!'

But it is not money but the *love* of money which is at the root of evil in society. There is no suggestion, as Shaw would have it, that Dickens was a revolutionary who regarded 'the existing social order as . . . transitory, mistaken, objectionable, and pathological: a social disease to be cured'. Pip is redeemed by his generosity to Herbert in giving a start to his career by secretly buying him a partnership. The firm prospers, 'we had a good name, and worked for our profits, and did very well'. There is no objection to Matthew Pocket's inheriting £4,000 from Miss Havisham. If anything in society is seen as a disease it is the criminal class, encouraged by the Law to flourish like a well-tended garden. Not that Dickens, even then, wanted lenience. Pip may be supposed to be roughly contemporaneous with Dickens, and the time of his visit to Newgate about thirty years earlier than the date of writing the novel: 'At that time', Dickens writes, 'jails were much neglected, and the period of exaggerated reaction consequent on all public wrong-doing—and which is always its heaviest and longest punishment—was still far off.' Reform could go too far. Some men, like Compeyson and Orlick, are irredeemably criminal by nature. Some, like Magwitch, are unfortunate. Most need forgiveness rather than justice. But the whole point of Pip's progress is not that it is due to faults in society, but that he comes to know when he is wrong and that, in the end, he tries to do what is right.

So one may separate two or three strands of the novel; but the pursuit for complexity in Dickens may be driven much further. For it happens that, in *Great Expectations*, Dickens fully succeeds in creating a world of his own neither bounded by his own comments nor obviously limited by his point of view. He had reached the stage at which he could claim with Flaubert that he had 'cut the umbilical cord'; for, far from rushing to identify himself with Pip (the first-person narrator), as he tells the story, he did what Flaubert advised George Sand: 'One mustn't bring one's own personality on the scene. We must, by an effort of mind, go over to the characters, as it were, not make them come over to us.' When the tale is complete, it is felt to have an internal consistency as if it had a life of its own, and it is one capable of a variety of interpretations.

It is strange, in fact, how little Dickens's own remarks reveal about what the novel must have meant for him; for, whatever his purposes may have been other than the superficially obvious, he kept them from his friends more closely than the mystery of *Edwin Drood*. It is true that he added, when first writing about the story to Forster, that 'To be sure that I had fallen into no unconscious repetitions I read *David Copperfield* the other day and was affected by it to a degree you would hardly believe.' But to call this remark (as Hillis Miller does) 'our one important sign of the depths which Dickens was plumbing in the conception of the basic motif of *Great Expectations*', shows almost desperation in looking for a sign. After all, it was reading *Copperfield* that had moved him; and, at first conception, he speaks of *Great Expectations*, as merely different and 'droll'. Obviously the significance of the novel developed rapidly; but Dickens was tempted to no further comments. We should recognize that, even for his own times, he was exceptionally close about his imaginative life; however little he may have examined himself, he must have understood more than he says. We sometimes have Melville held up to us as an artist of dignified reserve—as he was. Even so, he could write such a letter as the one to Nathaniel Hawthorne in which he says of himself: 'It is but nature to be shy of a mortal who boldly declares that a thief in jail is as honourable a personage as George Washington.' Yet Dickens, though this might be thought to be the main implication of *Great Expectations*, hardly once looks out from under cover.

Yet we know that there was a tension between the life of the novel and the world in which Dickens was acquainted with men like Magwitch. For while, in the novel, our sympathies are swung from horrified fascination to something like Pip's final affection, Dickens's only stray comment (as p. 215 above) on contemporary prison conditions—rather than those of the previous generation, which is the time of the novel—shows a stern lack of compassion for the convicts who had mutinied against barbarous conditions only a few miles from his home (chapter xxxii; and Philip Collins, *Dickens and Crime*, chapter i). Dickens's attitude to crime is both involved and strong: Magwitch is a man whose aims are clear, his energies enormous, he strikes hard against his enemies, his generosity and love are open; his tragedy is that the hand of society has always been against him. On one level, in spite of a revulsion we may share with Pip, our admiration for Magwitch is expected to be in the same tradition as the earlier popular radical Victorian enthusiasm for its convict heroes in *Paul Clifford* and *Jack Sheppard*, with a new awareness that society is not divided simply into two classes but that we are all divided by contradictory impulses.

Similarly, while Magwitch is a victim of society's criminal law, Pip is caught within its social and moral laws. We sometimes hear too much, from various commentators, about Pip's sense of guilt, without enough allowance for the way it derives from his own sensitivity. For in his middle-class morality, in his authentic tones of self-depreciation, we hear almost nothing directly from Pip of what ought to be evident, of his astonishing transformation, his vigour, his honesty, his general decency which overcomes the selfishness of his snobbery, his help for the returned convict (after the first impulse to forsake him), and the self-abnegation of his love for Estella. Of course he is humanly frail, but to attempt to give the novel a deeper meaning dependent on accepting literally that his own sense of guilt is justified apart from his treatment of Joe and Biddy is to begin to write further subtleties into it.

Again to say, as one critic does for example, that Pip first becomes aware of the 'identity of things', as he is suspended heels over head by the convict, and that 'he is in a world turned literally upside down', is not only to attempt a slight revision of the text but to apply a kind of interpretation to the novel inappropriate to it. To take too seriously Pip's horror that, 'however undesignedly', circumstances had led him to provide the weapon for the attack on his sister, is as grotesque as to interpret Mrs. Joe's abasement before Orlick as a sign of her 'redemption'. Orlick may, perhaps, be more reasonably be thought a somewhat inadequate indication that however divided we are about social and moral law, evil does exist; and Mrs. Joe may show how thoughtless, loveless, broken humanity can be driven to regard it.

Yet even the most acceptable of all these interpretations makes less of the novel than the impression it ought to make directly for itself. In advice to a would-be contributor to *All the Year Round* Dickens was to explain, 'My notion always is, that when I have made the people to play out the play, it is, as it were, their own business to do it, and not mine.' *Great Expectations* is perhaps the only novel which completely realizes this aim.

Even so, no reading should ignore that it was also written for a particular culture and addressed to men of his own time. Pip's feeling of the 'taint of prison or crime' upon him immediately after a visit to Newgate, is at least partly an indication of a simple sense of decency shared by many at a time when a high court judge could write that the Old Bailey (in or out of the dock) was 'a very cesspool for the offscourings of humanity', when the law at each assize was 'like a tiger let loose', and when his greatest delight as an advocate had been 'the obtaining of an acquittal of someone whose guilt nobody could doubt', Similarly, the ironies about money in a Christian society were ripe for a world in which an Attorney General could address the young men of a Y.M.C.A. and assure them: 'I am perfectly confident that the principle of mutal benevolence, of a universal desire to do good, derived from Christianity . . . is one of the best and most sure modes of securing even temporary success in life (Cheers).'

It is even not too fanciful to think that in writing of Pip, Dickens had his elder sons in mind. He was worried about their future, and tried to encourage them to expect as little from him as possible. They showed little inclination to help themselves. While he was writing, he had taken his third son, Francis into the office of *All the Year Round* because he was in 'a desultory unprofitable state of mind' and unwilling to work in the City; Walter was in the army, in India, showing a tendency to run into debt; Charley was on a voyage to the East to study the prospects for trade in the manner of Messrs. Clarriker & Pocket. He came back looking for a partnership just as the story was finished. The book came closer to Dickens's heart than the novels written immediately before and after it; and though he had probably learnt something about women from Ellen Ternan which helped him write with a greater understanding about them from now on, he may have learnt something about Pip from his own family.

It is even possible that too much has been made about Dickens's new-found skill in writing about women. It is true that Estella and Biddy are better than anything he had done in portraying women before. The way in which Dickens wove snobbery and sexual passion together, as House pointed out, is skilfully convincing: 'the irony of the book turns on the fact that both the money and the girl derive from Magwitch'. But almost everything in *Great Expectations* is done better than before. It is written with much greater ease and grace than anything since *David Copperfield*, and always with power. It is full of good scenes to which justice has never been done because there are so many. Dickens seems to write with a new pride in his mastery. There is no fine writing: there are no set scenes. Graham Greene speaks of Dickens's mature style as a 'secret prose' which gives us 'that sense of a mind speaking to itself when there is no one there to listen', and describes *Great Expectations* as written in 'delicate and exact poetic cadences, the music of memory that so influenced Proust'. Far from agreeing with the belief that even by this time Dickens took no thought for 'the art of the novel', it is almost impossible to imagine how *Great Expectations* could have been written without it. In the previous ten years critics such as G. H. Lewes had begun to think and write about the art of the novel. Presumably under Lewes's influence, George Eliot had even devoted half a chapter in writing *Adam Bede* to justify her preference for writing about things as they are, and (with an eye on Dickens) to attacking those who let their 'facility' lead them into exaggeration. Like almost every other novelist of his time, Dickens was not to be lured into publicly discussing critical theories and generalities. But there can be no doubt of the advance he made, and that it was largely a matter of technique. Without calling attention to all that was new in the novel, Dickens produced his greatest work only to have it hailed by the critics as a welcome return to the old manner.

What was new was that he had completely mastered the skill of construction, and that everything in the novel —even the humour—was completely under his control. The story was built round the simple irony of Pip's expectations being due to a convict, but the structure itself was far from simple. The part-plan which Dickens drew up to help him is a mere sketch, and much was roughed out in his mind. It is almost impossible to be sure that any incident was left until Dickens sat down to write. Even Wemmick's wedding is prepared for: his character never needs forgiveness or redemption just because in spite of his work in Little Britain and Newgate he has never been shut off from the 'natural and healing influences' of Walworth and the Castle. Yet the plot opens out, stage by stage, until we know all. One of the best scenes is the chapter in which Herbert is carefully taking a bandage off Pip's arm while he tells him, bit by bit, what he has learnt from Magwitch of his earlier life: it means little to Herbert, who apologizes for his clumsiness as Pip winces and starts at the discovery that Estella's mother was a murderess and that Magwitch is her father. As Dickens has wished when writing *A Tale of Two Cities*, not only the dialogue but the story expresses the characters, 'pounding them . . . in its own mortar and beating the interest out of them'.

Above all, in spite of its complications, there is an inevitability in the plot to which Dickens did draw some attention in the course of the story. His use of the first person gave him a legitimate opportunity to comment on the course of events, which he used with restraint. He ends the description of Pip's first day at Satis House with the fancy of what his life might have been without this first link in a chain; and, as he comes to the return of Magwitch, he compares the approach of the catastrophe with an incident from his favourite *Arabian Nights*, one like Pip's own case, like the planning of the novel, in which 'all the work near and afar, that tended to the end had been accomplished; and in an instant the blow was struck, and the roof of the stronghold dropped'.

'It is a pity that the third portion cannot be read all at once,' Dickens wrote to Forster, 'because its purpose would be much more apparent; and the pity is the greater because the general tone and turn of the working out and the winding up, will be away from all such things as they conventionally go.' Forster was delighted with its freshness and novelty; and Dickens himself wrote to Macready, 'the work has been pretty close. But I hope that the book is a good book.' He was busy at the same time in reading the proofs of one of Lytton's stories for *Household Words*; and on exchanging the proofs of his own new work, Lytton replied to say, 'I am deep in the back numbers of your tale with which I am literally *enchanted*. What freshness & gusto. In point of interest I know none even of yours more enchanting.' When he went on to the final chapters, however, he wrote to Dickens again, objecting to a conclusion that would leave Pip quite alone.

Without discussing it once more with Forster, Dickens thought the matter over carefully, and altered the ending in order to unite Estella and Pip. It is not an improvement. As Dickens said, he 'put in as pretty a little piece of writing' as he could; but it is no more than that. It is deftly done. It even gives too neat a twist that both having deserved forgiveness after suffering they should be rewarded by being brought together. But it was too conventional, and spoils the force of what had gone before.

A new series of readings outside London (delayed until *Great Expectations* was finished) started in October 1861 and went on, in prolonged spells, all through 1862 and up to January 1863, when Dickens gave some readings for charity at the British Embassy in Paris. Once again, they were a tremendous success. 'The Reading so stuns and oversets the Parisians', he wrote to Wills, 'that I shall have to do it again. Blazes of Triumph!' Appearance in his own character and reading his own stories had come to mean far more to him than mere acting; the money meant much, with so many dependent on him; and now that he was no longer compelled to write, he meant to make the most of his freedom.

Chapter Thirteen

OUR MUTUAL FRIEND

ANOTHER short series of readings was given in London from March to May 1863, and later the same year Dickens wrote one of his best-known Christmas numbers, *Mrs. Lirriper's Lodgings*, for *All the Year Round*. Mrs. Lirriper is one of the few characters in the later Christmas numbers who are still remembered. The rest of them sold well enough, but she alone, says Forster, 'took her place . . . among people known to everybody'. Dickens declared, 'Mrs. Lirriper is indeed a most brilliant old lady. God bless her!' She was reserved for next Christmas, when she re-appeared in *Mrs. Lirriper's Legacy*, but many readers will prefer the number which followed it, *Dr. Marigold's Prescriptions*, the story of the cheapjack (1866).

Once the Christmas number for 1863 was out of the way, Dickens tried to settle to a new serial in monthly numbers, his last complete novel. He had fixed on the title of *Our Mutual Friend* as early as 1861 but, for a while, he had found that he had nothing new to say. 'Alas!' he wrote a year later, 'I have hit upon nothing for a story. Again and again I have tried.' Recognizing that his old inspiration had gone, he made up his mind not to launch the new serial until he had at least five numbers in hand. 'I have grown hard to satisfy', he told Forster, and write very slowly. And I have so much—not fiction—that will be thought of . . . that I am forced to take more care than I once took.'

He had greater difficulty in writing than ever before. The story was not popular at first, and after only three months he began to fall behind. 'Although I have not been wanting in industry', he wrote, 'I have been wanting in invention. This week I have been very unwell . . . and, as I know from two days' slow experience, have a very mountain to climb before I see the open country of my work.' As he went on, however, he was able to write to his publisher, 'I regard No. 4 as certain to pick up, and I have the strongest faith in the book's doing thoroughly well. I believe it to be GOOD, full of variety and always rising in its working out of the people and the story. (I know I put into it the making of a dozen books.)' Meanwhile, he was depressed and ill, and while his illness seems to have made it more difficult for him to write, it was partly his difficulties in working that helped to make him ill.

That spring and summer he felt sure he would break down if he did not go away and, as he left for France in May, he confided in Forster, 'no one knows . . . how near to it I have been'. His crowning misfortune was to be in a terrible railway accident when he came back in June. He had a narrow escape, and worked for hours among the dead and dying. What made it worse was that he had to look after Ellen Ternan, who had been in the same compartment. When he sat down again at his desk he turned sick and faint after writing only a few notes; and, for the first time for years, he misjudged the length of one of the monthly numbers, and left himself with an extra two-and-a-half pages to write. He rallied and worked hard; but once the end was in sight he wrote and told an American publisher that it was unlikely that he would 'fall to work upon another novel yet awhile'.

Written under these conditions it is not surprising that *Our Mutual Friend* is not entirely successful. It shows a sense of strain and a lack of coherence in its development. The wheels of the story do not grip. the enormous folds of the nineteen-number novel hang loosely over the characters and plot, which are not expansive enough to fill them out. Dickens had complained bitterly of the difficulties of weekly serialization, yet under its discipline he had done some of his best work. Now he wrote, to Wilkie Collins, that he felt like an amateur actor suddenly thrust on the stage of the giant San Carlo opera-house they both knew at Naples. 'Strange to say,' he said, 'I felt at first quite dazed at getting back to the large canvas and big brushes.'

Nor is it surprising that the total of subscribers dropped five thousand after the first number. Gaffer Hexam's trade of collecting dead bodies from the Thames was not only depressing but Dickens showed none of his old gusto in describing it. Hexam himself is half dead. The Veneerings seem to have been designed to play an important part in the novel, but they are never filled out as they ought to be. Podsnap is the only member of their circle we can remember, because he is the only one who has anything interesting to say. The wooden-legged Wegg begins well, but ends as a dreary bore; and his friend the taxidermist, Mr. Venus, who is described as swilling tea in his dirty little shop, finding old teeth in the coffee-pot, and toasting greasy muffins with an arrow extracted from one of his stuffed birds, is typically odd without being amusing.

There is no drive behind the story. On the one hand, Dickens was obviously in a state of depression and even despair. He had been growing increasingly critical of his times, of the government and the governing classes, of the empty frivolities of society, and of the dreariness of contemporary life everywhere from the schoolroom to the City. Yet, even in his private life, he felt it his duty to conceal his feelings. As a writer, he thought it his business to entertain. As he had told Miss Burdett Coutts, 'If *I* were soured, I should still try to sweeten . . . the lives of others.' This had always been his philosophy as a writer; but once it had come naturally, now it went against the grain of his imagery and much of his characterization. Unwilling to let himself go in describing the darker side of life, he took care that it should be balanced by rather strained attempts at humour. Many of his old fanciful comparisons were now unpleasant and even repulsive. Yet evidently Dickens did not mean to give this effect. For even well after he had started, he told Collins that he meant the work to be 'a combination of drollery and romance'; but the humour is forced and there is little romance.

This is not to say that there are not fine things in *Our Mutual Friend*, only that it can as well be enjoyed as a loose collection of pieces that might have appeared in the pages of a magazine. Some of them, in fact, were similar to articles that had already been published in *All the Year Round*; and, once again, Dickens felt a need to resort to the same notebook that he had used when writing *Little Dorrit*. He got little of importance from it. It is a sign of the slackness of his vitality and his self-distrust that he felt he had to pick it over like Boffin on the dust-heap.

Yet if it were not his last complete work, one might say it held out great promise. The Veneerings are not the only characters who are 'new'. Bella Wilfer is natural and fresh; the most natural and attractive woman in Dickens's novels, in fact the only one. Bradley

Headstone's fierce passion is something not to be found elsewhere in his works, and it was admired by Stevenson as 'one of Dickens's superlative achievements'. The sketch of Betty Higden is slight, but her story is told with controlled intensity and power. The Lammles are something untried before: for they and their friends represent an attempt to enter Thackeray's country, left open by his recent death. Dickens even seems to anticipate Wilde in describing Eugene and Mortimer, who are so new that they remind one of a pallid, mid-Victorian Algy and Jack. Eugene actually goes Bunburying and is reproached by his friend for not being earnest; and, in the same chapter, he and Headstone meet face to face in a manner which even Henry James, with characteristic reservations, felt forced to admire. Much of the writing, too, is done with tremendous skill, as if Dickens were aware that, deprived of his old vitality, every word must be made to tell.

Dickens himself rarely discussed his works once they were completed; but once again we can get some idea of what he thought of it from a review which was written by one of his friends, E. S. Dallas, for *The Times*. Dallas was a thoughtful and intelligent critic whom Dickens had just tried to help by recommending him to Lord John Russell for a Chair at one of the Scottish universities. Shortly afterwards, Dallas wrote his review of *Our Mutual Friend*, and it seems that Dickens was so pleased with it and grateful for some other service Dallas had done for him, that he made him the valuable present of the original manuscript. Trollope expressed his disapproval of such transactions; but, as it was the only time Dickens did anything of the kind in his life, we may assume that he was disinterested. A remarkable thing about it is that the review is not entirely favourable.

Dallas had some fairly hard things to say about the way in which there was, at first, 'an appearance of great effort without corresponding result'. He thought that:

> The first few chapters . . . are very heavy, and . . . that *Our Mutual Friend* has defects we not only allow, but shall ruthlessly point out. The weak part of the work is to be found in what may be called 'The Social Chorus'. This is the title which Mr. Dickens gives one of his chapters. . . . We can divide the tale distinctly into two parts, like a Greek drama—one part truly dramatic and given to the evolution of the story which Mr. Dickens has to tell; the other a sort of social chorus having no real connexion with the tale in which we are interested. Now the idea here is a great one, but it has not been worked out with details of sufficient interest. Of Mr. Dickens's main story . . . we cannot speak too highly; it is a masterpiece, but . . . [in writing about the chorus] the novelist has this further difficulty that he has to make us care about people who are remarkable for their nothingness . . . who, by the hypothesis are uninteresting. Now, it is in dealing with this cruel problem that Mr. Dickens falls short.

Dallas has much to say in praise of the naturalness of the characters in what he calls 'the main story', and he especially extols the novel for 'the immense amount of thought which it contains. . . . In all these six hundred pages there is not a careless line'. Dickens was apparently happy to accept his strictures as well as to enjoy his praise.

Another contemporary critic, whose remarks, if Dickens ever saw them, would have pleased him much less, was the young Henry James. He was then only twenty-one, but in reviewing the novel for the *Nation* he made some clear-headed comments; and although the maturer James's critique of fiction is quite inadequate as a means of judging Dickens's works, this early review was very much to the point. In his opinion the novel was wanting in inspiration: '*Bleak House* was forced; *Little Dorrit* was laboured; the present work was dug out as with spade and pickaxe.' He even felt tempted to congratulate the author 'on his success in what we should call the manufacture of fiction. . . . Seldom, we reflected, had we read a book so intensely *written*, so little seen, known, or felt.' The characters, including Wrayburn and Headstone, he thought were superficial and 'essentially small'. So far, his view is just.

At the same time, although it is true that *Our Mutual Friend* has usually been thought of as one of the least successful of Dickens's works, a number of recent critics have placed it among his best. Ever since Shaw wrote his two Dickens prefaces and told Frank Harris that the 'great period' began with *Hard Times*, some writers have been determined to see it as a unified work designed as a consistent study of an acquisitive society. Edgar Johnson, for example, seems to think it, 'in certain ways', the chief of his later books, 'and one of the supreme works of English fiction', while Jack Lindsay even proclaims that it is 'one of the greatest works of prose ever written'. The first opinion, at least, deserves an answer.

Certainly if *Our Mutual Friend* is even to be considered as among Dickens's greatest works, it is largely because of the way in which it may be interpreted as a study of an acquisitive and possessive society. Clearly this is one of the chief themes in the book. 'A man may do anything lawful for money', says the Genius of the Social Chorus, summing up the general view. He can undoubtedly buy his way into Parliament, buy a wife, buy friends, buy flattery and praise. And not only are the people in society the slaves of money: Bella is afraid of being so, Boffin pretends to be, and Silas Wegg certainly is. Above all, if one wants to make one's way in the world, one must have Shares: 'As is well known to the wise in their generation, traffic in Shares is the one thing to do in the world.' The Veneerings' gold camels, Podsnap's massive plate, and Shares all help to show society's blatant worship of property and wealth.

Yet as well as these symbols there is another which is never lost sight of throughout the whole book: the great Dust-heaps, left by the miserly John Harmon. They have their place on the monthly cover and on the frontispiece to the second volume, and apart from the age-old significance of muck as wealth, there are several references to Dust and the Dust-heaps which show they are meant to have some special meaning. It is argued by those who believe that the thought and feeling of the book are consistent, that they image wealth, 'the supreme goal of nineteenth-century society', and that they ultimately symbolize the dust and ashes of all misdirected human effort in a society in which true values have been distorted by an all-pervading greed for money.

All this is true. The only objection is that this chief symbol is used ambiguously. The foul dust-heap, composed of vast quantities of refuse, does represent wealth. But, in the first place, its more unsavoury aspects are glossed over, whatever critics may have since done to emphasize what might have been said of them, but what is not said of them, in the novel. Then, secondly, we are not allowed to forget that the golden-hearted Boffin also helped to build them up, that he inherits them, and that they are passed on to Bella Wilfer and the miser's son with the evident approval of the author. If any deduction is to be drawn from this ending it is that there is no objection to inheriting wealth without working for it, and that it is only wrong for a man like old Harmon to build it up by providing an honest service for the community. In its place in the usual outline of Dickens's analysis of society this is obviously absurd. The image is misapplied. Yet it is made perfectly clear that when the happy pair come into their inheritance and drive up to their new home, we are meant to be as delighted as the Boffins.

On this interpretation the whole book is flawed, and the ending slightly ridiculous. As John and Bella enter their new house and ascend the stairs, they find them 'tastefully ornamented with the most beautiful flowers. . . . Going on a little higher, they came to a charming aviary, in which a number of tropical birds were flying about; and among those birds were gold and silver fish . . . and a fountain, and all manner of wonders.' They look all over it: 'And a dainty house it was, and a tastefully beautiful; and they went through it in procession . . . And on Bella's exquisite toilette table was an ivory casket, and in the casket were jewels the like of which she had never dreamed of.' *Tastefully* is rather overworked throughout, and leaves the wrong impression.

Obviously this is not how it should be read, even though the way this scene is written makes it show through other intentions. The story is another 'morality', in which we are really meant to apply the Ruskinian teaching of *Unto This Last*, that is of the New Testament parable of the workers in the vineyard. The unearned wealth of 'great expectations' is now shown to be as good as, or better than, Pip's working 'for our profits'; just as, seen diagrammatically, the situation of the Headstone–Wrayburn rivalry reverses the Pip–Drummle opposition. But though the angle is new, the view is the same: that the worth of the man or woman is what matters, however involved it is with class or money.

Yet it is not only in the relations of John and Bella that there are flaws in coherence. The relationship between Eugene and Lizzie has an obviously special meaning. In fact, it is nearly all meaning: it shows that money, again, does not matter, and that love and humanity do; and that someone who feels purposeless can find a new meaning through a girl of the people.[1] If this were thoroughly worked out through the characters, as a criticism of society, the novel might have been the explosive force that some wish to find in it. But it is true in more ways than one that (as John Forster says of Betty Higden and the Poor Law) *Our Mutual Friend* finishes what *Oliver Twist* began. Headstone takes the place of Sikes; the Jew, Riah, is even an apology for Fagin; and Oliver's function, as 'the principle of Good, subsisting in things evil', is taken over by Lizzie. But in too many ways the later novel is much more insistently realistic, self-conscious and profound; it feels contemporary, its characters speak more naturally, its scenes are familiar. The 'allegory' is harder to accept. Apart from this, the function that had been fitting for a child-figure is false for the woman whom Headstone tells, 'You draw me to you. If I were shut up in a strong prison, you would draw me out. I should break through the wall to come to you. If I were lying on a sick bed, you would draw me up—to stagger to your feet and fall there.' For forcibly projected as Headstone is, and intriguing as

[1] It seems as though one response to the share-pushing sixties was a renewed popular demand for the fable that true love takes no account of class or money—especially if one can have it both ways—as in the popular dramas, *The Colleen Bawn* (1860) and *Caste* (1867).

Wrayburn may be, Lizzie is weak as a representative of her sex and her class. The attempted organization and sophistication of the novel no longer quite match either Dickens's rather hard and pointed style, his intensely vital scenes and characters, or its appeal to 'fancy' in such figures as those of the Doll's Dressmaker and the Golden Dustman. It is too diffuse and too ambitious. After a quarter of a century of development, Dickens was now pushing his aims beyond his means.

For again the novel is one which tries to be everything, and which with the generous reader succeeds. It is an analysis of society, a romantic justification of humanity, a fierce comment on contemporary society, and a profounder study of his response to life than Dickens had yet attempted. The emphasis of any one of these to the exclusion of others is a distortion. But a sense of man's precarious presence in life and the nature of his being is distinctly to be found. Here the river focuses our attention; for, as always in the novels, it is the dark centre of life, whether simply the 'portal of Eternity' of the *Chimes*, or representative of life itself. Gaffer's trade, Rokesmith's resurrection from the river, Wrayburn's escape from drowning, Headstone's death, Riderhood's and Gaffer's are generally less remarkable for any mythic potency than because Dickens uses them as the occasion to say something directly. He does not always say it as well as he does through Jenny Wren (II, iii; II, v). But, undoubtedly Dickens sees our situation in life as like Rokesmith's, one with a fanciful aspect we should be able to forsake, and with 'a real side, so difficult that, though I think of it every day, I never thoroughly think it out. . . . I know I evade it, as many men,—perhaps most men—do evade thinking their way through their greatest perplexity.' In assuming a second personality,

Rokesmith is forced to think what the nature of his own is; and he finds himself at last, as we are told Wrayburn does, and as Dickens himself was probably trying to do.

No single statement sums up the novel; it is varied and complex enough to invite responsive enthusiasm. As a study of the times it ought not to be read as an attack on the whole of nineteenth-century society. Dickens's sketch of the Veneerings and his remarks on Shares go no further than many of the jokes in *Punch*, Trollope in *The Way We Live Now*, or Tennyson in 'Maud'. He did not object to wealth, but to the way it was applied. Dickens wanted to show how a love of money might corrupt men, not necessarily a whole society. It is partly brought out at the end of the chapter in which John and Bella arrive at their new house. The Boffins gaze at Bella with the baby in her arms:

> 'It looks as if the old man's spirit had found rest at last; don't it?' said Mrs. Boffin.
>
> 'Yes, old lady.'
>
> 'And as if his money had turned bright again, after a long, long rust in the dark, and was beginning to sparkle in the sunlight.'

All is well now. The money can be put to good use, because it is in good hands. A simple theme in a complex novel, which is not least intriguing if one begins to try to relate the way its author looks at life, to the life he was then leading.

Chapter Fourteen

LAST YEARS AND *EDWIN DROOD*

WHEN *Our Mutual Friend* had been completed, Dickens decided to give a third series of the Readings, and this was arranged to continue throughout 1866. He was now beginning to suffer bouts of ill-health, although so far the doctors were unable to diagnose anything serious. Then, when this series was drawing to a close, his agents tempted him with a further engagement and, at sixty pounds a night for forty-two nights with all expenses paid, Dickens felt unable to resist it. At this rate he would almost reach the magnificent sum that Thackeray had forecast of twenty thousand a year!

This is a period of his life of which relatively little is known. When he was not giving the Readings, Dickens probably spent much of his time with Ellen, even though we still do not know exactly what their relations were. Years later, after she had married a schoolmaster and had two children, she is alleged to have said that she loathed the thought of her intimacy with Dickens; but whether this was merely in recollection, or whether she was unhappy at the time, must remain unknown. Again, although there is a story that they had a child which is probably impossible to disprove, there is no *reliable* evidence in its support.

Yet ridiculous and distasteful as some of the arguments about Dickens's association with Ellen have been, it cannot be dismissed lightly. It genuinely looks as if the greatest public figure of the age delighted, at times, to escape to the domestic privacy of Peckham and Slough. Incredible yet inescapable as this conclusion is, it shows a need to see Dickens as driven to seek to escape from a world in which he was continually playing a part, and yet showing amazing self-command at keeping this to himself so that he was not forced to go the way the world wished. It must have been as demanding as his public performances, and as skilful.

It would be a mistake, however, to imagine that Dickens was noticeably depressed at this time, in spite of the more sombre character of his writings. George Dolby, his new Reading manager, gives a very attractive picture of him, 'always cheerful and good-humoured' when on tour, even 'in the most trying situations', and a delightful host with a never-failing radiance about him that made 'the most ordinary things in life' seem 'special in his presence'. One person after another has testified to Dickens's possession of this exceptional quality. The Duke of Devonshire had written in his diary, in 1851, after meeting Dickens to arrange for the performance of *Not So Bad As We Seem*, 'I am bewitched by him'. The Hon. Richard Watson also recorded in his diary, after being his neighbour for five months, in 1846, 'It is impossible to describe the feelings of regard and friendship with which he has inspired us. He is certainly the most natural, unaffected, distinguished man I have ever met.' Sir George Russell wrote (in his manuscript reminiscences), 'As a charming companion, I never knew his equal', and Charles Eliot Norton, in a letter on hearing of his death, 'I never knew a famous and flattered man so utterly unhurt by it all. . . . The better one knew him, the more one loved him.'

The unfailing praise of such friends appears to have

irritated many who never knew him, but even men who thought they disliked him found him irresistible. Anthony Trollope was certainly no admirer, yet he wrote, 'Of the general charm of his manner I despair of giving any idea . . . he warmed the social atmosphere with that summer glow which seemed to attend him', and even Disraeli, who met him in 1870 probably for the first time for thirty years, spoke of the charm of Dickens's conversation, his brightness and his humour.

A great tribute to his popularity was shown in 1867, when a farewell dinner‘’ was organized in his honour, after he had decided to pay a second visit to the United States in order to pursue his Readings. Nearly four hundred and fifty guests attended, Lord Lytton took the chair, and there was a long list of eminent speakers. For once in his life, Dickens was almost overcome when he rose to reply. Towards the end of his speech he made it clear that though he was going to the United States mainly to fulfil a professional engagement, he also wanted to renew his acquaintance with a great country, and 'a kind, large-hearted, generous and great people'. A week later he sailed for America.

Before he left he arranged with Wills that Ellen should follow him there, if it were at all practicable for her to do so without its being generally known. It was soon obvious that this was impossible, and so the arrangement was reluctantly cancelled. The Readings themselves, however, were all that he had hoped for, except that as they went on they began to take a terrible toll of his health. Towards the end of the tour, Dickens wrote to Forster to confess 'I am nearly used up. Climate, distance, catarrh, travelling, and hard work, have begun (I may say so, now they are nearly over) to tell heavily upon me' (30 March). An old complaint of lameness returned. He could only just keep going, and yet, according to Dolby, he never once complained. Before he left he attended a banquet in his honour, given by the New York Press, in which he expressed his thanks for the way in which, throughout the tour, he had been 'received with unsurpassable politeness, delicacy, sweet temper, hospitality' and consideration.

On the return voyage he made a marvellous recovery, but when his friends saw him they noticed that there was a change. 'There was manifest abatement of his natural force', wrote Forster, 'the elasticity of his bearing was impaired, and the wonderful brightness of eye was dimmed at times.' One has only to look at a chronological series of photographs to see how strikingly he aged in the last three years; though those in which he looks ill have seldom been printed by his biographers. Although Dickens lived longer than his father or his brothers, or than most of his sons, almost everyone connected with the Readings thought that they ultimately shortened his life. This was also the opinion of his doctors. Yet still Dickens would not listen to advice. He took over the running of *All the Year Round* while Wills was ill, and concluded a final agreement with his agents to give a series of a hundred Readings for £8,000. He intended it to be the last, and it was.

It would be wrong to make out that this was due simply to a desire for money, a love of applause, or a reasonable wish to provide for the future. They all played their part: he enjoyed his public appearances, he had come to value security, and his anxiety for the future was justified. Dickens was afraid that, after his death, some of his family might go back to the shiftless ways of his father: Charley had already gone bankrupt, and other sons were showing signs of the family failing.

Throughout his lifetime he had seen that the career of a writer was hard and precarious. Thackeray had had the same wish to provide for his family by giving Readings. Many of Dickens's friends and acquaintances, including Jerrold, Mark Lemon, Leigh Hunt, and Sheridan Knowles, had accepted charity or left their families unprovided for; and he merely thought it less undignified to read his works for money than to leave his family—as Thackeray put it—'to pass the hat round' after he was dead.

In order to make a great effect, on his last appearance, he now began preparing a reading he called 'Sikes and Nancy', which led up to the murder-scene in *Oliver Twist*. It was tremendous. Fainting women were carried out by the dozen, and old Macready called it 'two Macbeths'! Yet it seriously worsened his health. Dolby tried to persuade him to cut down the number of performances, and for the only time in their association Dickens turned on him in anger—and then burst into tears. The crisis came towards the end of April 1869, at Preston, when the tour was suspended.

Even so, by August, he could be persuaded to take the chair at a dinner given to a visiting Harvard rowing crew. A new friend, Robert Lytton, son of the novelist, was moved to write to him that he had 'rarely felt more genuine pleasure' than in reading the speech, 'the only utterance I have heard addressed in England to listeners in America . . . which has surpassed my ideal', and the more welcome because 'the general tone of most of our public utterances in reference to America' were usually so mischievous. In Birmingham (in September) Dickens addressed a great audience on Education, winding up with the Delphic remark, that 'My faith in the people governing is, on the whole infinitesimal; my faith in The

People governed, is, on the whole illimitable'. It was 'a little touch of Radicalism', he told James T. Fields, that 'with pride I observe . . . makes the regular political traders of all sorts, perfectly mad'.

A final series of Readings was given in London, from January to March 1870, and at the very last he took farewell of his audience, saying that he would henceforth devote himself exclusively to writing. In two weeks' time, he went on, he hoped that in the privacy of their homes they would join in 'a new series of his readings'. of his next novel *Edwin Drood*, 'but from these garish lights I vanish now for evermore, with a heartfelt, grateful, respectful and affectionate farewell'.

He had begun writing the novel the previous autumn, after thinking over and rejecting several ideas for the plot. The story was to be a *Mystery*, and few of the accounts of hints about it that he is alleged to have let drop to his friends, are to be trusted. It was to be issued in only twelve monthly parts, of the same length as before; and, according to the agreement signed on 1 February, the first instalment was to be published in March. The agreement contained proposals about what should be done in the event of Dickens's death; but, in spite of all that has been said to the contrary, it was not the first time that such a clause had appeared in one of his contracts.

Although it is hard, when discussing the last years of his life, not to be influenced by our foreknowledge of the imminence of his death, Dickens himself seems to have had no such foreboding until almost the end. Though undoubtedly ill, he was still full of life, and if he found it difficult to begin writing this was certainly nothing new. When the first number appeared, in April, he was able to report to an American friend—

with enthusiastic inaccuracy—that the sale had '*very, very far outstripped every one of its predecessors*'.

The novel itself is by no means what Bernard Shaw called it, 'a gesture by a man already three-quarters dead'. The fact that Dickens died when only six out of the twelve numbers had been completed has meant that critical attention has largely been concentrated on how the story would have finished. The writing itself does not show Dickens at his best, and if the novel had made its full effect it would have been through the novelty of the plot and its ideas. How it would have been concluded, therefore, is not mere idle speculation, or a detective-game, but an essential preliminary to any proper critical understanding.

In its unfinished state the story is rather confusing at first, and it may help to begin by giving an outline of the probable course of the plot. A whole library of books has been written about the *Drood* problem, and of course, it is impossible to go into it here in complete detail. The opening of the story, however, is clear. The scene is set in the cathedral city of Cloisterham, which may be identified with Rochester. Edwin Drood is a young man, studying to be an engineer, who is engaged to Rosa Budd, still a pupil at Miss Twinkleton's academy in Cloisterham. Both are orphans; and though they are fond of each other, soon after the opening of the story they decide that it would be better for the engagement to be dissolved.

Both Edwin and Rosa are relatively minor characters. The chief figure is Edwin's uncle, John Jasper, the lay precentor of the cathedral. He is a few years older than his nephew, but although outwardly just the respectable leader of the choir, he is a slave to opium. He is obviously villainous, passionately in love with

Rosa, and possesses a strange hypnotic power over her. He does not know that she and Edwin have decided to break off the engagement and, although he has a tigerish affection for his nephew, he plans to kill him.

He is assisted in this by the arrival of the twins, Neville and Helena Landless. Their parentage is mysterious, but they are known to have come from Ceylon, where they were brought up by a cruel stepfather. They are an unusually handsome couple, 'much alike; both very dark, and very rich in colour; she almost of the gypsy type; something untamed about them both'. Neville has come to Cloisterham as a pupil of Minor Canon Crisparkle and he, too, falls in love with Rosa. After his first evening at Mr. Crisparkle's, he and Edwin are invited back to Jasper's rooms at the Gatehouse, where Jasper doctors their drink and incites them to a violent quarrel. His purpose is to throw the blame on Neville. In his notes for this number Dickens made this memorandum, 'Jasper lays his ground.' The two young men are reconciled soon after, but a few weeks later they are both invited to dinner with Jasper on Christmas-eve. The next day Edwin is missing. Suspicion falls on Neville. He is arrested, and at length released because there is no evidence to convict him. Jasper swears to Mr. Crisparkle that he will never rest until he can 'fasten the crime of the murder of my dear dead boy upon the murderer'. and that he will devote himself 'to his destruction'.

Mr. Crisparkle, Neville's tutor, will not admit that his pupil is guilty, but he arranges for him to leave Cloisterham and to continue his studies in London. As his name suggests, Crisparkle is a vigorous and attractive character, and we have some reason to believe that he may already have fallen in love with Helena, although he is not as impetuous as the younger men. Neville is partly looked after in London by Mr. Grewgious, an old solicitor, who is Rosa's guardian. Rosa takes refuge with Grewgious in order to escape Jasper's attentions; but instead of falling in again with Neville, she rather avoids him and is introduced to Mr. Tartar, a young naval ex-officer, who is Neville's neighbour, and was Mr. Crisparkle's fag at school. It seems clear that Neville is to be neglected by Rosa, and Mr. Tartar to be favoured.

Meanwhile Jasper tries to find where Neville has gone, in order to incriminate him if he can; but he thereby only succeeds in drawing attention to himself. He also returns to an opium-den in the east-end of London which is run by a wretched opium-woman, between whom and Jasper there is some mysterious connection. It was in this den that the novel opened, and if we are right in assuming that Jasper is the murderer, he returns there because it is only after smoking a pipe mixed by the opium-woman that he can disburden his memory under its influence by re-living the crime. He does so, but evidently remembers something in his trance that he had forgotten in his waking state. The opium-woman, who both hates and fears him, listens eagerly to his mutterings, and when he comes to himself and returns to Cloisterham she follows him there—so the pursuer is now the pursued.

Jasper is also under observation in Cloisterham by a new arrival in the city, a Mr. Datchery, an old gentleman with black eyebrows and a white wig. He appears to be someone in disguise, and in all probability is Mr. Grewgious's clerk, Bazzard, whose chief foible we know is an interest in the stage and who presumably has some ability at make-up and in taking a part. Datchery meets the opium-woman, who is able to point out Jasper to him in the cathedral, and who tells him all she knows. He adds this information to what he has learnt from other chance witnesses, and with this he seems to be satisfied that he is well on the way to solving the mystery.

Thus far, though certain assumptions have been made, the story seems reasonably clear; and though this is where Dickens left off it is still possible to go farther without resorting altogether to guesswork. Jasper's recollection in his opium-trance that he has overlooked something was probably that (unknown to him in his normal state) his nephew was in possession of a gold ring which he was to have given to Rosa if they had decided to become formally engaged. This comes as a shock, therefore, since he had taken particular care to remove his nephew's only jewellery, his watch and tiepin, and to plant them where they might be found in a place which would cast suspicion on Neville. He now realizes that the ring is still with the corpse. This is serious, for though he has hidden the body in a tomb in the cathedral and buried it in quicklime, if it should ever be discovered it will still be possible to identify it as his nephew. This would draw attention to Jasper since he is known to have taken a suspicious interest in the tomb. It seems likely that the next time he takes opium he will make an attempt to recover the ring and be detected by Datchery. All this has been foreshadowed in the first half of the novel, for in one of his few intrusions into the narrative Dickens had solemnly declared that Edwin's decision to keep the ring in his possession was the vital link in a 'chain . . . rivetted to the foundations of heaven and earth, and gifted with invincible power to hold and drag'.

Exactly how Jasper was to be revealed as the murderer

it is impossible to say. It is evident from the story and from what Dickens told Charles Collins, his son-in-law, that Jasper's attempts to incriminate Neville were only to serve to fasten the guilt more strongly on himself. There is some reason to think that the design on the right-hand side of the cover (drawn by Collins) showing figures hurrying up a spiral staircase and led on by Jasper, was not merely emblematical of the pursuer pursued, but that the story might have culminated in a chase up the great Tower of the Cathedral and along the narrow galleries between the vaulting and the leaded roof. Jasper speaks in his opium-trance of 'a perilous journey over abysses where a slip might be destruction', and it may have been there that his nephew was murdered. In this pursuit the young naval officer, Tartar, would have taken the lead, since we have already been told that he was surefooted, had a head for heights, and 'the deftness of a cat'. It has been suggested, too, that Neville might have been killed in the same pursuit.

So many suggestions have been made about the probable course of the plot that it is foolish to be dogmatic. Only two main assumptions have been made in this outline, however, and the first is that Edwin was really murdered by Jasper. Although it is not conclusive, all internal and external evidence points this way, and Dickens took his relations with his readers far too seriously to mislead them unfairly. The other assumption, that the mysterious Mr. Datchery was Bazzard, hardly matters. The problem has bothered commentators on *Drood* to the exclusion of far more interesting questions. Indeed, as the outline stands, the plot is somewhat elementary. If this were the whole story it would almost justify Wilkie Collins's petulant dismissal of the book as 'Dickens's last laboured effort, the melancholy work of a worn-out brain'. The important questions are, what *else* was to come out, what was to be the main theme of the book, and how does it fit in with what we have seen to be Dickens's development as a novelist?

One thing is clear: that however closely Dickens had come to be concerned with plot, he had by no means given up the idea of having a unifying theme with a strong moral interest. In the past this morality had been a Christian one, and in several of the later novels certain key-phrases from the Bible or the Prayer book had played an important part in the thematic structure. This was seen most clearly in *A Tale of Two Cities* and *Great Expectations*. It also seems to have been foreshadowed in *Edwin Drood*. In the jottings on his part-plan for the very next number Dickens heavily underlined the phrase, 'Strike the key-note', and made it clear that this refers to the last paragraph of the first chapter, when Jasper hurries to the cathedral and joins the choir as it files in: they all hide their faces, 'and then the intoned words, "WHEN THE WICKED MAN—" rise among groins of arches and beams of roof, awakening muttered thunder'. No doubt, as was customary in Dickens's work, this phrase was to be repeated with a deeper meaning later on.

Now, as well as there being an uncertainty about the ultimate fate of Edwin Drood, there is also a mystery about the origins of several of the characters. The Drood family, we know, has long had business connections with the East. There are hints that Jasper has lived out there, where he has perhaps acquired his taste for opium and even learnt the art of murder in the manner of the Thugs. Certainly he has some closer connection with the opium-woman than that of a mere client. It seems likely that at the end of the story much more was to come out, revealed by Grewgious, and that it would all be in keeping with the theme of the book that Jasper Drood was to be revealed either as the brother (or half-brother) of Neville and Helena, or even as their nephew—'some uncles', we have been told, 'are even younger than their nephews'. The ground is prepared for this in the earlier chapters. All three are said to be unusually dark. It would not even have been unlike Dickens to have ironically underlined the relationship by making Mr. Honeythunder, Neville's preposterous guardian, hold forth to their coachman about all men being brothers whether they like it or not!

More important than this is the emphasis on the opening words of the morning and evening service with which Dickens meant to set the key-note, 'WHEN THE WICKED MAN'. The text goes on: 'When the wicked man turneth away from his wickedness that he hath committed and doeth that which is lawful and right he shall save his soul alive' (Ezekiel 18: 27). That Dickens intended Jasper to repent and be forgiven is extremely unlikely. It is more important that the verse comes from a passage in which the prophet Ezekiel teaches that what a man does is his own responsibility, and that we cannot lay the blame for our sins upon our fathers. He supposes that a just man has a son who is 'a robber, a shedder of blood': this son, then, 'shall not live . . . he shall surely die'. But supposing that this son has a son who is just and honest, 'he shall not die for the iniquity of his father, he shall surely live'. The teaching is not that man is entitled to forgiveness, but that God is just: 'The soul that sinneth, it shall die. The son shall not bear the iniquity of the father, neither shall the father bear the iniquity of the son.' This is Dickens's teaching in several of the novels: in *Martin Chuzzlewit*, for example, Jonas is a murderer in spite of his father's love, and in *Little Dorrit* Arthur Clennam is a good man in spite of his reputed mother's shame and hatred. There is the same sort of connection in almost all the novels, as in *Bleak House* (Dedlock—Summerson), *Great Expectations* (Magwitch—Estella), and *Our Mutual Friend* (Harmon: father and son). Exactly how Jasper and the twins were to be related it is impossible to say, but that they were to have been shown in some way as related, through their fathers, is extremely probable. Yet, whether this theory is true or false, no understanding admirer of Dickens can believe that, at this stage in his career, he would have sacrificed everything to plot and failed to bring the characters into some relationship that would have given the work a deeper meaning.

This is shown again in the way in which goodness and evil are depicted as existing side-by-side, with evil able to exert a strange attraction. As Dickens explained in the twentieth chapter, Jasper was intended to be the realistic study of an abnormal criminal, a class that had always fascinated him, especially in the way such men often exerted a strange power over women. It was something that he had returned to time after time, at first in the fantastic figure of Quilp, then in Jonas, in Murdstone, in Julius Slinkton (in the short story *Hunted Down*), and lastly in Jasper Drood. At each step he had gone farther from mere fancy and closer to something like realism. The strange conflict between good and evil is implicit in the whole idea of the book. Jasper warns Edwin, early on, that the cathedral service often sounds devilish to him, the echoes of his voice seem to mock him, and he wonders if he must take to carving demons out of his heart as the old monks used to carve them out of the stalls; and, on the very last page that Dickens wrote, the strange opium-woman who has followed Jasper to the cathedral is described 'as ugly and withered as one of the fantastic carvings on . . . the stall seats, as malignant as the Evil One'. Undoubtedly these aspects of the story would have been developed more powerfully in the second half of the novel.

It is not particularly interesting to judge the work solely as it stands. It has many of Dickens's characteristic faults and virtues. His power of creating odd and original characters is shown in Durdles, Deputy and, Sapsea, and there are still several flashes of his old humour almost unimpaired. The best writing is to be found in some of the descriptions of Cloisterham, and it was these, perhaps, which led Longfellow to declare, on Dickens's death, that it was 'one of his most beautiful works, if not the most beautiful of all'. This is an overestimate. Certainly it is to be understood best if it is seen in relation to the other novels, although in its unfinished state a full critical comparison is impossible.

For Dickens himself the end came suddenly and unexpectedly. On 8 June he spent all day working on the novel. At dinner he confessed that he had been feeling ill, then suddenly he rose and fell to the floor. Georgina Hogarth, his sister-in-law, was the only member of the family who was staying at Gad's Hill. She sent for the children, and (it seems) Ellen Ternan; Dickens lived through the night and all next day; but he never recovered consciousness. He died on the evening of 9 June 1870.

His death was felt as a devastating shock to those near to him. His eldest daughter Mamie wrote to her Bostonian friend, Susan Norton: 'You know how beautiful he was in life, & he was most grand and splendid in death. But he is never dead to us. Never can be as long as we live. We have all, I hope & think, tried to bear our sorrow patiently, & to behave throughout as he would have wished us to, but the light has gone from our lives. Life can never be the same to us as it has been, and our hearts are very sad and desolate. Every body loved him, but nobody knows what he was to us.' And John Forster wrote to Susan's father, Charles Eliot Norton: 'To you only I say this, my dear Norton. I have not been able, nor shall be, to have speech on these matters with any one. And to you for the present I will only further say that nothing in the future can, to me, ever again be as it was. The duties of life remain while life remains, but for me the joy of it is gone for ever more.'

His death was felt also as a national calamity. One of the less reverent members of his editorial staff later said, 'He had Westminster Abbey always before him.' At once a strong movement was launched to secure his admission, and he was buried there on 14 June. A fitting contemporary tribute was paid to him by Benjamin Jowett at a special evening memorial service:

> Men of genius are different from what we suppose them to be; they have greater pleasures and greater pains, greater affections and greater temptations than the generality of mankind, and they can never be altogether understood by their fellow-men. . . . We can hardly calculate the debt of gratitude which is due to a writer who has led us to sympathize with the good, true, sincere, honest English characters of ordinary life, and to laugh at the egotism, the hypocrisy, the false respectability of religious professors and others. . . . He whose loss we now mourn occupied a greater space than any other writer in the minds of Englishmen during the last thirty-five years.

SELECT ANNOTATED BIBLIOGRAPHY

Bibliographies

SHEPHERD, R. H., *The Bibliography of Dickens*, London, 1880.

KITTON, F. G., *Dickensiana. A Bibliography of the Literature Relating to Charles Dickens and His Writings*, London, 1886, and *The Minor Writings of Charles Dickens. A Bibliography and Sketch*, London, 1886. Both are still scrappily useful.

ECKEL, J. C., *The First Editions of the Writings of Charles Dickens and Their Values, A Bibliography*, London, 1903 and 1932. The later edition is much revised and enlarged. Entirely for collectors.

Charles Dickens. An Excerpt from the General Catalogue of Printed Books in the British Museum, London, 1926, and re-issued up to date, 1961.

HATTON, T. and CLEAVER, A., *A Bibliography of the Periodical Works of Charles Dickens*, London, 1933. For collectors only.

MILLER, W., *The Dickens Student and Collector, A List of Writings Relating to Charles Dickens and His Works, 1836–1945*, Cambridge, Mass., with two pamphlet *Supplements*, Hove, Sussex, 1947 and 1953 (privately printed). An amateur 'Pickwickian' publication. For a professional job on its many shortcomings see P. Calhoun and H. J. Heaney, 'Dickensiana in the Rough', *Papers of the Bibliographical Society of America*, XLI, 1947.

Victorian Fiction, A Guide to Research, edited by L. Stevenson, Cambridge, Mass., 1964, includes 'Dickens' by A. B. Nisbet: a discriminating and critical survey.

Victorian Studies, 'Victorian Bibliography' (in each annual, June, number), Bloomington, Indiana, gives the best current bibliography of Dickens, including numerous and important articles impossible to record here.

By Dickens

Novels

THE PICKWICK PAPERS, monthly numbers, April 1836 to November 1837.

OLIVER TWIST, serialized monthly in *Bentley's Miscellany*, February 1837 to March 1839, published in 3 vols. October 1838.

NICHOLAS NICKLEBY, monthly numbers, April 1838 to October 1839.

MASTER HUMPHREY'S CLOCK, weekly periodical, from 4 April 1840 to 27 November 1841.

THE OLD CURIOSITY SHOP, in *Clock* from 25 April 1840.

BARNABY RUDGE, in *Clock* from 13 February 1841.

MARTIN CHUZZLEWIT, monthly numbers, January 1843 to July 1844.

DOMBEY AND SON, monthly numbers, October 1846 to April 1848.

DAVID COPPERFIELD, monthly numbers, May 1849 to November 1850.

BLEAK HOUSE, monthly numbers, March 1852 to September 1853.

HARD TIMES, weekly in *Household Words*, 1 April to 12 August 1854.

LITTLE DORRIT, monthly numbers, December 1855 to June 1857.

A TALE OF TWO CITIES, weekly in *All the Year Round*, 30 April to 26 November 1859.

GREAT EXPECTATIONS, weekly in *All the Year Round*, 1 December 1860 to 3 August 1861.

OUR MUTUAL FRIEND, monthly numbers, May 1864 to November 1865.

THE MYSTERY OF EDWIN DROOD, monthly numbers, April to September 1870, uncompleted, six parts issued of twelve originally designed.

Short Stories, Essays, and Sketches

SUNDAY UNDER THREE HEADS, under pseudonym 'Timothy Sparks', 1836.

SKETCHES BY BOZ, first and second series, 1836.

SKETCHES OF YOUNG GENTLEMAN, Anon., 1838.

SKETCHES OF YOUNG COUPLES, Anon., 1840.

REPRINTED PIECES, articles contributed to *Household Words*, 1858.

CHRISTMAS STORIES, contributed to the Christmas numbers of *Household Words* and *All the Year Round*, often in collaboration with Wilkie Collins or in conjunction with other regular contributors, 1850–67.

HUNTED DOWN, short story, first published in the *New York Ledger* of 20 and 27 August and 3 September 1859; also in *All the Year Round*, 4 and 11 August 1860.

THE UNCOMMERCIAL TRAVELLER, essays from *All the Year Round*; the first edition had seventeen papers (1861); the next had an additional eleven (1868); a further eight were in the Illustrated Library Edition (1875); and one more, making it thirty-seven in all, in the Gadshill Edition (1908).

GEORGE SILVERMAN'S EXPLANATION, short story, first published in the *Atlantic Monthly*, Boston, January to March 1868, also in *All the Year Round*, 1, 15 and 29 February 1868.

HOLIDAY ROMANCE, children's story, first published in *Our Young Folks*, Boston, between January and May 1868, also in *All the Year Round* between 25 January and 4 April 1868.

MISCELLANEOUS PAPERS, published separately and also in certain editions of his works. They include his articles in *Household Words* and *All the Year Round* not collected in *Reprinted Pieces* and *The Uncommercial Traveller*, and others contributed to the *Examiner*, *Daily News*, *Cornhill*, etc. Almost, but not quite, complete. In the Nonesuch Edition of the *Works*, they are printed under the title of *Collected Papers*, elsewhere used for Dickens's Prefaces.

Christmas Books

A CHRISTMAS CAROL, 1843.

THE CHIMES, 1844.

THE CRICKET ON THE HEARTH, 1845.

THE BATTLE OF LIFE, 1846.

THE HAUNTED MAN, 1848.

Travel

AMERICAN NOTES, 1842.

PICTURES FROM ITALY, 1846. First published in the *Daily News* as 'Travelling Letters', between 21 January and 2 March 1846.

THE LAZY TOUR OF TWO IDLE APPRENTICES, first published in *Household Words*, 3 October to 31 October 1857, in collaboration with Wilkie Collins.

Dramatic Works

THE VILLAGE COQUETTES, libretto for comic opera, 1836.

THE STRANGE GENTLEMAN, comic burletta, 1837.

IS SHE HIS WIFE? OR SOMETHING SINGULAR, comic burletta, 1837.

THE LAMPLIGHTER, A FARCE, 1879.

Miscellaneous

A CHILD'S HISTORY OF ENGLAND, first published in *Household Words* between 25 January 1851 and 10 December 1853; 3 vols.: 1852, 1853, 1854.

THE LIFE OF OUR LORD, 1934. Written for Dickens's children, and not intended for publication.

SPEECHES, edited by K. J. Fielding, Oxford, 1960. The definitive text, based on more accurate sources, and much more complete, than the earlier collections.

Editorial Work

Dickens edited *Bentley's Miscellany* from January 1837 to February 1839; the *Daily News* from 21 January to 9 February 1846; *Household Words* from March 1850 to May 1859; and *All the Year Round* from April 1859 until his death. Separate works include *The Memoirs of Grimaldi* (1837); and *The Pic-Nic Papers*, edited for charity (1838).

Letters

The collection of Dickens's letters still most commonly to be met with is one edited by Georgina Hogarth and Mamie Dickens, in various editions, from 1880. There are many gatherings of letters to different correspondents, of which the most important are *Mr. and Mrs. Charles Dickens, His Letters to Her*, edited by W. Dexter, London, 1935, and *The Heart of Charles Dickens*, edited by Edgar Johnson, New York, 1952, a selection of Dickens's letters to Angela Burdett Coutts. The most complete collection is still the one edited by W. Dexter, in three volumes, for the Nonesuch edition of the Words, London, 1937–8. *The Selected Letters of Charles Dickens*, ed. F. W. Dupee, New York, 1960, has a fair introduction, but the texts are disappointingly familiar, uncorrected reprints. The first volume of a complete edition, edited by M. House and G. Storey, with (for that volume) W. J. Carlton, P. Collins, K. J. Fielding, and K. Tillotson as associate editors, will be published in 1964. The full edition will be in several volumes and will give a new and very much more complete and accurate text.

Books about Dickens

This is a highly selective list with a sparing commentary: almost all the works in it have merits, which will partly differ for each reader. Essays collected in book form but which have been included in the first three volumes of *Collected Articles* below, have not been separately listed but must be looked for there: students should find those selections indispensable.

ADRIAN, A. A., *Georgina Hogarth and the Dickens Circle*, Oxford, 1957. A useful and scholarly biographical study.

AYLMER, F., *Dickens Incognito*, London, 1959. About Dickens and Ellen Ternan. Certainly wrong about their supposed child, as it is based on an admitted misreading of certain records: see *Sunday Times* (London), 13 December 1959. Much of the rest of it stands.

BAGEHOT, W., 'Charles Dickens', in his *Literary Studies*, London, 1879, Vol. II.

BUTT, J. and TILLOTSON, K., *Dickens at Work*, London, 1957. Valuable study of Dickens's methods.

CARLTON, W. J., *Charles Dickens, Shorthand Writer*, London, 1926. The author deserves to be better known for his numerous and valuable biographical articles.

CAZAMIAN, L., *Le Roman Social En Angleterre*, Paris, 1904.

CHESTERTON, G. K., *Charles Dickens*, London, 1906, and *Appreciations and Criticisms of Charles Dickens*, New York, 1911. Perceptive as well as entertaining.

COCKSHUT, A. O. J., *The Imagination of Charles Dickens*, London, 1961. Thoughtful and strongly argued.

COLLINS, P. A. W., *Dickens and Crime*, London, 1962. Excellent scholarship, persuasive, and with critical implications that have still to be taken into consideration. *Dickens and Education*, London, 1963: new information and new insight into Dickens's thoughts and feelings.

DAVIS, E., *The Flint and the Flame. The Artistry of Charles Dickens*, Columbia, Missouri, 1963.

DOLBY, G., *Charles Dickens as I knew Him*, London, 1885.

ENGEL, M., *The Maturity of Dickens*, Cambridge, Mass., 1959.

FIELDING, K. J., *Charles Dickens, A Survey*, London, 1953, revised 1964. British Council booklet.

FORD, G. H., *Dickens and His Readers, Aspects of Novel-Criticism since 1836*, Princeton, 1955.

FORSTER, J., *Life of Charles Dickens*, London, 1872–4, 3 vols. Will always be indispensable partly as a source-book, and partly because of Forster's personal knowledge, though sparingly revealed. A useful edition annotated by J. W. T. Ley was published, London, 1926.

GISSING, G., *Charles Dickens*, London, 1898; and *Critical Studies of the Works of Charles Dickens*, New York, 1924.

GREENE, G., 'The Young Dickens', in his *The Lost Childhood*, London, 1951.

HOUSE, A. H., *The Dickens World*, London, 1941, should be read; and 'Dickens', Part III of his *All in Due Time*, London, 1955.

JOHNSON, E., *Charles Dickens. His Tragedy and Triumph*, New York, 1952. The best and essential biography.

KETTLE, A., 'Dickens: "Oliver Twist" ', in his *Introduction to the English Novel*, London, 1951, Vol. I.

KITTON, F. G., *Charles Dickens by Pen and Pencil*, with *Supplement*, London, 1890. For biography.

LEAVIS, F. R., 'Hard Times: An Analytical Note,' in his *The Great Tradition*, London, 1948. See above, p. 160; also 'Dombey and Son', *Sewanee Review*, LXX, 1962.

LINDSAY, J., *Charles Dickens*, London, 1950. Rewarding but wildly inaccurate.

MANNING, J., *Dickens and Education*, Toronto, 1950.

MILLER, J. H., *Charles Dickens and the World of His Novels*, Cambridge, Mass., 1948. It has sometimes been found difficult, but to the reader who knows the novels it should be thought-provoking and offer more insight into the novels than almost any work listed here.

MONOD, S., *Dickens Romancier*, Paris, 1953. An important study of Dickens's methods as a novelist.

NISBET, A. B., *Dickens and Ellen Ternan*, Berkeley, California, 1952.

ORWELL, G., 'Charles Dickens', in his *Inside the Whale*, London, 1940.

QUILLER-COUCH, SIR A., *Charles Dickens and Other Victorians*, Cambridge, Eng., 1925.

SHAW, G. B., Introduction to *Hard Times*, Waverley Edition, London, 1912, and to *Great Expectations*, Edinburgh, 1937, London, 1947. See also scattered references throughout his works.

SITWELL, SIR O., *Dickens*, London, 1932.

SPILKA, M., *Dickens and Kafka*, Bloomington, Indiana, 1962. Yields rewardingly to close study, though more Kafkan than Dickensian.

SWINBURNE, A. C., *Charles Dickens*, London, 1913.

TILLOTSON, K., *Novels of the Eighteen-Forties*, Oxford, 1954, particularly on '*Dombey and Son*'. See also J. Butt.

TRILLING, L., '*Little Dorrit*', in his *The Opposing Self*, London, 1955.

VAN GHENT, D., 'On *Great Expectations*', in her *The English Novel*, New York, 1953. Powerfully persuasive but difficult, if not impossible, to accept.

WAGENKNECHT, E., *The Man Charles Dickens*, Boston and New York, 1929. To be revised and re-issued.

WILSON, E., 'Dickens: The Two Scrooges', in his *The Wound and the Bow*, Boston, 1941, should need no recommendation.

ZABEL, M. D., 'The Revolutionary Fate', in his *Craft and Character in Modern Fiction*, New York, 1957.

Collected Articles

DISCUSSIONS OF CHARLES DICKENS, ed. William R. Clark, Boston, 1961. A most useful paperback selection of previously published current criticism.

THE DICKENS CRITICS, ed. G. H. Ford and Lauriat Lane, Jr., Ithaca, New York, 1961. A full and valuable collection of critical statements from Poe to Angus Wilson, with a good bibliography.

DICKENS AND THE TWENTIETH CENTURY, ed. J. Gross and G. Pearson, London, 1962. Twenty, mainly new, essays on the novels.

Between them these three volumes provide a wide-ranging, stimulating and long-needed examination of Dickens's work. See also the *Dickensian* (1905, in progress), now published thrice yearly, for a variety of articles; *A Review of English Literature*, Vol. II, No. 3 (1961), for a Dickens Symposium, ed. J. Butt;

and *Dickens Criticism, A Symposium*, ed. N. Peyrouton, Boston, 1962, a recorded discussion in which G. Ford, J. H. Miller, Edgar Johnson, and S. Monod took part.

Although many articles have thus been collected, many others deserve searching out and may be found by using the *Victorian Studies* annual bibliographies, records of publication in the *Dickensian*, or Ford and Lane's bibliography as above.

INDEX

Adam Bede, 140
Addison, Joseph, 3, 59–60, 127–8
Administrative Reform Association, 176
Ainsworth, William Harrison, 11, 25, 28, 57, 72, 217
All the Year Round, 197, 207, 219
Amalgamated Society of Engineers, 163
American Notes, 89–92
Andersen, Hans Christian, 64, 190
Arabian Nights, 2, 222
Arnold, Matthew, 143
Athenaeum, 136
Austen, Jane, 65

Bagehot, Walter, 50
Balzac, Honoré de, 172
Barnaby Rudge, 57; a traditional historical novel, 72–4; challenge to Scott, 73–4; and the riots, 74–6; social purpose, 76–7; weakness of plot, 77–8
Barrett, Elizabeth, 16
Barrow, John Henry, 7, 9
Battle of Life, The, 109, 115
Bayley, John, 35
Beadnell, Maria (later Mrs. Winter), 8, 10, 177
Beard, Thomas, 7
Bennett, Arnold, 131
Bentley's Miscellany, 27, 32
Berger, Francesco (musician), 196
Birmingham, 61; banquet to literature and art, 157
Birmingham and Midland Institute, 157–8; speech at (1869), 174–5
Birmingham Mercury, 158
Black, James, 9
Blacking-factory, 4–6, 130
Bleak House, 8; begun, 145; style or language, 146–8, 151–3; form, 145, 148; social satire, 148–50; themes, 154–6; Boythorn, 150; Skimpole, 150–1; reception, 156
Boston, Mayor of (J. Chapman), 87–8
Bradbury and Evans, 103, 110, 127, 195, 197
Bright, John, 175
Brown, Mrs. Hannah, 183
Browne, Hablot Knight ('Phiz'), 15, 47–8, 150
Browning, Robert, 30
Bryant, William Cullen, 97
Bulwer, Sir Edward B. Lytton, see Lytton
Bunyan, John, 36, 66–7, 69
Burdett, Sir Francis, 39–40, 44, 100
Burnett, Henry, 15, 32, 46
Bush, Douglas, 22
Butt, John, 132

Campbell, Thomas, 29
Carlton, W. J., 68
Carlyle, Thomas, 25, 64, 99, 108, 159, 174–5, 180, 197–9, 206
Carové, F. W., 68n.
Caste, 233 n.
Cattermole, George, 65
Cazamian, Louis, 103, 170
Chapman, Edward, 13–14
Chapman, Frederic, 111–12
Chapman, John, 120
Chapman and Hall, 13–14, 15, 16, 28, 47, 60, 93, 103
Chatham, 2–3, 141
Chimes, The, 105–8, 202
Chesterton, G. K., 17, 37
Chorley, H. F., 136
Christmas Carol, A, 102–3, 158
Civil Service, 180–3
Clark, Prof. G. Kitson, 171
Cockshut, A. O. J., 41, 258
Coleridge, Sara, 94
Colleen Bawn, The, 233n.
Collins, Charles, 246

Collins, Philip, 217
Collins, W. Wilkie, vii, 7, 20, 96, 126, 157, 172, 190, 196, 198, 226, 227, 246
Cornhill Magazine, 39
Coutts, Angela Burdett, 40, 100–2, 115, 125–6, 128, 183, 189, 194, 196, 208, 227
Cricket on the Hearth, The, 109
Crimean War, 173–4
Cruikshank, George, 11, 15, 27, 57

Daily News, 108–10, 127
Dallas, E. S., 228–9
David Copperfield, autobiography in, 5, 7, 9, 130, 140–1, 186; begun, 128–30; characterization and chief themes, 130–42; weaknesses, 140; praise for, 143
Dickens, Catherine Hogarth (Mrs. Charles Dickens), vii, 5, 10, 14, 15, 25–6, 45–7, 61, 62, 79, 80–1, 84, 86, 87–8, 130, 144, 185–6, 189–90, 192–4, 196
Dickens, Charles
Life:
Birth, 1; parentage, 1–2; first school, 2; life in London, 3–4; father's imprisonment, 4; blacking-factory, 5–6; and 'Murdstone and Grinby', 5; effect of experience, 6; further schooling, 6–7; learns shorthand, 7–8; as law reporter, 8; love for Maria Beadnell, 8–9; newspaper reporter, 9–10; first publications, 10; meets Catherine Hogarth, 10–11; *Sketches by Boz*, 11–12; arrangement to write *Pickwick*, 13; marriage, 15; *Pickwick* published, 15–16; success and new friends, 25; children, 26; moves from Doughty Street to Devonshire Terrace, 26; overwork, 27; relations with publishers, 27–30; friendship with Forster, 30–1; edits *Bentley's Miscellany*, 32; writes *Oliver Twist*, 32–3; death of Mary Hogarth, 45–6; field-work for *Nickleby*, 47–8; celebrates conclusion, 58; plans for *Master Humphrey's Clock*, 59–61; need for serial, 61–2; origin of *Old Curiosity Shop*, 62–3; death of Nell, 63–4; writes *Barnaby Rudge*, 72–4; visits Scotland, 73; visit to America, 79–89; voyage, 80–1; first impressions, 81–2; speeches on coypright, 83–5; New York, 84–5; disillusion, 86–8; Canada, 89; letters home, used for *American Notes*, 89–90; work for international copyright, 90; attacked by American press, 88–91; holiday, 92; begins *Martin Chuzzlewit*, 92; poor sales, 93; tory reaction, 98; friendship with Miss Burdett Coutts, 100; ragged schools, 101–2; writes *Carol*, 102; its effect, 103; discontent with novel-writing, 104; moves to Italy, 105–6; writes *Chimes*, 105; dreams of Mary Hogarth, 105–6; reading of *Chimes*, 108; return to England, 109; other Christmas books, 109; work for *Daily News*, 109–10; Switzerland and *Dombey*, 110–11; difficulty of writing, 114–15; in Paris, 115; 'Dombey dinner', 123; Guild of Literature and Art, 124; amateur theatricals, 124–5; Home for fallen women, 125–6; starts *Household Words*, 127–8; visit to Gt. Yarmouth, 129; starts *David Copperfield*, 129–30; its reviews, 142–3; work for Guild, 144; death of father, 144; and of daughter, Dora, 144–5; begins Bleak House, 145; its reception, 156; holidays, 157; with Guild in Birmingham, 157; first public reading, 157–8; visits Preston and begins *Hard Times*, 158–9; visits to France, 172; admiration for French, 173; increasing interest in Politics, 173–4; influenced by Carlyle, 174–5; joins in demand for administrative reform, 176; *Little Dorrit*,

176 ff.; radicalism or 'restlessness', 183, 187; view of life, 183–7; self-questioning, 186; failure of marriage, 188–9; increased unrest, 189; Mrs. Dickens, 189–90; *The Frozen Deep*, 190–1; the Ternan family, 191; holiday with Collins, 191; events leading to separation from wife, 192–4; arrangements for separation, 194; the 'address' in *Household Words*, 195; quarrel with *Punch* proprietors and staff, 195; probable relations with Ellen Ternan, 195–6; start of *All the Year Round*, 197; begins *Tale of Two Cities*, 197; at Gad's Hill Place, 207; sombreness of *Uncommercial Traveller*, 207; idea for *Great Expectations*, 207–8; the altered ending, 222; more public readings, 223; Christmas numbers, 224; difficulties of writing *Our Mutual Friend*, 224–225; illness and railway accident, 225; reviewed by E. S. Dallas, 228–9; and Henry James, 229–30; further readings, 236; relationship with Ellen Ternan, 236–7; his general charm, 237–238; second visit to United States (1867–8), 238–9; signs of strain, 239; reasons for readings, 239–40; last readings, 240–1; arrangements for *Edwin Drood*, 241; death and burial, 250; public and private sense of loss, 250–1; Jowett's tribute, 251

As Novelist:

characterization, 21, 49–50, 64–65, 70, 95, 98, 114–4, 118, 123, 131, 137–8, 201, 203, 215–16; style, 68–9, 109, 121, 151–3, 201, 207, 220, 229, 250; fancifulness, 11, 146–7; poetic life of writing, 121–3, 138–9, 160; restraint, 114, 147, 224; form of novels, 17–19, 78, 93–4, 111–14, 116, 129–30, 132–6, 145–6, 156, 176–7, 197–8, 220–2, 242–6; serialization, 19, 59, 61–2, 77, 129, 137, 197–8, 208, 226; as improviser, 18–19; use of themes, imagery and symbols, 38–9, 51–52, 64–8, 72, 78, 109, 118–20, 133–5, 148, 153–6, 178–9, 198–200, 210–14, 247; comedy, 21, 49–50, 52–4, 69–71, 137–9, 209; optimism, 23–4, 38–9, 51, 56–7, 143, 227; seriousness, 33, 37–8, 49, 54–6, 140–1, 186–7, 209–10, 216, 227, 234; his religious sense, 142, 169–71, 184–6, 200, 204, 210–14, 248–249; satirist, 97, 148–9, 176; as social critic and reformer, 33–35, 39–45, 47, 76–7, 98, 101–103, 107, 119–20, 128, 149–50, 160–8, 173–6, 180–3, 205–6, 217–19, 230–3, 235

Works:

see separate entries and Bibliography, pp. 253 ff.

Dickens, Charles Culliford Boz ('Charley'), 26, 194, 219, 239

Dickens, Dora Annie, 144–5

Dickens, Edward Bulwer Lytton (youngest son 'Plorn'), 169

Dickens, Elizabeth (Mrs. John Dickens), 1–2, 6, 49–50

Dickens, Frances Elizabeth (Mrs. Burnett), 1, 6, 49–50

Dickens, Francis Jeffrey ('Frank'), 219

Dickens, Henry Fielding, 129

Dickens, John, 1–8, 144, 178

Dickens, Mary ('Mamie'), 26

Dickens, Walter Savage Landor, 219

Disraeli, Benjamin, 43, 238

Dolby, George, 237–9

Dombey and Son, planning and construction, 110–17; pathos, 111–116; women characters, 116–19; and money-making, 119–20; and railways, 120; weaknesses, 120–1; 'poetic life' of prose, 121–2; Dallas's review, 122–3; Dickens's faith in, 123; 'Dombey dinner', 123–4

D'Orsay, Count Alfred, 25

Dr. Marigold's Prescriptions, 224

Edinburgh Review, 40, 64, 98
Edwin Drood, 175; begun, 241; outline, 242–6; new possibilities, theme as important as plot, 247–250
Eliot, George, 147–8, 220
Eliot, T. S., 131, 156–7
Evening Chronicle, 10, 11, 13
Examiner, 30
Eyre, Governor Edward John, 175
Ezekiel, 248

Fagin, Bob, 4
Féval, Paul, 172
Fielding, Henry, 2, 16, 38, 65, 93, 129
Fields, James T., 241
Fitzgerald, Edward, 64
Flaubert, G., 215
Foreign Quarterly, 91
Forster, E. M., 131, 137, 138
Forster, John, 5, 6, 78, 86, 104, 159; friendship with Dickens, 30–1, 63, 251; as an adviser, 33, 59–64, 104, 127, 132; and Dickens's letters from America, 89–90; article in *Foreign Quarterly*, 91; provides audience for *Chimes*, 108; takes over *Daily News*, 110; speech at Theatrical Fund Dinner, 144–5; reply to Lewes's criticism, 148; letters to Forster from Dickens, and F's *Life of Dickens* are quoted throughout.
Fortnightly Review, 148
Fox, Henry, 40
Fraser's Magazine, 98
French Revolution, The (Carlyle), 199
Frozen Deep, The, 190–1, 201–2
Furley, Mary, 107

Gad's Hill Place, 3, 189, 192, 207
Garrod, H. W., 118
Gaskell, Mrs. E. C., 127–8, 165
George Silverman's Explanation, 202
Gil Blas (Le Sage), 2, 94
Giles, William, 2–3
Gissing, George, 48, 50, 178
Gladstone, W. E., 90, 149, 170, 175
Goldsmith, Oliver, 3, 10, 59, 84
Gore, Mrs., 77
Grant, Daniel and William, 50
Grant, James, 15
Graves, Robert, 136
Great Expectations, 'tragi-comic conception', 208–10; a Christian 'moral Fable', 210–14; the 'world of the novel', 208–10; study of society, 214–17, 219; and Dickens's sons, 219; shows advance in skill, 219–21; ending, 221–3
Greene, Graham, 220
Guild of Literature and Art, 124, 150

Hall, Samuel Carter, 95–6
Hall, William, 13–14
Hard Times, 44, 230; begun, 158–9; Dr. Leavis's criticism, 160–1; as criticism of industrial society, 161–5; and on capital and labour, 162–4; and relation to contemporary scene, 164–7; Christian morality, 167–9
Harley, James Pritt, 25
Haunted Man, The, 109
Hawthorne, N., 216
Helps, Sir Arthur, 45
Hogarth, George, 10, 123
Hogarth, Mrs. George, 193–5
Hogarth, Georgina, 110, 193, 250
Hogarth, Helen, 193
Hogarth, Mary, 26, 45–6, 64, 67, 105–6
Hollingshead, John (member of *All the Year Round* Staff), 251
Holloway, John, 164n.
Hood, Thomas, 20, 28–9, 59, 66, 107; his biography, 207
House, Humphry, 34, 76, 170–1, 220
Household Words, 60; started, 127–8; articles in, 128; 'The Finishing Schoolmaster', 75; 'Child's Dream of a Star', 68, 120, 128; 'On Strike', 158, 163, 165; 'To Working Men', 171, 173–4; 'Monument of French Folly', 172; personal 'Address' (1858), 194
Howitt, Mary, 128
Hudson, George, 120, 180

Hunt, James Henry Leigh, 25, 49, 150–1, 240
Hunted Down, 249

Irving, Washington, 59–60, 64, 84–5, 97
Italy, 104–5, 108–9

Jamaican rising, 175
James, Henry, 131, 160, 210, 229–230
Jane Eyre, 145
Jeffrey, Francis, Lord, 64, 103, 116
Jerrold, Douglas, 95, 108, 190, 240
John Bull, 16
Johnson, Edgar, quoted, 149, 166, 230, 259
Johnson, Dr. Samuel, 3, 25
Jowett, Benjamin, 251

Kettle, Dr. Arnold, 36, 39
Knowles, James Sheridan, 124, 240

Laing, Mr. (magistrate), 34–5
Lancet, The, 41
Landor, Walter Savage, 25, 30, 62–3; (as Boythorn), 150
Laurie, Sir Peter, 107
Layard, A. H., 182
Lazy Tour of Two Idle Apprentices (Dickens and Collins), 191
Leavis, Dr. F. R., 121–2, 160
Leech, John, 15, 129
Lemon, Mark, 129, 194–5, 240
Lever, Charles, 208
Lewes, George Henry, 48–9, 147–8, 220
Lindsay, Jack, 148, 230, 259
Little Dorrit, 23, 175–6; subject, 176–178; construction, 179–80; purpose, 180; strength and weakness of social satire, 181–3; 'religious dimension', 183–8
Liverpool, 44
Lockhart, John, 40
Longfellow, H. W., 91, 250
Lover, Samuel, 25
Lytton, Sir Edward George Earle Lytton Bulwer (Lord Lytton), 25, 30, 35, 43, 72, 124, 147, 222, 238
Lytton, Robert, 240

Macaulay, Thomas Babington, Baron, 64, 159
Maclise, Daniel, vii, 25, 62, 92, 108
Macready, William Charles, 25, 58, 63–4, 86–7, 103, 105, 108, 117, 201, 240
Macrone, John, 11, 27, 29, 30
Marryat, Captain Frederick, 16, 28, 83
Marshalsea, 4, 176, 178, 184
Martin Chuzzlewit, 86, 87, 100, 102–103; begun, 92–3; bad sales, 93; weakness of plot, 93–4; moral purpose, 94–5; Pecksniff and S. C. Hall, 95–6; development, 96–7; satire, 97; reception in England, 97–8; power of characterization, 98–9
Martineau, Harriet, 41, 83
Marx, Karl, 168, 214
Master Humphrey's Clock, 59–61, 72
Melbourne, William Lamb, Viscount, 40
Melville, Herman, 91, 216
Memoirs of Grimaldi, 45
Metropolitan Magazine, 12, 16
Mill, John Stuart, 9, 175
Miller, J. Hillis, 43, 142, 184, 216, 259
Mirror of Parliament, 9
Mitford, Mary Russell, 16
Monod, Sylvère, 17, 19, 259
Monthly Magazine, 10, 13, 15
Moonstone, The (Collins), 156
Morning Chronicle, 9, 26, 68
Mrs. Lirriper's Legacy, and *Mrs. Lirriper's Lodgings*, 224

Napoleon III (Louis N.), 173
New York Herald, 88
Nicholas Nickleby, and Yorkshire schools, 47–8; its success, 48; seriousness, 49; characters, 49–50; its sanity, 51–2; theme of 'love', 51–2; comedy of shams, 53; reformism, 56–7; concluded, 58
Norton, Charles Eliot, 237, 251
Norton, Susan, 250–1

O'Connell, Daniel, 91
Old Curiosity Shop, idea for, 62, 65–6; writing of, 62–4; Little Nell, 64–66; a dream, 65–6; 'a kind of allegory' or fairy tale, 66–9; characters, 69–72
Oliphant, Mrs. Margaret, 40, 64
Oliver Twist, 12, 27, 29, 47–8, 52, 56; progress in writing, 32; 'startling' implications, 33–4; and the Law, 34–5; 'the principle of Good', 35–6; and of evil, 35–7; optimism, 38; power, 39; reception, 39–40; and Poor Law, 41; its relationship (as with other novels), to own times, 41–5
Once a Week, 197
Orwell, George, 50–1, 75, 169, 181–182
Our Mutual Friend, 184, 186; difficulty of writing, 224–5; unpleasing, 226–7; but skilful, 227–8; reviewed by Dallas and James, 228–30; structural flaw in, 230–2; aims exceed means, 233–5; view of life, 234

Palmer, Samuel, 109
Palmerston, Henry John Temple, Viscount, 149, 169, 176
Paul Clifford (Lytton), 35, 232
Perils of Certain English Prisoners, The (Dickens and Collins), 175
'Phiz', see H. K. Browne
Pickwick, Mr. S., 14, 19–21, 24; reappearance in the *Clock*, 61
Pickwick Papers, 28, 33, 41, 47, 85, 115; arrangements for, 13–15; progress, 15–16; as a novel, 17–19; Mr. Pickwick, 20; humour, 21–4; interpolated stories, 24; variety, 24–5
Pictures from Italy, 108–10
Poe, Edgar Allan, 78
Prayer, Book of Common, 200, 211, 247–8
Proust, Marcel, 220
Punch, 195

Quarterly Review, 16, 40, 98
Quiller-Couch, Sir Arthur, 19

Rambler (1854), The, 170
Reade, Charles, 28
Robinson, Henry Crabb, 89
Rogers, Samuel, 25
Roosevelt, Theodore, 97
Ruskin, John, 64, 159, 164–5
Russell, Sir George, 237
Russell, Lord John, 149, 228

St. James's Theatre, 27
Sand, George, 215
Sartre, J. P., 42
Saturday Review, 182
Scheffer, Ary, 173
Scott, Sir Walter, 10, 16, 45, 65, 72–74, 83, 104
Seymour, Robert, 13–15
Shaftesbury, Earl of, 108, 169
Shaw, G. Bernard, 149, 159, 164, 210, 214, 230, 242
Shaw, William, 47–8
Sketches by Boz, 10–12, 27–29
Sketches of Young Gentlemen, 45
Smith, Arthur (Readings manager), 195
Smith, Rev. Sydney, 25, 64, 169
Smollett, Tobias, 2, 16, 49, 65
Spectator, 22, 156
Stanfield, Clarkson, 92
Staplehurst railway accident, 225
Stephen, Fitzjames, 182
Sterne, Laurence, 16, 63, 64
Stevenson, Lionel, 163
Stevenson, Robert Louis, 228
Story Without a Beginning, The (Carové), 68n.
Sunday Under Three Heads, 26
Swinburne, A. C., 34

Taine, Henri (Hippolyte), 96, 118, 159
Tales of the Genii (J. Ridley), 2
Tale of Two Cities, A, 197, 208; plot, 197; themes, 198–200, 203–5; theatricality, 201–2; identity of Dickens with Dr. Manette, 202–3; duality in characterization, 203–4
Talfourd, Thomas Noon, 25, 34, 85–86
Tennyson, Alfred, Lord, 30, 175, 235

Ternan, Ellen Lawless, 191–2, 195–196, 202–3, 219, 225, 236–7, 250
Ternan, Francis Eleanor Jarman (Mrs. Ternan), 191, 196
Ternan, Frances Eleanor (eldest daughter), 195–6
Ternan, Maria, 191, 196
Thackeray, W. M., 15, 29, 40, 53, 80, 103, 116, 142–3, 180, 190, 197, 228, 236, 240
Times, The, 7, 143, 175–6, 194, 228
Trilling, Lionel, 184–5
Trollope, Anthony, 1, 12, 43, 73, 131, 228, 235, 238
True Sun, The, 9

Uncommercial Traveller, 207–8
United States, first visit (1842), 79, ch. Five; second visit (1867–8), 238–9

Victoria, Queen, 144, 191
Village Coquettes, The, 46

Warren, Samuel, 98
Washington Globe, 88
Watson, Hon. Richard, and Mrs., 151, 187, 237
Way We Live Now, The (Trollope), 235
Webb, Beatrice, 171
Weller, Mary, 2
Wellington, Duke of, 101
Westminster Review, 165
Whitehead, Charles, 13
Wills, William Henry, 127–8, 223, 238
Wilson, Edmund, 18, 119, 153